MARKETING THE REGULATED COMMODITIES

MARKETING THE REGULATED COMMODITIES

C. S. Bhanumate
Lecturer in Economics Department of Economics,
Shivaji University, Kolhapur

SERIALS PUBLICATIONS
NEW DELHI (INDIA)

First Published - 2008

ISBN: 978-81-8387-170-9

Published by

SERIALS PUBLICATIONS
4830/24, Prahlad Street, Ansari Road
Darya Ganj, New Delhi-110002 (India)
Phone : 23245225 Fax : 91-11-23272135
E-mail: serials@satyam.net.in

Dedicated

to the

Beloved Memory of

My Mother

SUGALABAI S. BHANUMATE

CONTENTS

FOREWORD

Since the signing on the AoA under WTO, a viable strategy to make agriculture sector compatible is considered so far. Focused and structural studies are required to stand in the world market. Market oriented agricultural reforms are being introduced widely and comprehensively. Agriculture sector comes under the State's agenda, obviously the State initiatives in designing the marketing strategy becomes an arena of state level reforms. The states based on local character can design a local marketing system for the benefit of the agriculturists. Elimination of middlemen cannot solve the marketing problem, since they have been accepted as inevitable part of our agricultural marketing. Competency with the APMC will not solve the seriousness of the marketing. Reforms in the sense may not and should not concentrate only on exports. The Doha Declaration reconfirmed the long-term objectives of setting up of "a fair and market oriented trading system through fundamental reforms ... to correct and prevent restrictions and distortions in the world agricultural markets." AoA thus, is a challenge if nothing is activated and is an opportunity if activated timely.

With the advent of liberalisation, agriculture sector has reserved for itself as a commercial niche and has attained a new dimension. Three types of technologies viz. biotechnology, eco-technology and IT have been considered worldwide. Precision farming has been a new trend in agriculture. Food standard programmes can be handled for attaining competency through precision farming. This has been proved to be an important means to harmonizing standards with a view to satisfy consumers of different countries, country-wise opportunity in formation by market survey is being provided to the farmers through I.T.

The restrictions imposed on the movement of agricultural produce have to be removed through Central Legislations, making it a fundamental right. There are around 6 Central Legislations and 3 State Acts regulating various commands through marketing and processing. Besides there are 25 control orders issued under Essential Commodities Act, 1955. Under the Central Legislations there are 5 Control Orders meant for defensive purpose, 3 temporary Control Powers and 2 for industrial development executed there under.

Commodity-wise strategies and arrangements for protecting the growers from adverse impact of undue price fluctuations in the domestic and world market and for promoting exports through various measures have to be implemented. Conversion of Essential Commodities Act into Emergency Legislation, which can be invoked only for a limited period with prior approval of the Central Government, is judicious. The restrictions imposed on licensing of processing of agricultural commodities should be withdrawn.

Multi-state Co-operative Marketing Law should be passed immediately. All states be asked to bring their co-operative laws in conformity with the Central Legislation. Central assistance for development of co-operative should be made contingent on this requirement. Unlike the Ministry of Company Affairs, Ministry of Co-operative Affairs be formed.

Developing the infrastructural facilities based on commodities and farmers is essential for enhancing the marketing and processing activities. There should be an effective link between marketing, storaging, transportation and processing activities framed in the co-operative structure unlike the China model of agricultural marketing.

Thailand Model can be adopted for export of quality produce. Development of mega-commodity based markets under joint venture will be an incentive and will work as a growth centre alongwith agri-parks. For performing most of national significant activities, some portion of marketing activities should be brought under the Central Subject.

Cost and quality imperatives for improving productivity, reducing wastage, standardizations and the prócessing are required for global competitiveness. Vertically co-ordinated demand driven value chain is the necessity of the hour.

The Indian diet has to be diversified with fewer cereals and more fruits, vegetables, milk, meat with knowledge intensive production systems. Alternative models reflected in the Model Act like contract farming, private mandies, direct marketing should be enhanced.

Virtual business through virtual team and among the virtual teams is more suitable to agribusiness industry. This idea has been developed in 1990s. Virtual Teams are common place among most global agricultural companies. Most large companies, for instances Syngenta and Pioneer have a teams working on specific programmes and projects from geographically dispersed locations. Input companies including John Deere and Monsanto have conducted virtual operations for years with remote soles.

Need to develop agribusiness model with local public-private partnership for comprehensive and perspective agricultural development is necessitated for developing domestic agri-markets. Agri-business centres can be initiated by the financial institutions under tripartite arrangements. Unlike entrepreneurs, we should develop Agri-preneurs for overall development of agriculture sector. Morarka Foundation has come out with this new idea.

The commodity approach (aspect) of agricultural development has to be incorporated in our Plan Model. Agricultural Economics should be pursued as a basic and fundamental for developing a Model of country's development. Agricultural fundamentalism must be integrated and co-ordinated with rural productive development. Cash and income-transfer schemes are just temporary patches to the sky torn areas. Precision farming is the only alternative to enhance the agricultural growth.

Dr. C. S. Bhanumate has tied to justify the case of APMC with reference to the Solapur. This in fact, reviews the status of APMCs in the State. It is worth research work adding to the economic literature.

Place: Kolhapur
Date: 14-1-2007

V.B. Jugale
Professor,
Department of Economics,
Shivaji University, Kolhapur.

ACKNOWLEDGMENT

I must consider myself a most fortunate enough to have received an opportunity to work under the guidance of Dr. V.B. Jugale, Professor and Head, Department of Economics, and Dean of the Social Science Faculty, Shivaji University, Kolhapur. I owe a great in debt of gratitude to him for his advice and encouragement regarding my research work.

I am greatly thankful to R.G. Dandge from Shivaji University, Kolhapur who rendered me in application of quantitative techniques, which facilitated my data processing work smoothly. I will be failing in my duty if I do not express my deep gratitude towards my teachers Dr. A. A. Dange, Dr. P. A. Koli, Dr. V. B. Kakade, Dr. P. N. Gavade, Dr. V. P. Katti, Shri A. N. Sabale, and all from the Economics Department, Shivaji University for their timely help and suggestions.

I wish to express my thanks to Late Shri Baburao Chakote, Ex-Chairman, and Shri Mahadev B. Chakote, Chairman and Shri D. V. Kamalapure, Secretary of Agricultural Produce Market Committee, Solapur for financial support to publish research work in the book form as well as their inherent help in providing the required statistical data and information of APMC.

I must express my heartiest feelings to my mother Sugalabai and my elder brother Shankar and family members for sparing me to afford the higher education and research activities. My thanks are due to my wife Sheela and my father-in-low Shri Mahadev Rampure who gives me moral support for completing this research work. I have no words to express my sentiments towards Hemant, Gautam, Ravi and my all friends for their support and encouragement.

C. S. Bhanumate

1

RESEARCH METHODOLOGY AND DATA BASE

INTRODUCTION

Well-regulated markets create a feeling of confidence and receiving fair play in the minds of the cultivator and his mood in which he is most ready to accept new ideas and strive to improve his agricultural practices. Keeping in view the significance of regulated agricultural markets, the present study was under taken to examine the performance of marketing of regulated commodities in Solapur. The APMC, Solapur is established in the year 1959 located in Solapur City on the Mumbai-Hydrabad Highway. It covers two talukas out of eleven; viz. North Solapur and South Solapur with a population cover of 969000 and 1931 Sq. Km of area. It covers 187800 hectares of geographical areas and 175100 hectares of cultivable area remaining 12700 hectares as non-cultivable area.

Indian farmers suffer due to his weak bargaining position in relation to the middlemen who have been exploiting the farmers over the decades. Governments at state level have therefore, stepped in to prevent this by providing a framework of regulatory measures in relation to the marketing of farm produce. The major steps initiated by the Government in this direction are related to: (1) The establishment of marketing co-operatives. (2) Buying of farm produce and price fixation and (3) Regulation of Markets.

Co-operative marketing has not been able to achieve the expected results as these societies have proved to be inadequate in helping the rural farmers on expected lines while government purchases and implement price support policies in favour of the farmers too. But these efforts have not been able to provide adequate protection against the middlemen in villages where nearly 65 per cent of rural produce is locally disposed off. Stronger organizations of middlemen have made the farmers face many odds in selling their produce. These deficiencies in the marketing of farm produce have led to the emergence of a structure of regulation framework of an agricultural marketing in India. Establishment of Regulated Markets with necessary facilities can be the answer to the marketing problems of the cultivator. The main objectives of establishment of Regulated Markets are to ensure fair prices to producer, elimination of malpractice and providing marketing facilities. "Well Regulated Markets create in the mind of the cultivator a feeling of confidence and receiving fair play and his mood in which he is most ready to accept new ideas and strive to improve his agricultural practice."[1]

Production function is incomplete without proper arrangements for the marketing of the product. In fact, production and marketing are intertwined and have symbiotic relationship. Agricultural marketing is a process which starts with a decision to produce saleable farm commodity and it involves all aspects of market structure or system, both functional and institutional, based on technical and economic considerations and includes pre and post-harvest operations-assembling, grading, storage, transportation and distribution. The objective of an efficient marketing system encompasses: (i) providing the best possible benefits to the primary producers, (ii) creating facilities for lifting all the produce of the farmers who are willing to sell at an incentive price, (iii) consumer, and (iv) making available all products of farm origin to consumers at a reasonable price without and deterioration in their quality (National Commission on Agriculture, 1976).[2]

The marketing of farm products is a matter of great interest to the farmers, the consumers and the middlemen. To the farmer, it provides a channel of communication between him and the society and gives him continuous information about the demand for his product. The consumer views it as a means of supply of farm product, since marketing helps in raising the standard of living of the people by satisfying a multitude of needs and desires of the consumers. The middleman depends upon it for his livelihood. These diverse interests lead the farmer to seek a high priced market for his products, the consumer a low prices market and the middleman, a margin between the farm price and consumer's price that reward him for his service. The basis of agricultural marketing is that, farm products are stored, transported to a place where wanted, at the desired time and transferred to those desiring them. It is for that reason that marketing has become part and parcel of the modern production process. It is marketing, which helps making goods useful to the society by getting them where consumers are wanted, when they are wanted and by transferring them to those people who want them. Marketing in this sense, has been defined as, "all the activities involved in the creation of place, time and possession utilities." To emphasize all these aspects of marketing, Clark and Clark wrote that, "Marketing consists of those efforts which effect transfer in ownership of goods and care for their, physical distribution."

According to Richard Kohl's, "Marketing is the performance of all business activities involved in the flow of goods and services from the point of initial agricultural production until they are in the hands of the ultimate consumer."[3] Committee of the American Marketing Association has given a comprehensive definition of marketing. According to the committee, "Marketing includes all activities having to do with effecting changes in the ownership and possession of goods and services. It is that part of economics which deals with the creation of time and place and possession utilities and that phase of business activity through which human wants are satisfied by the exchange of goods and services for some valuable consideration". In the light of the above definitions of the marketing, we can now define agricultural marketing in a simple language. Agricultural marketing is a process by which the producers and buyers of agricultural goods are brought together. Such a definition emphasis two things:

(i) The buyers of agricultural goods, and

(ii) The chain through which buyers and sellers of agricultural products are connected with each other.

Buyers of agricultural commodities can be divided into three main categories:

(i) Those who purchase agricultural goods for direct consumption;

(ii) Those who demand agricultural goods for use as intermediate goods;

(iii) Those who buy agricultural goods for sending them abroad i. e. exports.

Marketing is of great importance for the economy in several ways. We mention the principal ones as under.

(i) For Production,

(ii) For Development and

(iii) For Economic Welfare

Marketing provides several avenues of employment to various types of people. The various marketing operations spread across the country and outside, give rise to other activities like insurance, banking etc. Since marketing, as we have described above, raised production, productivity of agriculture, as also the economy's growth, the employment generation in this service sector is considerable and an expanding one.

The population in general benefits in two important ways. The marketing up downs the fluctuations of prices. It also keeps the price level of agricultural produce, and through it, the price level of the economy, uniform as among regions and generally nearer to the real costs which decline as the surpluses rise and the scale of marketing increases. Another benefit accrues specially to the poorer section through a public distribution system (PDS), which is fed by procurement of agricultural goods through markets and buying operations of the government as in India.

Moreover marketing of agricultural goods is more complicated than the marketing of other non-agricultural goods for the following reasons.

(i) The output of agriculture is largely a raw material, which is used for further processing. This processing may be simple as in converting livestock into meat or it may be highly complex as in converting wheat into flour. Regardless of the complexities, it is true that in most cases, the product sold by the farmer soon loses its identity as a farm product and simply becomes "food".

(ii) Compared to most other products, agricultural products are both bulkier and more easily perishable. When things are bulky, marketing functions concerned with their physical handling are very much affected. In the case of those products, which occupy a lot of space in relation to their value, the unit cost of transportation and storage is automatically raised.

(iii) Similarly, many agricultural products are exceedingly perishable. The degree of perishability, no doubt, varies from product to product but perishability remains a distinct characteristic of agricultural goods.

(iv) Most of agricultural production is highly seasonal. Most of the agricultural goods are ready for the market in certain fixed periods of the year only.

(v) The quantity as well as the quality of agricultural products is beyond the control of the producer. During some years, the growing conditions are such that the crop in general may be of high quality and more in quantity. In other years, unfavorable conditions may result in lower quality and lower production. Variations are quality and quantities of agricultural goods give rise to the following problems.

(a) Due to imbalance in supply and demand of agricultural goods, prices fluctuate from time to time.

(b) Variations in the quality of products make it very hard to apply uniform standards for grades from year to year.

(c) Variations in quantity of agricultural goods throw transport and storage arrangements out of year.

(vi) Agricultural output comes from many small units operating independently. Since the product is made available in relatively small amounts in the hands of many individual owners, the concentration process becomes very important in the case of agricultural marketing.

(vii) In the case of most agricultural goods, the demand is relatively inelastic; consequently, their prices rise steeply during the period of short supply and fall sharply in the period of excess supply. It is for this reason that marketing of agricultural goods has to face the problem of price instability.

The main characteristics of agricultural goods which make agricultural marketing much more elaborate and complex has been summaries as below.

Production Characteristics	*Product Characteristics*	*Consumption Characteristics*
1. Small Scale	1. More bulky and less value	1. Continuous
2. Scattered	2. Perishable	2. Regular
3. Specialized	3. Varying, Uncertain quality, quantity	3. Small quantity
4. Seasonal	4. Elastic supply	4. Inelastic demand

These characteristics have their effect on the facilities necessary to market farm products. Bulkiness, plus varying production, necessitates large storage capacities and higher cost of transportation. Perishable products require speedy handling as well as special refrigeration. Due to these characteristics, agricultural marketing sometimes is costlier than the marketing of industrial goods.

THE SIGNIFICANCE OF THE STUDY AND ROLE OF AGRICULTURAL REGULATED MARKETS

The S.L. Guru Expert Committee on "Strengthening and Developing of Agricultural Marketing' has recommended a complete revamp of the present marketing structure which, it said, would require funds of over RS 2,600 billion. The revamping would include repeal of the Essential Commodities Act allowing private sector to set up 50 mega agro-markets. Highlighting the inadequacies in the marketing infrastructure, the expert committee has estimated requirement of funds of RS 2,687.42 billion. It has recommended inclusion of more commodities under futures trading, linkages of forward and linkage markets and introduction of electronic warehousing system. The committee said large funds would be required for introducing irradiation system on semi-perishables, providing rural connectivity, developing market at all levels, storage, reefer vans, cleaning, grading, value addition centres and processing. It also highlighted he need to evolve agricultural marketing credit policy to meet the growing needs of funds.for agricultural marketing operations.

But, an important contribution of the Government of the improvement of agricultural marketing is the establishment of regulated markets in several parts of the country. A market committed consisting of the representatives of growers, traders, local bodies and Government manage regulated market. The market committee standardized the various market practices and charges, keeps standard weights and encores correct weighment. The committee issues licenses to the various market functionaries and punishes those among them who are guilty of fraudulent practices. Moreover, it constructs warehouses, rest houses and the other market ancillaries. Thus, with the help of Regulated Market, the government can avoid the defects of agricultural marketing by establishing orderly conditions within the market yard. Market should try to attract more and more quantities of commodities and maximum number of agricultural commodities. Moreover, farmers too should prefer to sale agricultural commodities in the market yard rather than private markets.

The establishment of a regulated market is meaningful only if it is sensitive to the needs of the buyers, sellers and the traders. However, most of the regulated markets in the country are still devoid of basic infrastructure. Metallic roads, auction platform, rest houses, cart parks, and water facilities respectively were provided in 37,47,21,38 and 36 per cent of regulated markets only in 1959-60. As a result of measures taken by the governments, these percentages have gone up during last three decades. There is a need to bring all agricultural markets, including periodic rural markets, under market regulation effectively. The emphasis is also needed to provide necessary infrastructure in all markets, to ensure effective utilisation of infrastructure created (like rural godowns, grading facilities, mechanical handling units etc.) and to ensure effective monitoring of the functioning of markets. Instances are not few, where open violations of various provisions of the Regulation Act are noted. Nevertheless, positive impact of the reform is noted on elimination of mal-practices and on increase in the marketing efficiency in most parts of the country.[4]

Definition of Regulated Market

Regulated Market is wholesale market where buying and selling is regulated and controlled by the state government through the Market Committee.

FUNCTIONS OF MARKETS

'Marketing function' may be defined as a major specialized activity performed in accomplishing the market process. Modern marketing system has several functions. Its important function is to move the desired varieties of farm products to consumers in the desired forms and conditions at the lowest possible cost. There are three principal marketing functions. (1) Assembling (procurement, concentration), (2) Processing (preparation for consumption), and (3) Dispersion (distribution). In carrying out each of the three major functions of marketing certain other functions are performed which are termed as 'secondary services'. They include, (1) standardization and grading, (2) packing, (3) transportation, (4) storage, (5) financing, (6) risk-bearing function, and (7) selling etc.

MARKET STRUCTURE AND WORKING: MYTHS AND REALITIES

Regulated Markets aim at the elimination of unhealthy and unscrupulous practices reducing marketing charges and providing facilities to the producers and sellers in the market. The poor standards of primary and secondary markets where producer convert their produce into cash. The prevalence of various malpractices such as short-weights, excessive market charges, unauthorized deduction, adulteration of produce and the absence of machinery to settle disputes between sellers and buyers were recognized as the main hindrances in agricultural marketing. These defects and malpractices can be recovered by the establishment of regulated marketing being regulated either by local bodies or under state legislation, which was suggested first in 1928 by the Royal Commission on Agriculture. The movement of regulation of market gained momentum only after 1930. The Bombay Agricultural Produce Market Act of 1939 was passed in respect of all agriculture produce viz., cereals, fibers and fruits etc. Regulated markets usually handle tobacco, cotton, groundnut, grains, coconuts, areca nuts, potatoes and turmeric etc.

MAIN FEATURES OF REGULATED MARKETS

Market Committee: Market Committee is comprised of representatives from different sectors of society that is farmers, traders, government local bodies and co-operatives. In general, it is observed that Market Committee consists of 15 members 10 from farmers 3 from traders and 1 each from the government and local bodies.

Area of Operation: The concerned state government notifies that its intention to regulate trade practices in specified area, such an area of operation is laid down either as a municipal limit or district or even it may be a region. In Maharashtra, area of operation of each Regulated Market is restricted to one taluka.

Methods of Sales: In Regulated Market the sale of agricultural market functionaries undertake produce either by open auction or by close tender method. These sales methods ensure a fair and competitive price for the produce and prevent the cheating of farmers. By these methods, the sale is carried out under the supervision of an official of the Market Committee.

Licensing of Market Functionaries: All the market functionaries including traders working in the regulated market have to obtain a license from the market committee after paying the prescribed fee to carry on their business, the licensed traders have to keep proper record and maintain accounts in accordance with the buy-laws of the market committee.

Market Levies or Fees: Growers and traders have to pay market fees, which are calculated on the basis of value of volume of a commodity bought and sold in the markets. Sometimes it may be based on a cart or truckload. To meet its administrative expenditure and in order to create infrastructure facilities in the market area the Market Committees get funds from the following sources:

1. Market fees on the produce brought for the sales in the market yard.
2. License fee and renewal fee for middlemen functioning in the area.

Settlements of Disputes: The Sub-Committee of the Market Committee solves Disputes arising out of the misconduct of the producers, seller and traders for various reasons of the quality of the produce, accounts and deductions of unauthorized charges. This avoids the legal complication and unnecessary expenditure.

ADVANTAGES OF REGULATED MARKETS

Following are some of the advantages of Regulated Markets:

1. Market charges are clearly defined and specified.
2. Market practices are regulated and undesirable activities are brought under control.
3. Correct weighment is ensured by periodical inspection and verification of scales and weights.
4. A suitable arrangement for the settlement of disputes is provided.
5. Reliable and up to date market news is made available to the farmers.
6. Suitable quality standards and standard terms for buying and selling are conveniently enforced.
7. Reliable statistics of arrivals, stocks, prices are maintained.
8. Other facilities like shades for the sale of produce, space for parking carts, drinking water facilities and cisterns of cattle, rest houses, grading and warehousing facilities are provided.
9. Open auction method is strictly followed.
10. Propaganda for agricultural improvement is more conveniently carried out. Taking over all picture Regulated Markets have produced a wholesome effect on marketing structure and have generally raised the efficiency or marketing at the primary level.

ORGANIZATION OF REGULATED MARKETS AND CONSTITUTION OF MARKET COMMITTEE

The primary object of regulating the Market is to safeguard the interests of the producers and sellers, which raises the standard of the local markets where the first exchange of the goods takes place. With a view to achieve the objectives in each of the Regulated Markets, Market Committees are established consisting of the representatives of the growers, traders, local bodies, sellers, co-operative enterprises and the State Government nominees. Producers are generally in the majority on these Committees. The Market Committee should consist of 12 to 18 members depending on the size of the market and other considerations, which are responsible for utilizing the fund for:

(a) Maintenance and improvement of the markets and its buildings.

(b) Maintenance of standards of weights and measures.

(c) Pay and pension of the staff

(d) Payment of interests of loans.

(e) Collection and dissemination of market information.

(f) Propaganda for agricultural improvement.

Moreover, Agricultural Regulated Market enables the producers to reap the best possible benefits, to provide facilities for lifting all produce the farmers are willing to sell at an incentive price; to reduce the price spread between the primary producers and ultimate consumer; and to make available all farm products to consumers at reasonable price without impairing the quality of the produce and to protect the interests of both the producers and consumers.

REVIEW OF LITERATURE

Selected Studies on Regulated Markets

Regulated markets have not been a panacea for eradication of the market imperfections in many of the States in India. For example, though there are seven principal regulated and nine sub-markets in the state of Assam, as per a study by K.C. Talukdar of AAU, collected at the check gates, infrastructures worth of several lakh are lying idle at all the markets. Godowns have been rented out to JCI and STATFED. Sales vouchers were not issued properly. Traders were continuing their business without license (Talukdar, 1988).

A study by Subba Rao(1987) in Bihar using the data of 144 sample farmers served by both regulated and non-regulated markets collected by Agro-Economic Centre, Allahabad found that small farmers incurred much higher cost per quintal of produce both at the regulated and unregulated markets than large farmers. Subba Rao examined the situation under four different marketing conditions, i.e., (a) sales at the door in hinterland villages served by Regulated Markets; (b) direct sales at the Regulated Market; (c) sales at the door in hinterland village served by non-regulated market; and (d) direct sales at the non-regulated markets. He drew the following conclusions: (1) the net price realized by farmers at door is roughly equal to or higher than the price realized when the produce is sold at the market in village served by Regulated Markets, (2) the net prices realized in the Regulated Market yard are also not better, in fact, worse in many cases than net prices realized for sale in the villages served by non-regulated markets, and (3) the net prices realized for sale in market yard, rise with the size of holding in both regulated and non-regulated markets. No tangible benefits seem to have percolated to small farmers by regulation since they realized more remunerative prices by sales at the door in the villages.

In another study conducted at Kanpur Regulated Market has a the new market yard constructed at a distance of 8 km from the present market on the Hamirpur Road, with a covered auction platform, three types at shops with godowns, cattle shed, canteen, rest houses, etc., but the yard is lying unused or least used for nearly one decade as the trade has been resisting to shift from old market Collectorganj and other grain markets functioning in and around the area due to various reasons, such as, (1) the marketing functions are performed in the old market (Collectorganj) by dealing in local primary produce and bringing commodities from outside the Kanpur Regulated Market, (2) the arrival from outside market for local sale is usually not permitted in the new market yard resulting in less of business and (3) the old market is well laid out and adequate for handling business.[5]

Prof K.N. Rai[6] and others were paper present on "Growth and Development of Regulated Markets in Haryana". The study was based on the secondary as well as primary data collected exhaustively from different sources. Detailed time series data on total production of principal agricultural commodities and the quantities arrived in the regulated markets for sale were collected from different issues of the 'Statistical Abstract of Haryana' published by the Economic and Statistical Organization, Government of Haryana. Similarly, data on number of Regulated Markets, number of sub-yards, average number of villages served buy Regulated Markets and sub-yards, square kilometer of area served per Regulated Market, capacity of state owned warehouses, capacity of cold storage and road length per square kilometer of area were also collected from 'Statistical Abstract of Haryana'. Information on state-wise average area served per Regulated Market at different point of time were scanned from different issues of the publication 'Agriculture in Brief' published by the Directorate of Economic and Statistics, Government of India. Data on income of Market Committees for different years were accumulated from Agricultural Marketing Board, Haryana, Chandigarh. Detailed data on administrative setup and amenities available in Agriculture Produce Market, Hisar were collected through personal visit to the office of Executive Officer, Market Committee, Hisar. Data were subjected to the tabular analysis and compound growth rate to draw inferences of the study. Conclusions of the study were made as under.

In Haryana all the agricultural produce markets and market sub-yards have been brought under the umbrella of the Punjab Agricultural Produce Act 1961. Over the years, it is not only that number of Regulated Markets have increased but, the infrastructure facilities required for orderly marketing of agricultural produce have grew at much faster rates. It is interesting to note that all the infrastructure facilities available in Regulated Market of Hisar fulfill the requirements of the Market Regulation Act, a rare phenomenon. Contrary to the general belief that arrivals of agricultural produce in regulated markets have failed to keep pace with increased production, in Haryana. Over the years, production of different agricultural commodities and their arrivals in Regulated Markets have had a close relationship. The significant growth in market arrivals of principal agricultural commodities and the significant correlation in production and market arrivals presented in the text are the testimony of the direct relationship between production and market arrivals in the state. Over the years, with increased arrivals, the income of Market Committees have also increased significantly which is being ploughed back for further expansion of infrastructure facilities including development of rural roads conducive to the interest of primary producer and ultimate consumers.

Dr. Dibakar Naik[7] studied a sustainable agriculture needs a strong regulatory measures for agricultural marketing in Orissa. Orissa is rich in agricultural resources with wide climatic diversity. The farm mechanization is marginal and adoption of yield raising technology is at the take-off stage. In such environment, provision of a dependable market support to the farmers of Orissa has played a key role for sustaining agricultural development. Orissa, which is far behind from the other states in respect of its agricultural productivity, needs strong regulatory measures for the marketing of its farm produce.

A large number of intermediaries are involved in the process of marketing of farm produce in Orissa and they are appropriate in paying a major share of the price paid by the consumers. With the rise in the number of intermediaries in the market channel, the share of the producer gets reduced. In the existing marketing scenario, the producers receive 61.63 per cent to 75.42 per cent of the price paid by the consumers for rice, 53.78 per cent to 72.56 per cent for groundnut, 21.57 per cent to 54.44 per cent for turmeric, 48.75 per cent to71.76 per cent for ginger, 52.94 per cent to 68.26 per cent for inland fish, 40.68 to 53.57 per cent for marine fish and 50 to 77.5 per cent for milk in Orissa market.

The number of markets brought under regulation is 31.40 per cent in Orissa as compared to 100% in Panjab, 62.52 per cent in Haryana, 72.15 per cent in Gujarat and 73.80 per cent in Andhra Pradesh. Through the Regulated Markets have been the major instruments of protection to the farmers against non-ethical market practices employed by the traders, many of the markets have shown uneven results, as the farmers, particularly the small ones, continue to sell their products within the village itself to the local traders. Those who bring the produce to the markets do not often sell in the market yard, resulting in the expected regulated markets not being realized by the farmers.

Markets and market practices in Orissa are more traditional. As estimated, there are about 1250 Primary and 76 Wholesale Market (including terminals) in the state as against 26,806 Primary and 6934 Wholesale Assembling Markets in India.

The strategy of Regulated Market should cover the facilitating functions, which includes:

(i) Regulated Market Committee should expand its activities of procurement, processing, grading and even exporting directly at the market committee level so that the farmers can be benefited in getting remunerative prices.

(ii) The Market Committee should give guarantee for the purchase of farmer's produce advancing money for their immediate needs, processing of the produces and arranging for marketing at the next point and making the final payment.

(iii) The growers should have major representation on the committee-determining price of the produce in the Regulated Market.

(iv) Facilities like market-yard, bank, trading floor, grading and storage for all commodities should be improved in the Regulated Market.

(v) The commodities like milk, egg, poultry, fruits and other agricultural produce should come to the Regulated Market.

Dr. S. Swamidoss[8] paper published on "Regulatory Framework for Agricultural Marketing". The paper suggests that the Market Committee should establish market yards at village level that is easily accessible to the farmers to market their produce. Further during the harvest seasons the government and publicity media should emphasis on the importance and benefits of Regulated Markets with the view to motivate the farmers to market produce through Regulated Markets. The importance and functions of the Regulated Markets should be discussed at the Grama Saba meeting in order to create the awareness among the Farmers (Meeting at the Panchayat Level). Thereby the Regulated Markets would achieve success in its functioning as the important markets channel of farmers.

Dr. M. N. Waghamare[9] and others have published a paper on Seasonal Variations in Arrival, Disposal and Prices of Crossbred Cows in Regulated Markets. The Marketing of livestock is complicated by religious and sentimental considerations especially in the case of cows. The glut of marketable crossbred cow in market may lower their prices and so the farms return. The paper has made an attempt to analyze seasonal variation in arrival, disposal and prices of crossbred cows in Regulated Markets of Western Maharashtra. The Krishna Valley (Satara and Sangli districts) considered for the study is a developed region for crossbred cows in Western Maharashtra. Out of the 18 cattle markets controlled by APMC in the Satara, Sangli Districts, only two Regulated Markets viz; Karad and Phaltan from Satara and Islampur from Sangli district were selected purposively selection based on sizeable transactions. The data obtained from APMC were analyzed by working out averages of arrivals, disposal and prices of crossbred cows. Correlation analysis between arrival, disposal and pries of animal was carried out.

The arrivals of crossbred cows in Regulated Markets were higher in winter but the disposal and prices were higher in summer. The arrival and prices showed positive correlation. The prices and disposal showed opposite direction indicating increasing relationship between price and demand for crossbred cows. The positive partial correlationship between price and arrivals indicate that supplies of crossbred cows were increased with prices. The negative partial correlation between disposal and prices of crossbred cows in summer of 1991-92, 1992-93 and rainy season of 1991-92, 1992-93 indicate a decreasing trend in disposal for increased prices. The multiple correlation analysis of arrival, disposal and prices revealed that the arrival and disposal of crossbred cows were determined by non-price consideration.

Dr. K.D. Sharma[10] and others studies a research topic on 'Market Regulation for Agricultural Growth and Food Security in Hills'. The study pertains to the hill state of Himachal Pradesh and examines the marketing scenario of food grain commodities and supports the argument how the efficient marketing can enhance the purchasing power of the farmer which is so crucial for increasing farm production and it has been observed that Green Revolution technology has made little headway in hill agriculture due to lack of complementary market infrastructures. The study is based upon the primary data collected from 120 farm households and 50 traders selected randomly from six potential food grain producing regions and markets located in Paonta, Nalagarh, Una, Indora, Bilaspur and Mandi regions in Himahchal Pradesh. The data on various aspects of production and marketing of food grain commodities were collected through survey method during the year 1997-98 and analyzed by employing tabular as well as functional techniques. The authors have also analyzed the existing and future demand and supply scenarios of food grain commodities and estimated that the state has a substantial exportable surplus of around 2 lakh tones of maize, which may increase further in the future. However, the state has remained moderately deficit in wheat that can easily be mopped up through regulated and efficient marketing. Ironically, the shortages in the rice and pulses would continue to aggravated further unless timely efforts are put forth to arrest the declining trends in these commodities.

The study further contemplates the inbuilt inefficiencies in the marketing of different food grain commodities as most of the commodities are being marketed through unorganized channels dominated by local traders. These channels, notwithstanding lower price, get preferences over organized functionaries owing to merits of outright purchases, prompt payments and personal contacts with the farmers. On the contrary, the regulated and established food grain markets within the state are found beset with number of imperfections and wanting amenities and infrastructural facilities for promoting orderly and efficient marketing. Consequently, the Regulated Markets have been attracting low arrival despite substantial farm surpluses recorded around. The authors have tried to design an organized and efficient marketing model in which inputs delivery and sale of farm commodities can be integrated at one place. According to them, the formation of a multi-purpose co-operative society at the village level at the behest of Panchayats or dedicated NGO may go a long way in delivering farm inputs and conducting outright assembling and marketing of farm commodities. Further, the infrastructural facilities in the Regulated Markets also need to be improving for achieving efficiency in operations and prompt clearances. Moreover, the State Marketing Board should be strengthened. More autonomy and adequate staff should be provided to monitor and promote orderly marketing in the state.

B.C. Nair[11] and others "Regulated Marketing Network for Farm Produces in Goa: An Analysis" have attempted to examine the Regulated Markets' structure and composition, growth performance of market functionaries, viz., commission agents, trader (Class A, B & C), weighmen and assistants to traders, market arrivals and prices of selected commodities-namely coconut, betel nut and cashew nut and the association between market arrivals and prices of those three commodities. The study was based on secondary data for a period of 10 years (1990-1999). The necessary data were gathered from the yearly-published annual reports of Goa Agricultural Produce Market Committee, Margao-Goa. In order to achieve the objectives of the study, a log-linear regression model as well as correlation technique has been employed to compute the growth rates and assess the relationship between markets arrivals and prices respectively.

The analysis revealed that all the market functionaries except commission agents and weigh men have registered a positive annual average growth over the study period. Similarly, a positive correlation was found between market arrivals and prices with regard to coco9nut and betel nut and a negative relationship was observed between market arrivals and prices of cashew nut. The overall analysis have come to the conclusion that the farmer producers were benefited with the regulated markets and the regulated markets seem to have been working in the interest of the farmers producers in the State of Goa. It was further noticed that the cashew nut producers were not much encouraged by the regulated markets. Some of the important suggestions made in this paper were; to introduce co-cooperative marketing societies and to establish some more sub-market yards at the different important agricultural producing areas so as to enable the farmer producers to avail the regulated market facilities and better returns for their produces.

B. B. Beohar[12] and others "Performance of Krishi Upaj Mandi in the Context of Arrival and Price of Agricultural Commodities in Madhya Pradesh" have conducted a study keeping in view the two specific objectives (1) Position of marketing functionaries (Strength). (2) To study the arrival and price of selected commodities. (Inter and Intra years variation in arrivals and prices).

Krishi Upaj Mandi, rahli of Sagar distt. (MP) was selected purposively for investigation. The study was based on secondary data related to year 1986-87 to 1996-97. Two major crops, Paddy (Kharif) and Gram (Rabi) were selected for study. Simple average and percentage statistical tools were applied for analyzing the data.

It was observed from the study that the increasing number of different market functionaries was observed in the mandi, which shows good performance of arrival quantity of different commodities and found in the increasing order during the last decade.

It was found that the arrival of soybean was directly related with the annual production of soybean in the study area. The lowest and highest arrivals of soybean in the mandi were recorded in the year 1987-88 and 1996-97 respectively (2592 qtl. and 306479 qtl.). The study further revealed that, during a peak season, the quantity of soybean arrival was maximum (35%) as compared to mid and off seasons. It was also derived from the study that the continuous hike in prices of soybean can be attributed to increasing demand of soya oil and also changes in demand due to increase in real income of people and the general inflationary trend of the economy.

For gram crop, it was observed that intra year arrivals varied from 69.4 per cent in November to 114.80 per cent in the month of August, indicating a very wide rage in inflow of gram in selected months. The annual quantity of arrival was directly co-related with the production. It was also found that variability in arrivals was much higher than those of prices, indicating that, the quantity of market arrivals was not the only factor, which determines the prices in the region. The study suggested that there must be a good infrastructure in the mandi. A committee be constituted to negotiate the problem/disputes occurred with farmers and marketing officials/agents and other functionaries. There mush is an arrangement of immediate payment to the farmers.

J. P. Misra[13] and others have studied, "Study of Regulated Markets in Utter Pradesh and Role of Rajya Krishi Utpadan Mandi Parishad in Development of the Markets". 265 Regulated Markets and regulated sub-markets are 382 of UP. Out of which 184 main market yards, 72 fruit and vegetable market yards, 165 hat/pats (rural markets) and 3 fish market were constructed.

The total arrivals of agricultural produce varied from 199.91 lakh M.T. in 1988-89 to 249.05 lakh M.T. in 1998-99 while the total income receipt by Regulated Markets was observed to be 45.99 crore rupees in 1988-89 and Rs. 248.12 crore in 1998-99. Commodity wise arrivals of agricultural produce in U.P. was 6.34 lakh M.T. for Rice, 28.94 lakh M.T. for paddy, 0.07 lakh M.T. for Jowar, 1.53 lakh M.T. for Bajra, 1.54 lakh M.T. for Maize, 21.16 lakh for wheat, 3.01 lakh M.T. for Gram, 7.85 lakh M.T. Gur, 5.47 lakh M.T. Mustard and 2.02 lakh M.T. Arhar during the marketing season of 1997-98.

Several welfare schemes were implemented by the Mandi Samittee to assist the producer-sellers like personal accident, insurance scheme, Khalihan Fire Insurance Schemes, distribution of store bins, scholarship to the meritorious son/daughter of farmers for the agricultural education etc. In all the constructed mandies different facilities were also made available to the producer sellers/traders namely weight bridges, drinking water, cattle shed, cleaning and sanitation, auction platform, storage facilities, bank, post office, police station, kisan bhawan, telephone, primary health centre etc. but still there were certain problems existing in these markets which need quick reform.

On the basis of forgoing discussion, the major problems identified are (i) Limited posts in large infrastructure of Mandi Parishad affect adversely the smooth functioning related markets, (ii) Functions of Directorate of Agricultural Marketing Board may be demarcated, (iii) Separation of the posts of Director Agricultural marketing and Director Mandi Board may be more useful for Agricultural Marketing Department in the State, (iv) Disputes between Government and traders may be tried to settle quickly. It is suggested that the Government should take action to remove these problems so that farmers and consumers may get full benefits of the regulatory measures.

Nasir Husain[14] and others studied, "Impact of Regulation of Markets on Price Spread of Potato: A Case Study in U.P.", 50 potato growers and 20 traders from Kidwai Nagar Regulated Market and Barra unregulated market in Kanpur district (UP). The main objectives of the study were (i) to estimate the price spread and producer share in consumer's rupee and (ii) to ensure remunerative prices to the producers.

The main findings of the study were that the price spread of potato i.e., producers share in consumer's rupee in Regulated Market was higher. The producer's share in consumer's rupee in Regulated Market was 71.25 per cent and 62.72 per cent in unregulated market. The wholesaler's margin cost of marketing and retailers margin in Regulated Market were 5.54, 13.35, and 9.86 per cent respectively and corresponding figures were 9.15, 16.34 and 11.79 per cent respectively in unregulated market. The marketing efficiency in Regulated Market was 2.48 per cent and 1.68 per cent in unregulated market. The farmers faced major marketing problems higher in unregulated market than that in Regulated Market.

It has been concluded that the Regulated Market was able to get higher producer share in consumer's rupee and marketing efficiency due to all facilities available in the Regulated Market. Thus, even after positive impact of the new wholesale market yards on farmer's share, the implications for further improvement in the marketing system through regulatory measures were not over looked. In this regard the following policy has been suggested.

Firstly, government policy must be rationally modified and clearly spelt out. The market must have storage and transportation facilities necessary to handle the increased marketable surpluses and to reduce marketing margins. The operations of the government agencies and co-operatives need to be made effective. Comprehensive measures were directed to reduce the cost and margin of intermediaries, improving marketing condition and strict enforcement of regulatory measures, which were needed to ensure correct weighment, standard weights and measures, proper grading, competitive price etc. to help to the producers for the production of several agro-products.

B.V. Pagire[15] and others studied, "Progress and Performance of Rahuri APMC: A Case Study", the market development activities in the States of Maharashtra, which have made an impact on structure, conduct and performance of Regulated Markets. The evaluation of these markets focuses a light on success and achievements. The study was carried out to evaluate the progress and performance of Rahuri APMC, in Ahemdnagar district. In this district, there are 13 Regulated Markets of which Rahuri is forefront in business activities. The Rahuri APMC has been ideally outlined in an area of 5.24 ha. The market provides all essential amenities to the farmers and traders. The market has spacious auction-platform, sale hall and cattle shed. The Rahuri APMC has two sub yards with all amenities.

The Rahuri APMC provides the marketing services to about 50,000 cultivators spread in more than 87 villages. The APMC is famous for cereal and vegetable marketing. Recently, it has come up as a major onion market in the district. The APMC Rahuri has brought up 41 commodities within its orbit of regulation. It has made a steady progress since its establishment in 1950 in both the arrivals of agricultural produce and turnover. The percentage share of the Rahuri APMC in the total district turnover showed a steady progress. Increasing trend was observed in number of market functionaries over the year. The APMC, Rahuri is accruing good profits since 1995-96. It has planned the developmental works worth Rs. 1.08 crore with an expectation of Rs. 5 to 6 lakhs annual increase thereafter in income. Thus, the Rahuri APMC is successful in fulfilling the aspiration both of agriculturists and traders and progressing steadily and rapidly with an eye on future development.

RESEARCH METHODOLOGY

Keeping in view the significance of regulated agricultural market, the present study tries to examine the performance of Siddheshwar Market Yard, Solapur established in Solapur city on the Mumbai-Hydrabad Highway. It provides a number of services to agricultural produces such as transportation, storage, processing, grading, standardization, packaging, credit supply, market information, insurance, advertisement etc.

Agricultural commodities, fruits and vegetables, flowers, dry straws and cattle are the main arrivals in the market yard from surrounding area of Solapur city, district and other adjacent states such as Karnataka and Andhra Pradesh. Siddheshwar Market Yard is being managed by Krushi Utpanna Bazar Samitee (Agricultural Produce Market Committee). APMC fixes the market charges, prices of agricultural commodity, involved to solve the complaints from buyers and sellers. This market yard provides vegetables, fruits and flowers to the sub-markets in the Solapur city; thereby residents get fresh agricultural commodities at reasonable prices. It is beneficial for agricultural producer, traders and consumers also.

STATEMENT OF THE PROBLEM

Efficient marketing of farm produce is vital to the economic development of a predominantly agricultural country like India. Incentive in the form of a ready market and a remunerative price for all produces are essential to enthuse the farmer to produce more with quality. The defects and malpractices in existence in most of the market can be removed by the exercise of proper control over the markets and the establishment of Regulated Markets in the country could do this. About 90 percent of agricultural markets all over the country are regulated under the Agriculture Produce Market Acts provide this incentive. The cultivator can now enter the market with confidence, offer his produce for sale on his own terms and get the maximum return from it. In such Regulated Markets selling of his produce is no longer an ordeal for the cultivator.

There has been a considerable improvement in the field of agricultural marketing. Rationalization of market changes, protections of the regulation, increase in the number of sellers bringing their produce to these markets, a change in the socialistic behavior, powerful and economically well trading sections towards the illiterate, ignorant, indebtedness and economically back-ward cultivators be constant diversion of their attention to the canons of fair trading. Market practices are regulated and market functionaries are brought under the control, correct weighment is ensured by periodical inspections and verifications, machinery too the settlement of disputes between traders and sellers reliable and up to date market news are available to the sellers, proper market yard nearby with full facilities like sheds, cart parking, water and water tanks, cisterns and troughs for cattle water huts, with taps, rest houses, latrines, canteens, bathrooms to the farmers, better grading and warehousing facilities the open auction sale method, unjustified trade deductions are eliminated, suitable quality standards, and standard terms for buying and selling, reliable statistics of arrivals, stock and prices are easily maintained marketing societies which render all assistance to the needed agriculturists. Thus regulation of markets has been a boon to the agriculturists. It has not only introduced a system of regulated market but has also developed area of North and South Solapur. North and South Solapur talukas have been treated as one unit.

OBJECTIVES OF THE STUDY

Following were the main objectives of the study:

1. To overview the progress of agricultural Regulated Market in India and to access the urge of policy measures.
2. To study the perspectives of market regulations.
3. To study the historic needs, structure and operations in general and Solapur in particular.
4. To study the progress of arrivals of major food grains, fruits and vegetables.
5. To study the progress of value transaction of major food grains, fruits and vegetables.
6. To study the variations in the arrival of major food grains, fruits and vegetables.
7. To study the variations in the sales of major food grains, fruits and vegetables.
8. To examine trends behavior in the price of major food grains, fruits and vegetables.
9. To study the performance of sub-markets in the market yard.
10. To examine the financial performance of APMC, Solapur.

HYPOTHESES

The following hypotheses are set forth in the present study.

1. An arrival of the food grains and their prices are negatively associated during the study period.

   H_0 : $r = 0$

   H_1 : $r < 0$ (one way)

2. An arrival of the fruit and their prices are negatively associated during the study period.

H_0 : $r = 0$

H_1 : $r < 0$ (one way)

3. An arrival of the vegetables and their prices are negatively associated during the study period.

   H_0 : $r = 0$

   H_1 : $r < 0$ (one way)

4. Arrivals of the major food grains in the regulated market have shown positive trend (performance) during the study period.

   H_0 : $b = 0$

   H_1 : $b \neq 0$ (two way)

5. Arrivals of the fruits in the regulated market have shown positive trend during the study period.

   H_0 : $b = 0$

   H_1 : $b \neq 0$ (two way)

6. Arrivals of the vegetables in the regulated market have shown positive trend during the study period.

   H_0 : $b = 0$

   H_1 : $b \neq 0$ (two way)

7. Value transaction of the major foodgrains in the regulated market have shown positive trend during the study period.

   H_0 : $b = 0$

   H_1 : $b > 0$ (one way)

8. Value transaction of the fruits in the regulated market have shown positive trend during the study period.

   H_0 : $b = 0$

   H_1 : $b > 0$ (one way)

9. Value transaction of the vegetables in the regulated market have shown positive trend during the study period.

   H_0 : $b = 0$

   H_1 : $b > 0$ (one way)

10. The total turnover of Sub-markets have shown positive trend during the study period.

    H_0 : $b = 0$

    H_1 : $b > 0$ (one way)

11. The Solapur Agricultural Produce Market Committee has financially sound during the study period.

    H_0 : $b = 0$

    H_1 : $b > 0$ (one way)

12. Price fluctuations of the food grains, fruits and vegetables has controlled or minimized by Solapur APMC in the regulated market during study period.

This hypothesis will be studied by employing sub-period analysis.

SELECTION OF THE COMMODITY

Foodgrains, fruits, vegetables, flowers, straw and cattle are the main arrivals in the market yard. Out of these foodgrains, fruit and vegetables arrivals are considerable and selection of the commodities was based on their volumetric sharing in the total turnover of the market yard. The selected of regulated commodities were as under:

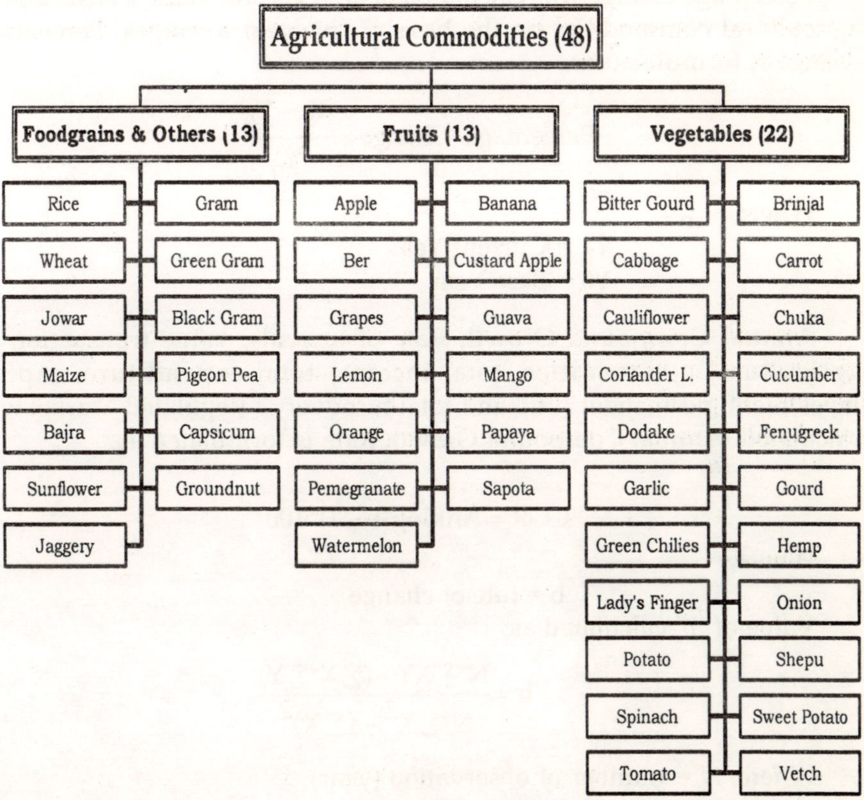

PERIOD OF THE STUDY

As pointed out earlier, the present study aims to examine the progress made by the APMC, Solapur. In this direction the period, from 1983-84 to 2002-03 is selected for analysis. The entire time series is divided into four periods; each period carried five years, viz., 1983-84 to 1987-88, 1988-89 to 1992-93, 1993-94 to 1997-98 and 1998-99 to 2002-03.

DATA BASE ANALYSIS

The analysis is mainly based on secondary sources of the data. The statistical data on relevant information was collected from the Annual Reports published by APMC, Solapur. Additional information was also collected from the books, journals, Govt. publications library and Internet etc.

DATA ANALYSIS

Keeping in a view the objectives of the study, some appropriate statistical techniques such as five-year average of arrivals, value transaction, etc. (Y1+Y2+Y3+Y4+Y5 divided by 5, Where, Y = year).

Percentage change was calculated of arrivals and value transaction of agricultural commodities on the basis of five-year averages. Percentage change is formulated as,

$$\text{Percentage Change} = \frac{Y_1 - Y_0}{Y_0}$$

Where,

Y1 = Current Year,
Y0 = Base Year

Annual Compound Growth Rate of arrivals, value transaction of agricultural commodities, total income, total expenditure, capital investment, permanent fund and total turnover of Regulated Market was calculated. Annual Compound Growth Rate is formulated as,

$$\text{CGR} = \text{Antilog}(b - 1)*100$$

Where,

b = rate of change

Value of 'b' calculated as:

$$b = \frac{N*\Sigma XY - (\Sigma X*\Sigma Y)}{N*\Sigma X^2 - (\Sigma X)^2}$$

Where, N = number of observation (year)

Dispersion analysis is used for measuring the fluctuations in the prices of agricultural commodities. Standard deviation shows a absolute variability and co-efficient shows relative variability use for the analysis. Coefficient of range is defined by the ratio:

$$RR = \frac{X_{max} - X_{min}}{X_{max} + X_{min}}$$

Standard deviation calculated as:

$$S.D.=\sqrt{\frac{\sum X^2}{N}-\left(\frac{\sum X}{N}\right)^2}$$

Coefficient of variation, abbreviated as C.V. Thus,

$$C.V.=\frac{\sigma}{\bar{X}}*100$$

Where,

σ = Standard Deviation

$\bar{X}$ = Mean

Pearson's Coefficient of Skew ness calculated as:

$$PSk=\frac{\bar{X}-Mo}{s}$$

Co-relation analysis is used for studying the relationship of the variables and explained how strong or weak relationship between these variables (i.e. variables are, total income and total expenditure, prices and arrivals) exists. Karl Pearson's formula is used for measuring the coefficient of correlation (r) between two variables as,

$$r=\frac{N^*\Sigma XY-(\Sigma X^*\Sigma Y)}{\sqrt{N^*\Sigma X^2-(\Sigma X)^2}*\sqrt{N^*\Sigma Y^2-(\Sigma Y)^2}}$$

Regression analysis studies relationship between independent and dependent variable. In this study, linear regression (bet. X and Y) relationship was calculated as:

Regression Equation Y on X,

$$Y = a + bx$$

$$byx=\frac{\Sigma(x-\bar{x}^*y-\bar{y})}{\Sigma(x-\bar{x})^2}$$

$$a=\frac{\Sigma Y}{N}-byx^*\frac{\Sigma X}{N}$$

or

$$a=\bar{Y}-byx^*\bar{X}$$

Where,

Y = dependent Variable (i.e. arrivals, total exp. etc,)

a = intercept
b = slope of the line
X = independent variable (i.e. time, prices, income etc.)
y bar = arithmetic mean of y series,
x bar = arithmetic mean of x series

Regression Equation X on Y,

$$X = a' + b' Y$$

b′ calculated as:

$$bxy = \frac{\Sigma(x-\bar{x}^{*}y-\bar{y})}{\Sigma(y-\bar{y})^2}$$

a′ calculated as:

$$a' = \frac{\Sigma X}{N} - bxy^{*}\frac{\Sigma Y}{N}$$

Where,

X = dependent Variable (i.e. arrivals, total exp.etc,)
a′ = intercept
b′ = slope of the line
Y = independent variable (i.e. time, prices, income etc.)
y bar = arithmetic mean of y series,
x bar = arithmetic mean of x series

Moreover, some graphic devices was used for data analysis i.e. progress of arrivals and value transaction by bar graph, regression trend line fit by line graph of arrivals and value transaction of agricultural commodities, pie chart was also used for showing the shear of each sub-market in the total turnover etc.

CHAPTERS IN BRIEF

First chapter is entitled 'Research Methodology and Data Base', it consists of role of agricultural regulated markets and significance of the study, main features of regulated markets, advantages of regulated markets, organization of regulated markets and constitution of market committee. It has also included research methodology and review of literature.

Second chapter is on, 'Market Regulation Act in Maharashtra', this chapter has included composition of market committee as per 1939 and 1963 acts, staff schedule of market committee, and license fee for market functionaries. This chapter also involved the progress of regulated markets in Indian in general and Maharashtra in particular.

Third chapter explains, 'The Profile of APMC, Solapur', this chapter deals with the jurisdiction of APMC, staffing pattern, composition of the executive body, working charges, regulated agricultural commodities and agricultural regulated market committee in Solapur.

Fourth chapter deals with, 'Analysis and Interpretation of Marketing Activities of APMC, Solapur: Foodgrains', this chapter consists of progress of arrival as well as value transaction in respect of foodgrains. This chapter also deals with the price behaviour of food grains and variations among the major foodgrains during under the study.

Fifth chapter is relating to, 'Analysis and Interpretation of Marketing Activities of APMC, Solapur: Fruits', this chapter consists of growth of arrival as well as value transaction in respect of fruits in the regulated market. This chapter also deals with the price behaviour of fruits and variation among the major foodgrains during under the study.

Sixth chapter is on, 'Analysis and Interpretation of Marketing Activities of APMC, Solapur: Vegetables', this chapter has analyzed the progress in arrival as well as value transaction in respect of vegetables. This chapter also deals with the price behaviour and variations among the vegetables during the under the study.

Seventh chapter explains, 'Analysis and Interpretation of Marketing Activities of APMC, Solapur: Correlation between Arrival and Prices', this chapter has been analyzed the association with arrival and their prices relating to the foodgrains, fruits and vegetables in the regulated market during under the study.

Eight chapter deals with, 'Analysis and Interpretation of Marketing Activities of APMC, Solapur: Regression Analysis of Regulated Commodities', this chapter has been tested some hypotheses like arrival of regulated commodities in the regulated market have shown positive trend, value transaction of regulated commodities also have shown positive trend during the study period. Some other hypotheses have been tested in respect of financial performance of sub-market of APMC.

Ninth chapter is entitled, 'Financial Turnover of APMC, Solapur', this chapter has been analyzed the growth rates and variations in the financial turnover of sub-markets in the APMC. This chapter also deals with average share of sub-markets in the total turnover in the Solapur APMC during the study period.

Tenth chapter is on, 'Conclusion and Suggestions', in this chapter some conclusions have derived on the basis of earlier chapter and also some suggestions have been made for better performance of APMC.

NOTES

1 L. D. Vaikunthe, Regulatory Frame work for Agricultural Marketing: A Case Study of APMCs in Karnataka, *Indian Journal of Agricultural Marketing*, Conf. Spl., Vol. 14, No. 3, pp. 1-2, Sept-Dec., 2000.

2. P.C.Bansil, Regulated Market System in Meeting Urban Food Needs, *The Bihar Journal of Agricultural Marketing.*, Vol. V, No. 3, p. 270, July-Sept., 1997.

3. Sadhu & Singh, Fundamental of Agricultural Economics, Himalaya Publishing House, p. 254, Mumbai, 1999.
4. V.P.S.Arora, Agricultural Marketing Scenario in India, *The Bihar Journal of Agricultural Marketing*, Vol. V, No. 3, p. 281, July –Sept., 1997.
5. P.C.Bansil, "Regulated Market System in Meeting Urban Food Needs", *The Bihar Journal of Agricultural Marketing*, Vol. V, No. 3, p. 278-279, July –Sept., 1997.
6. K.N.Rai, S.P. Singh, S.N.Singh & V.P. Mehta, research article on, "Growth and Development of Regulated Markets in Haryana", *Indian Journal of Agricultural Marketing*, Conf. Spl., Vol. 14, No. 3, p. 25, 31 & 32 Sept-Dec. 2000.
7. Dibakar Naik, research article on, "Sustainable Agriculture Needs a Strong Regulatory Measures for Agricultural Marketing in Orissa", *Indian Journals of Agricultural Marketing*, Conf. Spl., Vol. 14, No. 3, p. 33 & 34, Sept-Dec., 2000.
8. Dr. S. Swamidoss, research article on "Regulatory Framework for Agricultural Marketing", *Indian Journal of Agricultural Marketing*, Conf. Spl., Vol. 14, No. 3, pp. 34 & 35, Sept-Dec., 2000.
9. Dr. M. N. Waghamare, research article on "Seasonal Variations in Arrival, Disposal and Prices of Crossbred Cows in Regulated Markets", *Indian Journals of Agricultural Marketing*, Conf. Spl., Vol. 14, No. 3, p. 35, Sept-Dec., 2000.
10. Dr. K.D. Sharma, Research Article on, "Market Regulation for Agricultural Growth and Food Security in Hills", *Indian Journals of Agricultural Marketing*, Conf. Spl., Vol. 14, No. 3, p. 35, Sept-Dec. 2000
11. B.C. Nair, Research Article on, "Regulated Marketing Network for Farm Produces in Goa: An Analysis", *Indian Journals of Agricultural Marketing*, Conf. Spl., Vol. 14, No. 3, p. 37, Sept-Dec. 2000.
12. B.B.Beohar, Research Article on, "Performance of Krishi Upaj Mandi in the Context of Arrival and Price of Agricultural Commodities in Madhya Pradesh", *Indian Journals of Agricultural Marketing*, Conf. Spl., Vol. 14, No. 3, p. 39, Sept-Dec., 2000.
13. J. P. Misra, Research Articule on, "Study of Regulated Markets in Utter Pradesh and Role of Rajya Krishi Utpadan Mandi Parishad in Development of the Markets", *Indian Journals of Agricultural Marketing*, Conf. Spl., Vol. 14, No. 3, pp. 39 & 40, Sept-Dec., 2000.
14. Nasir Husain, Research Article on, "Impact of Regulation of Markets on Price Spread of Potato: A Case Study in U.P.", *Indian Journals of Agricultural Marketing*, Conf. Spl., Vol. 14, No. 3, p. 42, Sept-Dec. 2000.
15. B.V.Pagire, research article on, "Progress and Performance of Rahuri APMC: A Case Study", *Indian Journal of Agricultural Marketing*, Conf. Spl., Vol. 14, No. 3, p. 42, Sept-Dec., 2000.

REFERENCE

Agrawal A.N. and Kundan Lal (1996), "Agricultural Problems of India", Vikas Publishing House, New Delhi.

Desai R.G. (1998), "Agricultural Economics", Himalaya Publishing House, Bombay.

Jugale V.B. (2000), "Sugarcane Pricing: Policy, Procedure & Operations", Atlantic Publishers & Distributors, New Delhi.

Govil R.K. & Tripathi B.B. (1996), "Agricultural Economy of India", Kitab Mahal, New Delhi.

Khusrao A.M. (1968), "Leading in Agricultural Development", Allied Publishers, Bombay.

Kohls R.L. (1967), "Marketing of Agricultural Products", Macmillan, London.

Mathur P.N. & Kulkarni A.K., Some Observations on the Working of Regulated Market at Ghoti Dist. Nasik.

Memoria C.B. (1999), "Agricultural Problem of India", Kitab Mahal, New Delhi.

Sadhu & Singh (1999), "Fundaments of Agricultural Economics, Himalaya Publishing House, Bombay.

Soni R.N. (1992), "Leading Issues in Agricultural Economics", S. Chand & Co., Delhi.

Bhatia D.K. & Gupta Vijay (1986), "Business Statistics", Vikas Publishing House Pvt. Ltd., New Delhi.

Puri V.K. (1992), "Elements of Business Statistics", Himalaya Publishing House, Bombay.

Rangaswamy R. (2000), "A Text Book of Agricultural Statistics", New Age International (P) Limited, Publishers, New Delhi.

Monga G.S. (2000), "Mathematics and Statistics for Economics", Vikas Publishing House Pvt. Ltd., New Delhi.

Indian Journals of Agricultural Marketing (2000), Vol. 14, No. 3, (Conference Special), Nagpur.

Indian Journal of Agricultural Economics (2000), Vol. 55, No. 3 (Conference Number), Mumbai.

The Bihar Journal of Agricultural Marketing (2000), Vol. VIII, No. 1, Patna.

Solapur Agricultural Produce Market Committee, Solapur, Annual Report for the year (1995-96).

http: www.agmarket.nic.in/reforms.htm.

http: www.agriwatch.com/statichtml/apmcreport.htm.

http: www.msamb.com/english/apme/default.htm.

2

MARKET REGULATION ACT IN MAHARASHTRA

EMERGENCE OF MARKETING REGULATION IN INDIA

Marketing legislation for regulating the marketing activities for the farm produce is traced to as early as 1886 when Hyderabad Residency Order led to the first Regulated Market in India. Berar passed 'The Cotton and Grain Market Law' in 1897. The Indian Central Cotton Committee appointed by the Government of India in 1918 recommended the regulation of cotton market on the lines of Berar Act. The Government of Bombay enacted 'The Bombay Cotton Market Act' in 1929. The first Regulated Market was established under this Act in Dhutia in West Khandesh in 1930. After that a series of regulated cotton markets were setup in Karnataka and Maharashtra.

The Royal Commission on Agriculture setup in 1926 by the British Government suggested for establishing the Regulated Markets on the Berar pattern. Market legislation was enacted by Bombay (1927, 1939), Hyderabad (1930), Central Provinces (1932, 1939), Madras (1933), Baroda (1934), Panjab (1941) and Patiala (1947). Reorganization of States (1956) resulted in the transfer of Regulated Markets operating under respective State Acts. Now all the States/Union Territories except Jammu and Kashmir, Mizoram, Sikkim, Andaman and Nicobar Islands, Daman and Diu and Lakshadweep have implemented APM(R) Acts in their respective states.

Various Committees and Commissions have stressed regulation of markets for agricultural products viz. The Banking Enquiry Committee (1931), The Congress Agrarian Reforms Committee (1947), The Rural Marketing Committee of the Indian National Congress (1948), The Planning Commission (1952), The All India Rural Credit Survey Committee (1954) and The Agricultural Production Team sponsored by the Ford

Foundation (1959) etc. Various Review Committees on the working of the Agricultural Produce Markets Acts have recommended to bringing all agricultural produce including horticulture, forestry and livestock under the scope of Agricultural Produce Market Acts.

AGRICULTURAL REGULATED MARKETING ACTS

Though the state intervention in marketing began in India with the promulgation of the "Regulation of the Branch of Judicature, Bombay" in 1829, the idea of regulation of markets could take practical shape only at the end of the 19th century. It was all, in the interest of cotton textile industry of the United Kingdom that the British Government in India went to regulate marketing of cotton only. The passing of the Berar Cotton and Grain Market Law 1897 envisaged for the first time regulation of other agricultural products in addition to cotton though in practice cotton alone remained regulated. In 1917, the Government of India appointed a Cotton Committee. It recommended regulation of cotton markets in India on the lines of Berar markets. In view of its recommendations the Government of Bombay enacted the Bombay Cotton Market Act in 1927, which could be considered the first piece of legislation in the country attempting regulation of market in order to evolve sound market practices for the benefit of both the producers and the traders. However, the provisions of this Act were applicable to cotton only; regulated markets for other commodities could not see in light.

The Royal Commission on Agriculture (1927) provided the torchlight for developing agricultural marketing. In its report submitted in 1928, enhanced the prosperity of the agriculturist. The success of any policy of general agricultural improvement was dependent on a large degree of the facilities, which the agriculture community had at its disposal for marketing to the best advantage. It recommended that the establishment of Regulated Markets for agricultural commodities could only remove the defects.

The Central Agricultural Marketing Department prepared a model bill in 1928 for regulation of agricultural commodities. The provinces were to draft their own legislation on this line. Accordingly, the erstwhile Bombay Province passed the Bombay Agricultural Produce Market Act in 1939. The feature of this Act was that, for the first time in the history of legislation on agricultural marketing, it has provided for regulation of marketing of a large number of agricultural produce including all produce of agriculture, horticulture and animal husbandry.

In order to assess the success of this Act, the Government of Bombay appointed a committee under the Chairmanship of M. L. Dantwala on 19th August 1950. The Committee recommended that the consolidation of gains accrued under the Act should be given priority over the expansion of the Regulated Markets. In 1955-56 another expert Committee under the Chairmanship of T.G. Shriname was appointed. The government accepted its report along with 173 recommendations. In 1963, the need was felt to amend the Agricultural Produce Market Act, because of the application of different Acts in different regions within the newly constituted Maharashtra State. On 12th December 1963, a comprehensive Act was passed in the State assembly. But the provisions of this modified act were brought in force from 15th June 1967. The Act of 1963 was amended first in 1968, and again in 1970.

The modified Act of 1963 has 66 sections and it is more precise in the matter of prohibiting trade allowances, penalties for the defaulters' market funds, etc. Its rules were amended in 1967. There are in all 122 rules.

OBJECTIVES OF MARKET ACTS

The Government of Bombay decided in 1929 to enact the Bombay Agricultural Produce Market Act with the avowed objective of securing the best possible price to which the agriculturists were entitled after deducting the legitimate expenses of marketing and after taking into account the price that could be realized for the same quality of the produce in the terminal market. The main objective of the Act was to quote the Finance Minister who moved the Bill was "to see that the agriculturist who takes his produce to the market is dealt with fairly by the dalal or the broker who stands between the agriculturist and the purchaser or the purchaser over the agriculturist."

The statement of objectives of the Maharashtra Agricultural Produce Market Act, 1963 was read as under: "At present there are different laws in force in different parts of the State relating to the regulation of buying and selling of the agricultural produce. The Bombay Agricultural Produce Market Act, 1939 is in force in the Bombay area of the State of Maharashtra. The Central Provinces and Berar Cotton Market Act, 1935 applies to the Vidarbha area of the State of Maharashtra and the Hyderabad Agricultural Produce Market Act (No. 2 of 1939 F) operates in the Hyderabad area of this State. Government had appointed in 1955 a Committee to go into the details of the system of the regulation of buying and selling of agricultural produce and advice government. The Committee made several suggestions for the effective implementation of the Bombay Agricultural Produce Market Act, 1939. After taking them into consideration the present bill is prepared.

AREA OF OPERATION

The Bombay Act, 1939 provided for the operational jurisdiction limits of regulation specifying 'market area' proper and 'market yard', 'market area' referred to the entire revenue limits of a taluka or a part thereof for which the market committee is created. 'Market Yard' means the principal market yard and sub-market yard where actual marketing takes place. The

Maharashtra Act 1963 continued with the some connotations. Moreover, The Bombay Act, 1939 covered with the marketing of 86 commodities in which 36 agricultural commodities, 11 fruits, 5 vegetable varieties, grass and fodder and 9 animal husbandry products for the purpose of regulation. The Maharashtra Act specified in its schedule; 40 agricultural commodities, 8 vegetables, 17 fruits mainly along with other commodities for the purpose of regulation. The Maharashtra Agricultural Produce Market Act, 1963 was amended in 1972 and the amendment regulated marketing of 110 commodities in which are 2 times, 15 cereals, 13 pulses, 12 oilseeds, 17 fruits, 10 animal husbandry products, etc.

COMPOSITION OF MARKET COMMITTEE

Table 1 refers to the composition of the Market Committee. The Bombay Act, 1939 did not provide equal representation to the farmers' and the traders' interests. Many a time the representative of the local self-authority happens to be a merchant. Under Bombay Act, 1939 the Mamlatdar was a government nominated member of the Market Committee. His nomination was cancelled in Maharashtra Act, 1963.

Table 1
Composition of Market Committee as per 1939 and 1963 Acts

		Legal Provision Made Under			
		Bombay Act, 1939			
Sl. No.	*Constituents*	*Minimum*	*Maximum*	*Maharashtra Act, 1963*	*Maharashtra Act, 1968 Amendment*
1.	Agriculturists	6	8	7	-
2.	Credit Co-Op. Societies	-	-	-	7
3.	Village Panchayat	-	-	-	3
4.	Traders	3	4	3	3
5.	Chairman Of Taluka Purchase Sale Union	-	-	1 or 2	1
6.	Chairman Panchayat Samiti	-	-	1	1
7.	Local Self Authority	1	1	1	1
8.	Zilla Parishad	-	-	-	1
9.	Govt. Nominee	2	2	-	-
10.	District Agriculture Officer	-	-	1	1
	Total	12	15	15 or 16	18

Only the representatives from traders' and farmers' constituencies got the voting right in Maharashtra Act, 1963. By the 1968 amendment the total membership has been raised to 18.

Tenure of Office

The nominated Market Committee would be of two years and that of the elected body three years. The elected body would come into operation from the date on which the names of the elected members of the market committee are published in the government Gazette. The Maharashtra Act, 1971 provided for publication of the names of the elected Market Committee in the Gazette as soon as the results are out. The Bombay Act, 1939 did not make provision for removal of any member of Market Committee but this was provided for in the Maharashtra Act, 1963.

Chairman and Vice-Chairman

No qualifications specified for both the posts. Their honorarium is fixed at Rs. 3,600- per annum. They hold the office for 3 years in the normal course.

Meetings

The Maharashtra Act prescribes that there should be at least one meeting within 60 days. There was no such legal binding in Bombay Act, 1939. The amended Act 1971, in addition to putting an obligation of holding a meeting at specified interval, prescribes a quorum of minimum 10 members for every meeting.

Sub Committee

The Maharashtra Act, 1963 provides for the appointment of various sub committees, for example, Committee for Recruiting the Staff, their promotions and construction of work as also a sub committee for settling disputes in the transactions arising on account of price, weight, payment, etc. The Vice-Chairman of the Market Committee is the ex-official Chairman of this sub committee. Disputes are to settle on the spot by a Board of Arbitrators.

Powers and Duties of Market Committee

The Market Committee has the following powers and duties to perform:

(1) To implement the provisions of the Act, the rules and Bye-laws;

(2) To regulate the entry of the persons and of vehicular traffic in the market;

(3) To supervise the behavior of those who enter the market for trading purpose;

(4) To grant, renew, refuse, suspend or cancel licenses;

(5) To provide for settling disputes arising out of any kind of transactions connected with the marketing of agricultural produce and all matters connected thereto;

(6) To prosecute persons for violating the provisions of this Act, the rules and Bye-laws made there under;

(7) To maintain and manage the market, including admission to and conditions for the use of the markets;

(8) To regulate marketing of agricultural produce in the market area and the payment to be made in respect thereof, weighment or delivery of the agricultural produce;

(9) To acquire, hold and dispose of any movable or immovable property including any equipment necessary for the purpose of efficiency carrying out of its duties;

(10) To collect and maintain, disseminate and supply information in respect of production, sale, storage, processing, prices and movement of agricultural produce, as may be required by the Director of Agricultural Marketing;

(11) To take all possible steps to prevent adulteration and to promote grading and standardization of the agricultural produce as may be prescribed;

(12) To enforce the provisions of this Act and Rules, Bye-laws and conditions of the license granted under the Act; and

(13) To perform all such other duties as may be prescribed.

Administrative Staff

The Market Committee is empowered to employ Secretary and other required staff. The Secretary is the Chief Executive Officer to implement the resolutions of the Market Committee. He is responsible to the Chairman for keeping the accounts and for rendering of all the returns. Also he lays down the duties of other members of the staff. He can attend the meeting of the Market Committee. He has power of inspection, seizure of material inspection of weights and measures and maintenance of account books and market premises. The success of the market depends much on the ability of the Secretary. Staff of the Market Committees is given in Table 2.

The other administrative staff consists of the deputy and assistant secretaries, accountant, treasurer, inspector, head clerk, clerks, peons, watchmen, drivers, gatemen, etc. Market Committee appoints them. Moreover, for each big sub-market yard additional posts of assistant secretary, one clerk, and one peon and for each small sub market yard one clerk and one peon are allowed on the establishment of the same by the Market Committee. It can be observed that for A and B class market committee grader, head peon and head watchman are the additional posts specially provided. Every Market Committee has to follow strictly the given staff schedule. The Director of Agricultural Marketing, Maharashtra State, Pune is empowered to approve the staff of the Market Committee, to accept the resignations if any, or to approve the termination orders issued in case of any incumbent of the Market Committee. Staff of the Market Committee is given in Table 2.

Table 2
Staff Schedule of a Market Committee

Sl. No.	Particulars	*Class of the Market Committee with Income Range*					
		A	B	C	D	E	F
		1 lakh & above	50,000 to 1 lakh	30,000 to 50,000	20,000 to 30,000	10,000 to 20,000	Below 10,000
1.	Secretary	1	1	1	1	1	1
2.	Asstt. Secretary	1	1	-	-	-	-
3.	Accountant	1	1	1	-	-	-
4.	Inspector	1	1	1	1	1	-
5.	Supervisor	1	-	-	-	-	-
6.	Jr. Cleark	6	4	3	1	1	1
7.	Stat. Asstt.	1	-	-	-	-	-
8.	Watchman	1	1	1	-	-	-
9.	Peon	3	2	2	1	1	1
	Additional Staff						
1.	Head Peon	1	1	-	-	-	-
2.	Head Watchman	1	1	-	-	-	-
3.	Grader	1	1	-	-	-	-
	Total	19	14	9	4	4	3

EDUCATION AND TRAINING

As per the recruitment rules (Maharashtra Agricultural Produce Market, 1967) the qualification of the officers' is graduation and that of senior grade staff matriculation. No qualification is prescribed for the junior grade staff. The Market Committee deputes its staff for training by taking a bond to serve the Market Committee for at least three years after completion of training.

FINANCIAL POSITION OF THE MARKET COMMITTEE

The Market Committee gets income mainly from the licence fee and market fee. The additional source of income includes subsidy and loan from the State Government and fine from the market functionaries.

License Fee

The Bombay Act, 1969 and the Maharashtra Act empower the Market Committee to charge license fee on the market functionaries as per the rates in Bye-laws. The Market Committee can cancel or suspend a license for a specified period for breach of law.

Market Fee

The Bombay Act, 1939 authorized the Market Committee to levy fees on the transactions in agricultural produce. The said fee was payable by the seller according to the weight of the produce. The Maharashtra Act 1963 authorized the Market Committee to collect the market fee from the purchases and the fee is charged as valorems.

Table 3
The Schedule of Minimum and Maximum Rates of Market Fee

Sl. No.	*Commodity*	*Minimum Rates*	*Maximum Rates*
1.	Agricultural Produce other than poultry	15 paise per Rs. 100	30 paise per Rs. 100
2.	Poultry	5 paise each	10 paise each
3.	Sheep and Goats	25 paise each	50 paise each
4.	Cattle	Rs 1 on sale proceeds	Rs. 1 per Rs. 100 sale

Supervision Charges

As per circular No. CMR/R/11/SUP/GESS dated 30-11-1972 of the Director of Agricultural Marketing, Pune and Section 34 of the Maharashtra Amendment Act, 1972 the supervision cost is to be recovered from every purchaser. This supervision cost is 5 paise per Rs. 100 of sale proceeds.

Other Sources

Section 17 of the Bombay Act and 48 of the Maharashtra Act limit the penalty upto Rs. 500 with imprisonment for the trader who trades without licenses. Market Committee earns income from its surplus amount invested in government securities. It sells specific forms and documents and gets a paltry sum.

External Source

A Market Committee raises money by way of borrowing. It gets loans for the expenditure incurred on acquisition of land, construction of building and provision of basic amenities in the market yard. The State Government sanctions loan after considering its technical and economic aspects and on the ground of its repayment in 15 annual installments at the interest rate of 5.5%. The Maharashtra Act 1963 provided for creation of Permanent Fund of the Market Committee to pay loan and interest. Market Committee gets subsidy to meet its initial expenditure. If the annual income of the Market Committee is below Rs. 10,000 it gets a subsidy of Rs. 3,000. If the annual income is more than Rs. 10,000, the subsidy is Rs. 5,000.

SETUP OF MARKET YARD AND SUB-MARKET YARD

The Bombay Act, 1939 and the Maharashtra Act, 1963 provided for the establishment of the principal market yard and, if necessary the sub market yard. The market area may be the revenue limits of taluka or more than one taluka, if necessary. Section 16 of the Bombay Act, 1939 empowered the government to acquire a suitable land for the Market Committee and to transfer the land to the Market Committee on payment of the acquisition cost. The Maharashtra Act continues the provision. The Market Committee is responsible for constructing buildings and providing other amenities in the market yard. It allocates plots to the licensed traders for construction of their shops and godowns.

BYE-LAWS OF THE MARKET COMMITTEE

Detail provisions regarding actual regulation of the agricultural marketing are made in the Bye-laws of Market Committee, which should be approved by the Director of Agricultural Marketing, Maharashtra State, Pune. The Bye-laws include objectives of the Market Committee and define and restrict its activities. Section 27 of the Bombay Agricultural Produce Act, 1939 authorized the Market Committee to make the Bye-laws for the regulation. The Maharashtra Agricultural Produce Market Act, 1963 is wider in scope. The Bye-laws pertain to the procedure regarding license, license fee, sale of agricultural produce, weighment, warehousing of the produce and the administration.

PRINCIPAL MARKET AND SUBSIDIARY MARKET

Every Market Committee is established according to the Maharashtra Agricultural Produce Market Act, 1963. The declaration to that effect and the notification of it in the gazette are also noted in the Bye-laws. The market area of the principal market and sub market area also laid down in the Bye-laws.

LICENSE FOR THE MARKET FUNCTIONARIES

In accordance with the provision of Section 6 of the Maharashtra Act, 1963 nobody is allowed to function in the market area in respect of the declared agricultural produce unless the license fee is obtained by him.; The Market Committee is authorized under Section 7 of the Maharashtra Act, 1963 to grant or renew a license for the use of any place in the market area for marketing of the agricultural produce or for operating therein as a trader, commission agent, broker, processor, weightman, measures, surveyor, warehouseman or in any other capacity in relation to the marketing of agricultural produce.

RATES OF MARKET FEE

Section 13 of the Maharashtra Act, 1963 prescribed the minimum and maximum rates of market fees. The Market Committee is competent to fix suitable rates within the said limits and make the provision for it in its own Bye-laws.

RATES OF LICENSE FEE

Rates of license fee for market functionaries are shown in Table 4.

Table 4
Rates of License fee for Market Functionaries

Sl. No.	*Market Functionaries*	*Rates of License Fee*	*Renewal Fee*
1.	Adatya (Commission Agent)	100	90
2.	Trader A Class	100	90
3.	Trader No. 1	100	100
4.	Trader B Class	50	45
5.	Trader C Class	80	80
6.	Trader D or No. 3 Class	75	75
7.	Broker (Dalal)	40	35
8.	Processor A Class	100	90
9.	Processor B Class	50	45
10.	Surveyor	15	14
11.	Warehouseman A Class	15	14
12.	Weightman A Class	10	9
13.	Weightman B Class	5	5
14.	Assistant to Trader/Adatya	5	4
15.	Cartman	20	19
16.	Assistant to Cartman	5	4
17.	Hamal A Class	3	2
18.	Hamal B Class	2	2

Source: Annual Report of the Agricultural Produce Market Committee, Solapur.

SALE, WEIGHMENT AND WAREHOUSING

Form No. 12; based on Section 18 of the Maharashtra Act, 1963 is the receipt of agricultural produce brought for sale to the Adatya. Standards of weighments are prescribed in the Bye-laws; they are presented in Table 5.

Table 5
Weight and Measurement

Sl. No.	*Produce*	*Weight & Measurement*
1.	Agricultural Produce	Quintals
2.	Fruit, Vegetables, Coconut	Numbers
3.	Eggs, Hens, Cattle, Goat	Numbers
4.	Wool, Black Pepper, etc.	Kilograms
5.	Butter, Milk	Kilograms/Litres
6.	Skin and Hides	Kilograms

The Bye-laws prescribe that every trader/licenser must have weights and measurements to weigh at least one quintal, other small weights up to 100 k.g. and one litre is essential for a trader.

MARKET CHARGES

Market functionaries such as trader Adatya, dalal, weighman, surveyor, cartman, etc have to charge their rates in accordance with the provisions in the Bye-laws. The market prescribes the rates of commission, dalali, weighing charges, hamali, godown rent, sieving and grading charges, etc.

per quintal or number. The market functionary is prohibited from charging more than the rates fixed.

ADMINISTRATION

Meeting

Procedure regarding the issue of notice of meeting, conducting the meeting, procedure of voting, minutes of the meeting and implementation of the resolutions passed in the meeting are laid down in the Bye-laws.

Sub Committees

The Market Committee is authorized as per the provisions in the Bye-laws, to appoint the following sub committees.

(i) Disputes Sub Committee

(ii) Staff Selection Sub Committee

(iii) License Sub Committee

(iv) Building Sub Committee

(v) Gradation Sub Committee

The Market Committee can determine the number of each of the Sub Committee and assign the duties.

Expenditure

In addition to the expenditure incurred by the Market Committee on permissible items under the provisions in the Maharashtra Act, 1963 and the rules there under, the Market Committee is authorized to spend from the market fund on the following items.

(i) Annual subscription of Maharashtra State Federation of the Market Committees, Pune;

(ii) Study tour;

(iii) Exhibition, wall papers, bulletins and magazines in the cause of regulated marketing; and

(iv) Market research.

Staff

The Market Committee employs a Secretary and such other officers and staff as may be necessary for the management of the market. The Market Committee makes Bye-laws for pay scales attached to various posts, for grant of leave including leave allowance, for maintaining the provident fund, for prescribing the conditions for pension and gratuity and for undertaking the welfare activities.

Others

The Market Committee prescribes various forms for conducting the marketing activity smoothly.

PROGRESS OF REGULATED MARKETS

The Royal Commission on Agriculture (1927) recommended regulation of the markets to help the farmers to do away with the rampant malpractices and help them to realize better returns. Many State Governments went in for Regulated Markets and there were about 250 such markets at the time of Independence[1].

After independence the Planning Commission in its first and subsequent Five Year Plans emphasized the vital role played by the Regulated Markets in promoting on orderly marketing of farm produce in the country and urged various states that had not enacted the necessary legislation to do so and to regulates the market there under.

The Five Year Plans visualized the regulation of new markets throughout country. In November 1955, an All India Conference on Marketing and Co-operation was held at Hyderabad. It made many recommendations for accelerating the progress of regulation during the Second Five Year Plan and for effective improvement in the working of the markets already established.

The Conference on Marketing and Co-operation held at Jaipur in February 1956, while endorsing the major recommendations of Hydrabad Conference, particularly stressed the need for accelerating the place of regulation of the uncovered marketing centres during the Second Plan period.

At the beginning of the Third Five Year Plan, legislation for establishment of markets was in force in nine states. Later on four, other states also had enacted the Agricultural Produce Markets Acts. During the Fourth and Fifth Plan periods, the remaining states viz. Assam, Kerala, Jammu and Kashmir also enacted legislation after reorganization and by the end of 1980; Agricultural Produce Marketing Acts were in force in 18 states and 4 Union Territories.

PROGRESS OF REGULATED MARKET IN INDIA

Keeping in view the significance of Regulated Markets emphasis was made to develop and expand agricultural regulated market in India during planning period. As a result, the number of regulated market has increased sharply. There were 283 regulated markets in 1950-51, which rose to 450 in 1955-56, indicating 59.0 percent change in the growth during 1950-56. Subsequent period showed that number of Regulated Markets increased rapidly. In 1960-61 there were 700 Regulated Markets in which further rise of 2803 had been added in 1971-72 and further addition was made by 3819 in 1980-81.

Moreover, it also showed the number of Regulated Markets in India further increased to 6217 and to 7177 in 2000-01. The progress of Regulated Markets in India is given in Table 6, which indicates that the overall progress of agricultural Regulated Markets indicated that agricultural Regulated Markets have been increasing in India.

Table 6
Progress of Regulated Markets in India

Year	*No. of RMs*	*% Change*
1939	122	—
1950-51	283	131.97
1955-56	450	59.01
1960-61	700	55.56
1965-66	1012	44.57
1970-71	2803	176.98
1975-76	2938	4.82
1980-81	3819	29.99
1990-91	6217	62.79
2000-01	7177	15.44
2003-04	7418	3.36
2005-06	7566	2.00

Source: Various Report of Economic Survey, Govt. of India.

However, it also indicates that uneven temporal growth rates in agricultural marketing during 1950-51 to 2000-01. For example number of Agricultural Regulated Markets have increased by 59.01 percent during 1950-51 to 1955-56, which were recorded to 176.98 during 1965-66 to 1970-71.

While the period 1990-91 to 2000-01 showed marginally improvement in the number of Regulated Marketing (15.44). However, overall performance of Regulated Markets showed impressive during 1939 to 2005-06 i.e. number of Regulated Markets raised from 122 to 7566. Thus, in relative term, the overall change recorded at 6102 per cent.

PROGRESS OF REGULATED MARKETS IN MAHARASHTRA

The Act provides for establishment of Market Committees in the State. These Market Committees are engaged in development of market yards for the benefit of agriculturists and the buyers. Various agricultural produce commodities are regulated under the Act. At present there are 290 APMCs with main markets and 593 sub markets. The map given bellow shows districts covered under various divisions.

APMC PROFILE

The MSAMB has 7 Divisional offices at Pune, Nasik, Aurangabad, Latur, Amravati, Nagpur and Ratnagiri for proper co-ordination of the activities of all APMCs in the State.

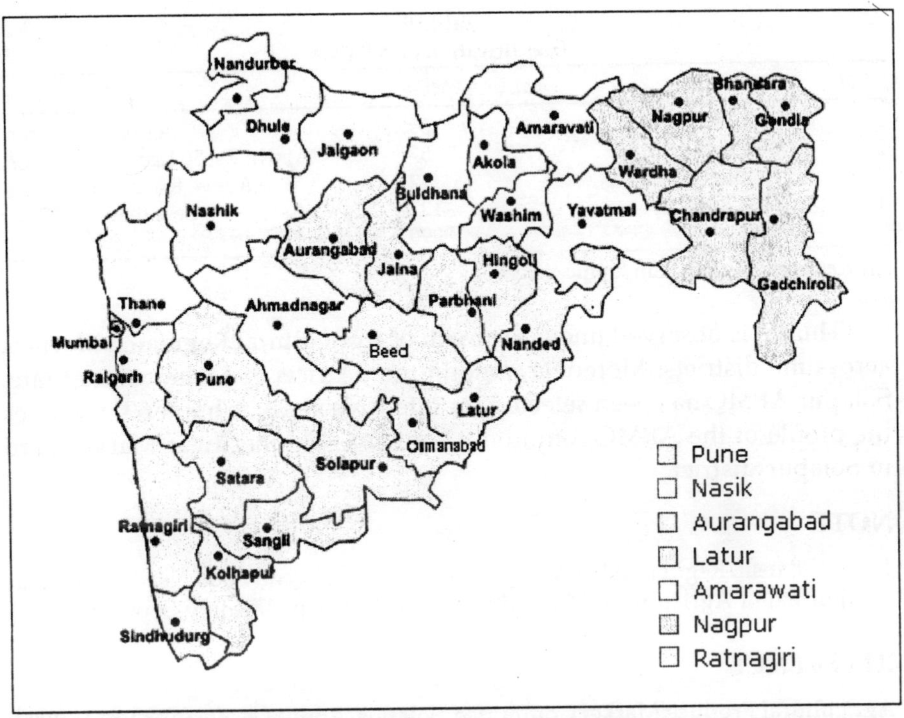

Source: www.msamb.com/apmc/profile.

Table 7
Division of APMC in Maharashtra

Ratnagiri Division	Raigad, Ratnagiri, Sindhudurg
Pune Division	Pune, Satara, Solapur, Sangli, Kolhapur
Nasik Division	Nasik, Ahmednagar, Jalgaon, Dhule, Nandurbar,Thane, Mumbai
Amaravati Division	Amaravati, Akola, Buldhana, Washim, Yavatmal
Aurangabad Division	Aurangabad, Jalna, Parbhani, Hingoli
Latur Division	Latur, Osmanabad, Beed, Nanded
Nagpur Division	Nagpur, Bhandara, Gondia, Wardha, Chandrapur, Gadchiroli

Source: www.msamb.com/apmc/profile.

Table 8
Division wise break-up of APMCs is as follows

No.	*Division*	*Main Market*	*Sub Market*
1.	Amravati	55	91
2.	Aurangabad	33	69
3.	Konkan	20	48
4.	Latur	46	86
5.	Nagpur	43	72
6.	Nasik	51	106
7.	Pune	42	121
	Total	290	593

Source: www.msamb.com/apmc/profile.

Table 9
Classification of APMCs

Sl. No.	APMC Class	No. of APMCs	Total Income
1.	"A" Class	39	Above Rs.1 Crore
2.	"B" Class	57	Above Rs. 50 Lac to Rs. 1 Crore
3.	"C" Class	72	Above Rs. 25to Rs. 50 Lac
4.	"D" Class	122	Less than Rs. 25 Lac
	Total	290	

Source: www.msamb.com/apmc/profile.

Thus, it is observed uneven growth of Agricultural Regulated Markets across the districts. Moreover, among the districts of Maharashtra State, Solapur APMC has been selected for intensive study. Chapter 3 discusses the profile of the APMC commonly known as Siddheshwar Market Yard in Solapur district.

NOTE

1. P.C.Bansil, Regulated Market System in Meeting Urban Food Needs, The Bihar Journal of Agricultural Marketing, Vol. V, No. 3, p. 271, July-Sept., 1997.

REFERENCE

Agricultural Produce Market Committee, Solapur, Annual Report 1982-83 to 2002-03.

Ambapkar G.B. (1986), "Functioning of Regulated Market-A Case Study of Shahu Market Yard, Kolhapur", M. Phil Dissertation, Shivaji University, Kolhapur.

Bhanumate C.S. (2000), "Functioning of Regulated Market: A Case Study of Krishi Utappanna Bazar Samiti, Solapur (Siddheshwar Market Yard)", M.Phil. Dissertation, Shivaji University, Kolhapur.

Kulkarni B.D. (1977), "Functioning of The Regulated Markets in Solapur District with Special Reference to Groundnut, Tur and Bajra", Ph.D. Thesis, Shivaji University, Kolhapur.

Rupanawar V.D. (1993), "A Study of Agricultural Marketing and Its Impact on Rural Development (Case Study of Agricultural Marketing of the Taluka Malshiras of Solapur District)", Ph. D. Thesis, Shivaji University, Kolhapur.

The Bihar Journal of Agricultural Marketing, Vol. VIII, No. 1, 2000, Patna.

Indian Journals of Agricultural Marketing, Vol. 14, No. 3, (Conference Special), 2000, Nagpur.

http: www.msamb.com/english/apmc/profile.htm.

http: www.msamb.com/english/apmc/default.htm.

http: www.agriwatch.com/statichtml/apmcreport.htm.

http: www.agmarket.nic.in/reforms.htm.

3

PROFILE OF THE A.P.M.C., SOLAPUR

AGRICULTURAL PRODUCE REGULATED MARKETS IN SOLAPUR DISTRICT

Maharashtra State has developed seven divisions for administrative purposes; viz. Ratnagiri (Konkan), Pune, Amaravati, Aurangabad, Latur, Nashik and Nagpur. Solapur district is one of the districts of Pune Division. Solapur district, situated on the south east fringe of the Maharashtra State, lying on the ridge in the Bhima and Sina basins and almost the whole of it is drained by either Bhima River or its tributaries. The district has an area of 15,057 sq. km. The area of Solapur district lies between latitudes 17^0 to 19^0 and longitudes 75^0 to 77^0, on the Southern border of Maharashtra. It lies in the centre of a large plain 1,800 feet above mean sea level. It is surrounded by Gulbarga and Bijapur districts of the Karnataka State to the South, Sangli district to the South-West, Satara district to the West, Pune district to the North-West, Ahmednagar district to the North and Osmanabad district to the East. The district headquarter, is situated at a Solapur city.

The State Government has established one Market Committee for each taluka. For this purpose North and South Solapur talukas have been treated as one unit so that there exist in all 10 market committees in the district. Except in case of Malshiras and Madha talukas respectively due to their importance as commercial centres. Details regarding the establishment of these Market Committee and the sub-markets in each taluka is presented in Table 1. It can be seen from Table 1 that in the whole of the district, there are in all 9 sub-markets, Barsi and Kurduwadi Market Committees each claiming one-third of the number.

It means that Solapur district has not made much headway in decentralizing the marketing activity through creation of market points, which can be regularly supervised.

Table 1
Agricultural Regulated Market Committees in Solapur District

Sl. No.	Sub-Divisions	Date of Establishment	Sub-market location
1.	*Solapur*		
	1. Solapur	12/08/1959	–
	2. Barsi	01/01/1948	Vairag, Yedsi, Talwale
	3. Akkalkot	15/11/1951	Dudhani
2.	*Pandharpur*		
	1. Pandharpur	01/07/1947	–
	2. Malshiras (Akluj)	02/03/1950	Natepute
	3. Sangola	25/07/1960	–
	4. Mangalwedha	19/05/1965	–
3.	*Madha*		
	1.Madha (Kurduwadi)	01/05/1995	Madha, Modnimb, Tembhurni
	2. Karmala	01/01/1948	Jeur
	3. Mohol	29/12/1954	–

Source: B. D. Kulkarni's, Ph.D. theis on "Functioning of The Regulated Markets in Solapur District with Special Reference to Groundnut, Tur and Bajra" page-32.

Moreover, it seemed that, on the basis of the respective date of establishment of the Market Committee, the order of seniority are: Pandharpur, Barsi, Karmala, Akluj, Kurduwadi, Akkalkot, Mohol, Solapur, Sangola and Mangalwedha. It is to be particularly noted here that though Pandharpur claims to be the oldest Market Committee, it lagged behind Barsi in making a headway in the regulation of market activities so that Barsi has come out to be the most developed Market Committee in the district.

Before the establishment of Siddheshwar Market Yard; Busar market of agricultural commodities was in Jodbhavi Peth and Mith Galli, Fruit and vegetable agricultural commodities market was in Kasturba Mandai and Rani Laxmibai Mandai. Cattle market was in Kanna Chowk. Moreover, Kadaba (fodder) market was in Balives, Bandanves. Agricultural producers were exploited in these markets. Therefore, it was felt to establish Agricultural Regulated Market in Solapur City. Consequently Solapur Krushi Utppanna Bazar commonly known as Siddheshwar Market Yard was established in 1967. After that market yard areas had developed and all type of agricultural commodities market migrated in Siddheshwar Market Yard, Solapur. Cattle market was migrated from Khanna Chowk in 1969, Kadaba (fodder) market was shifted from Balives and Bandan Ves, Jodbhavi Peth and Mith Galli in 1972 and Fruit and Vegetable market was shifted from Kasturaba and Laxmi Market in 1987. Buying and selling business of all above regulated agricultural commodities are being conducted in the place of Shri Siddheshwar Market Yard, Solapur.

COMPOSITION OF MARKET COMMITTEE

As per provisions of the Maharashtra Act, 1963, the executive body of the APMC consists of 18 representatives drawn from different constituencies as laid down by the Act and the Bye-laws.

The APMC thus, consists of representatives of agriculturists, traders, co-operative societies, local self-government and the State Government. Care has been taken in the Act itself to see that majority of the members of the Market Committee are agriculturists. The details are as given in Table 2.

CHAIRMAN OF THE MARKET COMMITTEE

Chairman is the executive head of the Market Committee. He provides leadership and shapes to the development of market yard. Normally, the persons prominent in public life try to assume this coveted position. Motives may be many. To gain leadership and thereby enhance one's image in public life may be the primary motive.

Table 2
Composition of the Executive Body of the APMC, Solapur

Sl. No.	*Name of the Constituency*	*Number*
1.	Agriculturists	10
	(a) Co-operative Societies	7
	(b) Gram Panchayat Constituency	3
2.	Traders	3
3.	Co-operative Marketing Societies	1
4.	Local Authority	2
	(a) Taluka Panchayat Chairman	1
	(b) Solapur Municipal Corporation Representative	2
5.	Government nominees	2
	(a) District Agricultural Officer, Z. P., Solapur	1
	(b) District Deputy Registrar Co-operative Societies, Solapur	1
	Total	18

Source: Annual Report of the Agricultural Produce Market Committee, Solapur.

Such people would like to 'hold on' to the position as long as possible, but may not put their head and heart into the development of the market. Continuation of such people for a long time into this high office, thus, causes a setback to the market development. On the contrary, assuming the office even for one term by a really interested and dynamic personality helps in changing the face of the market of the APMC, Solapur, should be assessed.

STAFF POSITION

As the scope and extent of the activities of the Market Committee widened with lapse of time, it recruited more persons to look after the routine work. Staff position can be seen from Table 3 with these additions, the APMC, Solapur had 109 persons on its staff looking after the principal yard and sub market yards.

Table 3
Staffing Pattern of the APMC, Solapur

Sl. No.	*Category*	*Number*
1.	Secretary	1
2.	Asstt. Secretary	1
3.	Accountant	1
4.	Supervisor	1
5.	Si. C. Com Sta. Asstt.	1
6.	Clerk	60
7.	Grader	4
8.	Peons	9
9.	Others*	31
	Total Staff	109

* Others includes Watchman, Labourer, Drivers, Servear, etc.

Source: As per Table 2.

JURISDICTION OF SIDDHESHWAR MARKET YARD (APMC, SOLAPUR)

The APMC, Solapur has a very wide geographical coverage. It covers two talukas out of 11. It covers 9, 69,000 population and 1931 sq. km. of North Solapur taluka and South Solapur taluka.

Table 4
Jurisdiction of A.P.M.C., Solapur

Sl. No.	*Particulars*	*Quantity*	*North Solapur Tehsil*	*South Solapur Tehsil*	*Total*
1.	Population	Number	783000	186000	969000
2.	Area	Square K.M.	736	1195	1931
3.	Area	Hectares	68300	119500	187800
4.	Cultivable Area	Hectares	63500	111600	175100
5.	Non-cultivable Area	Hectares	4800	7900	12700
6.	Irrigated Area	Hectares	3270	7046	10316

Source: Report of Agricultural Produce Market Committee, Solapur.

It covers 1,87,800-hectare areas, out of 1,75,100-hectare cultivable area and 12,700 hectare is non-cultivable area. Irrigated area is 10,316 hectare. Details are given in Table 4. Besides this Market Committee, there are 9 others at Barshi, Akkalkot, Pandharpur, Malshiras, Sangola, Mangalwedha, Madha (Kurduwadi), Marmala, Mohol in Solapur district. But Solapur is the biggest one on the basis of area covered as also the volume of transactions.

BENEFITS OF THE APMC, SOLAPUR

The objective behind the establishment of a Regulated Market is to establish orderly conditions in the agricultural markets and thereby create environment congenial to assurance of better returns to the producer-sellers of agricultural commodities. The traders under free market conditions free the producer from the exploitation.

Siddheshwar Market Yard of Solapur has a history of 40 years. Over such a long span of time, the market yard has grown quite well. The APMC, Solapur has been able to provide adequate infrastructural facilities in Siddheshwar Market Yard and volume of transactions of agricultural produce has increased multifold. Hence, by and large, Siddheshwar Market Yard has come out as a well-developed market yard. As such, it is worthwhile to take stock of the benefits it has conferred so far on the farmers and traders.

Benefits to the Farmers

The market yard has provided a free and carefully supervised platform for conducting sale operations by the producers-sellers with their personal involvement in the operations. Various features have contributed to this vital change.

Open Auction of the Produce

The traditional system of sales under cover has been totally done away with open auction system. Farmers remain present at the time of auction and play their part in deciding whether the highest bid is to be accepted or not. Thus, they became the partners with traders in finalizing the sale price of their produce.

It appears that the traders have become a part of this practice and have accordingly changed their methods of operations. They are only concerned on the occasions with adoption of different strategies in the auction either independently or in collusion with a few other traders with an intention to get the lots at lower prices. Traders engaged in purchase and sale activity on their own particularly indulge in such activities; commission agents are normally less inclined. It is reported by the APMC authorities that generally in the auctions farmers' interests are well protected and the APMC is always aware of this.

Correct Weighment of the Consignment

Prior to market regulation, farmers were losers even in the process of weighment of their consignments as the Diwanjis (Accountant) of the private traders did the weighments and they always saw that the produce was underweighed. With market regulations, the Diwanjis have been relieved from this work and it is entrusted to the licensed weighmen. Since any trader does not employ the persons, no vested interest is developed in them in order to favour the trader at the cost of the farmer. The licensed weighmen, therefore, are careful in doing correct weighments of the consignments. Moreover, as a check on them, the APMC has appointed inspectors who work as watchdogs. This arrangement has not only relieved the farmers of their losses in weighment but also created a confidence about just weighments under the eye of the representatives of the APMC.

Well Trimmed Market Practices

The APMC has streamlined the market practices by fixing the kind and quantum of deductions from the sale proceeds payable to the farmers by traders. Traditionally prevailing undesirable deductions have been discontinued and thereby the farmers are able to get at least about 10% higher net income. Now, deductions borne by the sellers of the produce are few, moderate and reasonable. As the trader to the APMC submits a copy of the sale note, the latter is able to know whether the norms of deductions are properly observed or not.

Prompt Payments

As per earlier practice, the farmer was seldom paid his due amount by the trader immediately on conclusion of the transaction and delivery of the produce. He had to make frequent trips to the shops and receive the money in installments. He thereby incurred expenses on bus fare and refreshments, which was an inevitable cost. He had to bear for collection of his sale proceeds. A relief from this torture has been provided by the APMC's insistence of immediate payment as an obligation on the traders. The APMC also ensures about it and promptly looks into the complaints in this behalf received from the sellers. As the traders also have a realization about their obligation, they normally see that payments are done quickly. In case the amount is big, they enter into tacit understanding with the seller regarding the time and installments of payment for these suitable book entries in account books of the trader are made with mutual consent to comply with the APMC's rule of cash payment.

Settlement of Disputes

The APMC has taken all precautions to see that the sale and purchase transactions are carried through smoothly and no room is left for conflict on any account between the seller and the buyer. In spite of this, sometimes differences crop up and dispute arised. It is particularly regarding the quality of the consignment actually received and money payments to the sellers. In the history of Siddheshwar Market Yard, such occasions have not been very frequent. Moreover, whenever differences could not be bridged mutually the matter was taken to the APMC. It has a Disputes Committee established as per provisions of the Rules. The matter was referred to the Committee and the parties in conflict accepted its decision. Thus has maintained the confidence of the farmers in the effectiveness of the authority of the APMC in giving protection to them in the market.

Storage and Godown Facilities

In the age old system of marketing both the producer and trader suffered in various ways for want of adequate storage facilities. The producers could not wait for an expected price due to non-availability of proper storage facility and hence were compelled to sell their produce at the going market price. The traders, on the other hand, faced the problem of spoilage and deterioration due to stacking of consignments in open space. In the market yard, private traders have provided their own storage accommodation. Besides the, Central Warehousing Corporation, Co-operative Marketing Societies have also established their own godowns. The farmers can make use of the godowns of the Warehousing Corporation particularly for the depositing their produce and get bank loans on the strength of the warehouse receipt till the market position improved.

Before the establishment of the market yard, the traders faced an acute shortage of storage facilities, as their own premises were insufficient to store their purchases. Open stacking of goods led to considerable losses. This problem has been solved to a great extent by construction of godowns by the traders in the market yard on the plots provided at cheap rate by the APMC. Besides, godowns by the co-operative marketing societies, APMC, the Central Warehousing Corporation also have provided considerable space for storage. Availability of extensive storage facility has helped the traders to wait for some time and sell their stocks to the up country traders' at the most opportune time.

Market Intelligence

Till the active functioning of the APMC, lack of market information was the most unsatisfactory feature of the agricultural market in Solapur. Dissemination of market information is an important responsibility of the APMC. It has been fulfilling this task quite satisfactorily details of daily arrivals, sales, stocks and prices of regulated commodities are displayed in the office of the APMC. Solapur is a major jaggery market in the country. Therefore, daily information about this products arrival, sales, stocks and prices grade wise is sent to the All India Radio for inclusion in daily broadcast of agricultural prices.

In addition such details for all the regulated commodities are sent regularly to the Deputy Director of Marketing, Government of Maharashtra. Apart from this, these details are published in local dailies too. Weekly trends are also indicated through the daily newspapers of this area. The farmers also have become regular visitors to the market yard and collect necessary market information through personal contacts with traders and officers of the APMC. As a sum total of the various ways in which market details are disseminated, producers of agricultural commodities now do not grope into dark, but are prone to take their decisions regarding the supply and price of their produce. The farmers have become alert, active and enlightened.

Market information also has made the traders better informed than before. Earlier, every trader adopted secrecy about his own purchases, sales, stocks and prices. Now all these facts become well known to all. The traders not only know the market rates and arrivals but also can have a broad scenario of the entire market. Their knowledge of the market now is first hand and broad based and as a result their market decisions are more realistic. They can view the market as an aggregate and make their micro level decisions. This is certainly a significant change in the marketing system itself.

Benefits to Traders

Traders are deriving benefits from the market yard. Though market regulation is aimed primarily at conferring benefits on the producer-seller, it aims also at providing adequate infrastructure required for growth of agricultural marketing activity. Therefore, automatically even the traders also derive certain gains which otherwise were not available to them.

Conveniences of Transportation

Siddheshwar Market Yard has been located at a strategic place from transportation point of view. Arrivals of almost all the commodities in the yard are by road mostly. Location of the market yard has a good road link for the purpose as it is situated on the Bombay-Hydrabad National Highway No. 9, which is well served by the district roads and State Highways. Farmers use bullock carts, tractor trolleys and trucks to bring the produce from farm to the yard whereas the produce is sent out to up country places by the traders in truckloads. Therefore, road links to and from market yard play a significant role in carrying trade and business activities in the yard. The road network closer to the yard has been an asset to the traders and farmers.

Incidental Benefits

Banking and insurance facilities are most vital for development of trade and business. Officers of banks and general insurance companies are located within the premise of the market yard. Traders have an easy access to these institutions in close proximity of their trading premises. Moreover, their existence has helped them to conveniently utilise warehousing facility of the Central Warehouses in the market yard.

REGULATED AGRICULTURAL COMMODITIES

Establishment of Siddheshwar Market Yard was planned to provide a regulated market for trade in jowar, rice, wheat and jaggery the principal agricultural produce of the area. But gradually the market yard facilities were extended too many other products like grains, groundnuts, onions, tobacco, sheep, chilies, vegetables, fruit, cattle, goats, etc. Consequently, with the same establishment in the yard, the traders can undertake business in one or more commodities; they can thus avoid cost multiplication due to separate establishments for different commodities in the absence of a single yard.

Of all the commodities traded in the market yard jaggery, rice, wheat, jowar, etc. are the most important farm produce. Among main commodities jaggery occupies major share. It is sent out in different parts of the country. Rail facility is more useful for this purpose. Jaggery and other exportable products, therefore, can be conveniently loaded in wagons and transported to the destinations in the country at the earliest.

Table 5 is the list of agricultural commodities regulated in the market area of this Market Committee. So long as the Bombay Agricultural Produce Market Act, 1959 was applicable to Siddheshwar Market Yard, only 18 commodities were regulated, as they were the principal agricultural products of the market area. With the implementation of the Maharashtra Agricultural Produce Market Act, 1964 additional one commodity dry fodder of Jowar (Kadaba) was covered for regulation effective from 2nd April 1964. In the 1965 three commodities were further added.

Table 5
Regulated Agricultural Commodities

Sl. No.	*Names of the Agricultural Commodities*	*Date of Regulation*	*No. of Agricultural Commodities*
1.	Pod, Groundnut, Tur, Karadi, Javas, Moong, Udid, Gram, Jawar, Wheat, Rice, Bajra, Jaggery, Chillie, Cotton, Sali, Jod, Rui	17/04/1961	18
2.	Kadaba (Straw)	02/04/1965	1
3.	Goat, Sheep, Buffalo, Cow, Ox, Horse	01/04/1966	7
4.	Onion, Banana, Leaves	10/12/1965	3
5.	Maize, Turmeric, Sezamum, Coriander, Mataki, Karal	01/10/1968	6
6.	Tomato, Potato, Lemon, Grapes, Sweet Potato, Mango, Guava, Chinch, Garlic, Water melon, Kalingade, Custard Apple, Vegetables and Fruits	18/11/1976	13
7.	Varai, Sava, Chavali, Methi, Vatana, Ambadi, Arandi, Mohari, Chinchoka, Sunflower seed	16/10/1983	10
8.	Sweet lime, Orange, Chikku, Papaya, Bor, Apple, Pomegranate, Ginger,	02/06/1986	10
9.	All types of Flowers	07/05/1992	1
	Total		67

Source: Reports of Agricultural Produce Market Committee, Solapur.

In 1966, seven commodities (cattle) were again regulated. Since 1968, six commodities were regulated. Further since 1973 additional 13 commodities were covered for regulation effective from 18th Nov. 1976. In 1983, ten commodities were regulated. In 1986, eight agricultural commodities were regulated and 1992, flowers (all types of flowers) have been regulated.

Thus, year after year the number of regulated commodities and therefore, administrative workload has increased. For the sake of convenience and efficiency in operation, the APMC has opened commodity sub-markets in Solapur city. Market complex in the principal market designed by the Market Planning and Design Centre, Government of India and FAO jointly have been undertaken and the work is in progress. But the development of foodgrains market is a huge task and the same is not undertaken yet.

LICENSE FEE/WORKING CHARGES/MARKET FEE AND OTHER CHARGES

In order to keep effective control over the market activities, the functionaries are required to take license from the APMC by paying stipulated license fee for a period of one year; the license has to be renewed annually. Rates of the license fee, functionary wise were in force in 1998-99 in Siddheshwar Market Yard are specified in Table 6. The functionaries have been divided into 15 categories as (1) Commission agents, (2) Traders 'A' Class and so on. Rate of license fee is maximum at Rs. 100 per annum and levied on commission agents, traders 'A' Class, Brokers and Processors.

Table 6
License Fee Payable by the Market Functionaries

Sl. No.	*Types of License*	*Annual license fee (Rs.)*	*Renewal fee (Rs.)*
1.	Commission Agents	100	90
2.	Traders 'A' Class	100	90
3.	Traders 'B' Class	50	45
4.	Traders 'C' Class	25	20
5.	Traders 'D' Class	10	9
6.	Oil Traders 'A' Class	50	45
7.	Oil Traders 'B' Class	25	20
8.	Brokers	100	90
9.	Carting and Clearing Agents	25	10
10.	Processors	100	90
11.	Warehousemen	15	14
12.	Weighmen	10	9
13.	Coolies (Male)	3	2
14.	Coolies (Female)	2	1
15.	Assistants	5	4

Source: Reports of Agricultural Produce Market Committee, Solapur.

Class 'B' traders and oils traders 'A' Class paid Rs. 50 per annum. Coolies paid only Rs. 2 for female and Rs. 3 for male, the least charge. It is observed that the rates of license fee on all the market functionaries as they exist today are very moderate and not at all burdensome to anybody. The APMC has adhered to the economic principle of 'ability to pay' while levying these charges.

WORKING CHARGES

The APMC is authorized to fix the various market charges that need to be paid either by the seller or the buyer for the specific functions performed. The details are laid down in the law 10, Bye-law 23 of the APMC, Solapur. In fact, this is quite an important function of the APMC to serve its objective of creating orderly conditions in agricultural marketing.

The APMC not only fixes them and revised at times as per need, but also exerts to see that the functionaries scrupulously adhere them to. Such charges are to be paid in the process of carrying on of trade and business and hence they are described as 'working charges'. A detail in this respect as are in force at present is presented in Table 7 and Rates on Weighment/ Measurement of Commodities is presented in Table 8.

The charges pertain to commission, market fee, entry fee, maintenance cost, weighment, coolie work, which are essential in the sale and purchase activities they have been listed in respect of all regulated commodities in all their details.

Table 7
Working Charges of APMC, Solapur

Sl. No.	*Commodities*	*Rate (Rs.) sale proceeds per Rs. 100*	*To be recovered from*
1.	Cotton, Wheat, Rice, Paddy, Jawar, Bajra, Maize, Pigeon pea, Gram, Black gram, Green gram, Chavali, Pod, Groundnut, Seasum, Sunflower, Gur, Turmeric, Coriander, Fodder (Kadaba) Rui, Jod, Varai, Sava, Chillie, Mataki, Javas, Karadi, Hemp, Arandi, Karal, Mohari, Fenugreek, Chinchoka,	3.00	One who entrusts the work
2.	Onion, Potato, Sweet Potato, Garlic, Chinch	5.00	
3.	Tendu leaves, Banana	6.00	
4.	Mango, Lemon, Grapes, Tomato, Sweet lime, Watermelon, (All types of fruits, Vegetables & Flowers) Papaya, Water melon, Custurd apple, Pomegranate, Sapota	8.00	

Source: Reports of Agricultural Produce Market Committee, Solapur.

There is no ambiguity as to who should bear them. Both the sellers and buyers have full knowledge of their burden.

MARKET FEE

As per Bye-laws of the APMC, market fee is fixed as valuorem at 80 paise per Rs. 100/-. For transactions of cattle the rate is Re. 1/- per Rs. 100/- value. For transactions of cotton (ginned/unginned) the rate is 70 paise per Rs. 100/- value. Many other Market Committees in Maharashtra and the neighboring State of Karnataka charge the current levy of market fee.

Table 8
Rates on Weighment/Measurement of Commodities

Sl. No.	*Commodities*	*Unit*	*Rate (Rs.)*	*To be recovered from*
1.	Groundnut, Moong, Bajra, Jawar, Rice, Wheat, Tur, Gram, Udid, Maize, Turmeric, Seasum, Cotton, Chavali, Sunflower, Karadi, Sal, Karal, Javas, Matki, Rui, Varai, Methi, Sava, Vatana, Arandi, Chinchoka	Quintal	0.90	
2.	Pod, Coriander, Chillies, Onion, Potato and Tur	Quintal	0.90	One who
3.	Banana	10 k g	0.20	entrusts
4.	Tendu leaves (Measurement)	Per 1000 nos.	0.20	the work
5.	Guava, Green Chillie, Gavari, Brinjal, Lady finger, Tomato, Flowers	10 k g	0.20	
6.	Grapes	Per box	0.20	
7.	Mango, Apple, Orange, Pomegranate	10 dozen	0.45	
8.	Watermelon	Per 100 nos.	0.50	
9.	Flower	Per 100 nos.	0.25	
10.	All types of Vegetables	per 100 bundle	0.50	

Source: Reports of Agricultural Produce Market Committee, Solapur.

CONCLUSIONS

Siddheshwar Market Yard, which is the main organ of the APMC, Solapur has been pioneered by the visionary founding fathers who had faith in co-operative action. The personalities that held the key position of Chairman guided the destinies of the market committee in true spirit and saw that a well-developed regulated market for agricultural commodities takes shape. The market has taken a good shape no doubt. Siddheshwar Market Yard has now attained the status of a key centre for important agricultural products of the region. The cause of concern, however, is that market arrivals of gur and groundnuts are depressing with time mainly because of new developments on production front. This commodity feature need not, however, depress anybody. Because, the market as a whole shows a signs of healthy development. This should be taken as a merit point.

REFERENCES

Agricultural Produce Market Committee, Solapur (2003-04), Annual Report.

Ambapkar G.B. (1986), "Functioning of Regulated Market-A Case Study of Shahu Market Yard, Kolhapur", M.Phil. Dissertation, Shivaji University, Kolhapur.

Kulkarni B.D. (1977), "Functioning of The Regulated Markets in Solapur District with Special Reference to Groundnut, Tur and Bajra", Ph.D. Thesis, Shivaji University, Kolhapur.

Bhanumate C.S. (2001), "Functioning of Regulated Market: A Case Study of Krishi Utappanna Bazar Samitee, Solapur (Siddheshwar Market Yard)", M.Phil. Dissertation, Department of Economics, Shivaji University, Kolhapur.

Memoria C.B. (1999), "Agricultural Problem of India", Kitab Mahal, New Delhi.

Sadhu & Singh (1999), "Fundaments of Agricultural Economics", Himalaya Publishing House, Bombay.

http: www.msamb.com/english/apmc/profile.htm.

http: www.agriwatch.com/statichtml/apmcreport.htm.

http: www.solapur.com.

http: www.agriwatch.com/statichtml/apmcreport.htm.

http: www.msamb.com/english/apme/default.htm.

4

ANALYSIS AND INTERPRETATION OF MARKETING ACTIVITIES OF A.P.M.C. SOLAPUR: FOODGRAINS

This chapter deals with the analysis and interpretation of marketing activities of Agricultural Produce Market Committee, Solapur in terms of growth in arrival, value transaction and price behaviour of foodgrains and other agricultural commodities and also in terms of variation and other economic variables performed during 1983-84 to 2002-03.

PROGRESS OF ARRIVALS OFFOODGRAINS AND OTHER COMMODITIES

It is observed from the Table 1 that Agricultural Produce Market Committee, Solapur has been making progress in the arrivals of foodgrains and other commodities over a period of time. Thus, it reflects the fact that agricultural producers in this region prefer to sale agricultural commodities this market yard, because it ensures the reasonable price to their products as well as it is convenient to sell their products in many ways in the market yard. Among the cereals, the performance of Rice arrival is significant. It is much better than Wheat, Jowar and Maize. The arrivals of Rice was recorded 1842.45 hundred quintals during first period (1983-84 to 1987-88), which raised to 2563.95 hundred quintals during second period (1988-89 to 1992-93) and in the third period (1993-94 to 1997-98) it has marginally raised by 2974.32 hundred quintals and rapid increase to 5077.78 hundred quintals during the fourth period (1998-99 to 2002-03). Thus in relative terms, it showed arrival of Rice increased by 39.16 per cent during first period, which raised marginally by 16.01 per cent in the second period, which rapidly increased to 70.72 per cent during the third period. The performance of Rice is very significant among the cereal crops as well as other crops in the fourth period (i.e. 175.60 per cent).

Table 1
Progress of Arrival of Foodgrains

(Figure of Arrival in '00' Quintals)

Sl. No.	Foodgrains	Period I	Period II	Period III	Period IV	Percentage Change 1st	Percentage Change 2nd	Percentage Change 3rd	Percentage Change 4th
1.	Bajra	99.05	49.34	36.27	87.98	-50.19	-26.49	142.58	-11.18
2.	Black gram	99.45	93.68	136.97	120.03	-5.78	46.20	-12.37	20.69
3.	Capsicum	159.48	145.22	102.37	100.79	-8.94	-29.53	-1.51	-36.80
4.	Gram	77.47	79.78	98.97	99.95	2.99	24.05	0.99	29.02
5.	Green gram	46.13	21.05	26.37	15.62	-54.37	25.27	-40.75	-66.13
6.	Groundnut	210.44	73.34	200.41	15.04	-65.15	173.28	-92.50	-92.85
7.	Jowar	1917.60	1305.17	1377.23	2126.54	-31.94	5.52	54.41	10.89
8.	Maize	39.07	67.22	78.16	56.00	72.07	16.27	-28.35	43.34
9.	Pigeon pea	459.29	343.53	187.57	341.78	-25.20	-45.40	82.22	-25.58
10.	Rice	1842.45	2563.95	2974.32	5077.78	39.16	16.01	70.72	175.60
11.	Sunflower	146.51	125.96	305.36	8.82	-14.03	142.42	-97.11	-93.98
12.	Wheat	1131.77	1276.33	2162.97	2554.33	12.77	69.47	18.09	125.69
13.	Jaggery	806.88	2360.33	1713.64	2826.75	192.53	-27.40	64.96	250.33

Note:
(1) Period: I=1983-84 to 1987-88, II=1988-89 to 1992-93, III=1993-94 to 1997-98, IV=1998-99 to 2002-03
(2) Percentage Change: 1st = {(II-I)/I}*100, 2nd = {(III-II)/II}*100, 3rd = {(IV-III)/III}*100, 4th = {(IV-I)/I}*100

Source: Processed data on the basis of Annual Report of APMC, Solapur, period from 1983-84 to 2002-03.

The main reason of better performance of Rice is not only due to arrival from surrounding area but the arrival from moffusil area of Andra Pradesh and Karnataka state.

Jowar is a main crop in this region. Consequently, in the total transaction of agricultural commodities occupy a major share among the cereals in the market during the first period with 1917.60 hundred quintals. But in the second period, it reduced to 1305.17 hundred quintals and marginally increased to 1377.23 hundred quintals in the third period and further increased with 2126.54 hundred quintals of Jowar was arrived in the market. There are ups and down in arrival of the cereals. The overall change of Jowar was recorded only 10.89 during the study period. In the case of Wheat, progress seemed to be quite satisfactory than Jowar. During first period, 1131.77 hundred quintals of Wheat was arrived in the market with a rise of 1276.33 hundred quintals during the second period and further increased to 2162.97 hundred quintals in the third period, and finally it was recorded with 2554.33 hundred quintals during the fourth period. It is much higher than the earlier period. In relative terms, it showed that the arrival of Wheat increased by 69.47 per cent in the second period, it was quite higher than the first period and it was marginally increased by 18.09 per cent during the third period. Overall change in Wheat arrival seems to be remarkable by 125.69 per cent. It is less than Rice but much higher than cereal corps and other crops.

In case of Bajra, there is ups and down in arrival like Jowar. During the first period, 39.07 hundred quintals of Bajra was arrived and increased to 67.22 hundred quintals in the second period with the repeated trend of increase by 78.16 hundred quintals during the third period, but the arrival had reduced to 56 hundred quintals in the fourth period. Bajra is produced in the sounding area but it is not important crops like Jowar, therefore, arrival of Bajra recorded much less than Jowar in term of quintals. But at the same time overall change in Bajra is quite higher than Jowar crop, i.e. 43.34 per cent.

Among the pulses, Pigeon Pea is important crops than other pulses like Gram, Black Gram and Green Gram. It occupies a major share in the market. In first period, 459.29 hundred quintals of Pigeon Pea was arrived in the market, which has reduced to 343.53 hundred quintals in the second period and further declined to 187.57 hundred quintals in the third period and significantly increased to 341.78 hundred quintals in the fourth period. But overall change was negative during the study period. Except Gram, Black Gram and Green Gram were negatively shown in the arrival. While arrival of Gram increased by 29.02 per cent. In the case of Groundnut and Sunflower showed a negative change in the study period. The arrival of Capsicum was continuously declining. It has recorded decline by 36.80 per cent. Among the processed goods, Jaggery occupies a major share of turnover in the market yard. Overall change in Jaggery is remarkable by 250.33 per cent. But Jaggery too experienced a negative growth in the second period as compared to first period.

ANNUAL COMPOUND GROWTH RATES IN ARRIVAL OF FOODGRAINS

Point to point annual compound growth rate was calculated for the analysis of growth of arrival of agricultural commodity in the market yard for twenty year. This period is further divided into four sub-periods with a unit of five years. Annual compound growth rate (CGR) is calculated as:

$$CGR = \text{Antilog}(b-1)*100$$

Value of 'b' calculated as:

$$b = \frac{N*\Sigma XY - (\Sigma X*\Sigma Y)}{N*\Sigma X^2 - (\Sigma X)^2}$$

In the above equation, value of b is indicated as the rate of change in the variables. Here Y notation taken for arrival of agricultural commodity and X for the time. The trends estimated in annual compound growth rates of arrival of food grains, fruits and vegetables are discussed below.

CGR IN ARRIVAL OF FOOD GRAINS

Table 2 accounts for the annual compound growth rates in arrival of food grains and other agricultural commodities. It is observed from the Table 2 that the arrival of Jaggery increased by 6.74 per cent per annum during 1983-84 to 2002-03, followed by Rice (6.34 per cent), Wheat (6.07 per cent), Maize (2.57 per cent), Black gram (1.94 per cent), Gram (0.91 per cent), and Jowar (0.51 per cent).

Table 2
Compound Growth Rates in Arrival of Foodgrains

Sl. No.	*Foodgrains*	*CGR Period* I	II	III	IV	V
1.	Bajra	28.05	-13.43	-9.26	-22.35	-1.67
2.	Black gram	2.74	-9.58	24.47	-19.17	1.94
3.	Capsicum	-11.73	-6.01	-5.13	-16.34	-3.87
4.	Gram	-7.46	-23.53	-26.49	11.84	0.91
5.	Green gram	-16.08	11.60	-0.80	-16.87	-5.31
6.	Groundnut	-32.01	-1.98	-3.72	-43.03	-14.07
7.	Jowar	-15.99	-4.44	2.90	-6.70	0.51
8.	Maize	-5.61	14.79	4.35	-13.46	2.57
9.	Pigeon pea	-6.22	-6.93	-2.96	12.55	-2.29
10.	Rice	-9.19	3.78	1.78	9.58	6.34
11.	Sunflower	5.52	52.31	-20.23	-24.30	-17.19
12.	Wheat	-12.99	27.01	-2.24	-0.17	6.07
13.	Jaggery	-0.01	-2.54	7.88	-7.39	6.74

Note: (1) CGR calculated as Antilog (b-1)*100.
(2) Period: I = 1983-84 to 1987-88, II = 1988-89 to 1992-93, III = 1993-94 to 1997-98, IV = 1998-99 to 2002-03, V = 1983-84 to 2002-03

Source: As per Table 1.

On the other hand arrival of Sunflower and Groundnut recorded a high negative growth rates by 17.19 per cent and 14.07 per cent respectively during the same period, followed by Green gram (5.31 per cent), Capsicum (3.87 per cent), Pigeon pea (2.29 per cent), and Bajra (1.67 per cent). Out of the total number of arrival of food grains and other commodities, some crops showed a negative trend during the study period.

Sub period wise position as indicated during Period-I showed that arrival of Bajra, Black gram and Sunflower has increased at varying rates. These three crops showed positive growth rates while other crops i.e. Capsicum, Gram, Green Gram, Groundnut, Jowar, Maize, Pigeon pea, Rice, Wheat and Jaggery have registered a negative growth rates during 1998-84 to 1987-88.

The position of arrival of agricultural commodities during Period-II showed some improvement in respect of some commodities, namely Green gram, Maize, Rice, and Wheat. These crops had a negative growth rates during Period-I, maintained positive growth rates during Period-II. Of special significance were the facts that sunflower recorded very high annual compound growth of 52.31 per cent followed by Wheat (27.01 per cent) and Green gram (11.60 per cent). While annual compound growth rates were negative with Bajra, Black gram, Gram, Capsicum, Pigeon pea and Jaggery.

The position of arrival of food grains and other commodities during Period-III showed some improvement in respect of some agricultural commodities, namely Black gram, Jowar and Jaggery. These three crops had negative growth rates during Period-II, maintained positive growth rates during 1993-94 to 1997-98. But on the other hand Gram had recorded a negative growth rate at the higher rate during Period-III than Period-II. While annual compound growth rate of Sunflower was also recorded negative with 20.23 per cent. Position of Sunflower was better in Period-I and II than Period-III.

The position of growth of arrival of food grains and other commodities during Period-IV showed disfavors to many commodities. Some of these crops registered a very high negative growth rates. During the entire period annual compound growth rate of arrival of foodgrains and other commodity is shown in the Diagram 1.

Growth of arrival of Groundnut has reduced by 43.03 per cent per annum followed by Sunflower with 24.30 per cent and Bajra with 22.35 per cent. Other crops like Black gram, Capsicum, Green gram and Maize were recorded a negative growth in between 10 to 20 per cent range. Only Rice, Gram and Pigeon pea recorded a positive growth rates at the lower rates during the same period. Groundnut is single commodity, whose performance is continuously negative in the sub-periods, and on the other hand, surprisingly, not a single commodity has recorded a positive trend continuously during study period.

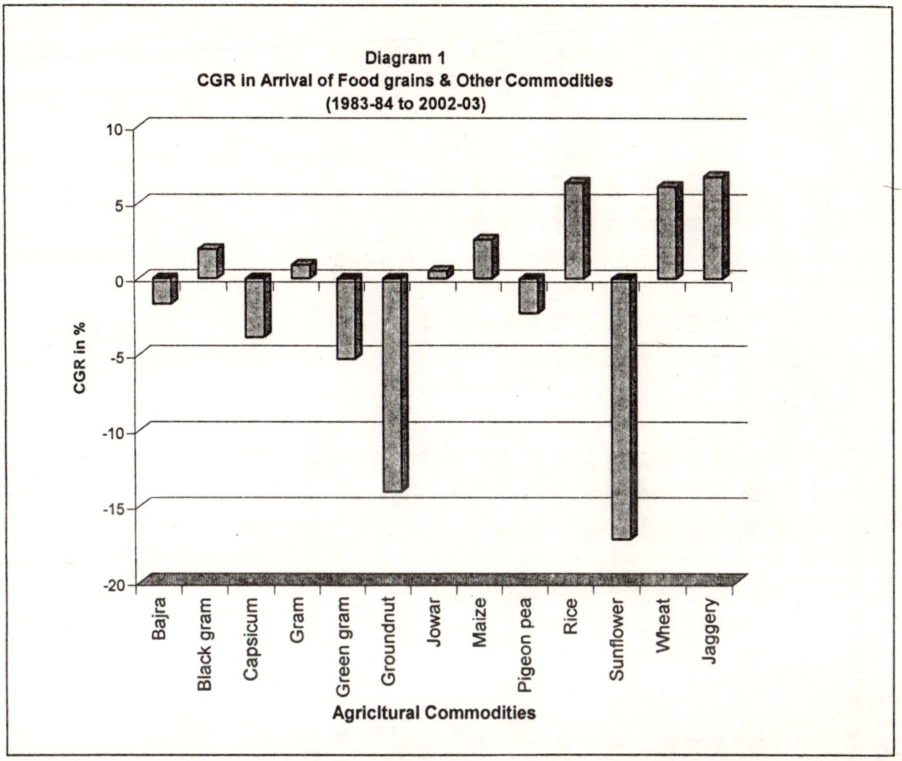

PROGRESS OF FOOD GRAINS IN VALUE TRANSACTION

It is observed from the Table 3 that value transaction of Foodgrains and agricultural commodities. Crop wise position in the first period showed that transaction of Rice was opened to the extent of 785.25 lakhs, followed by Jowar with Rs. 405.54 lakhs and wheat Rs. 326.30 lakhs. In the case of Jaggery, it was Rs. 266.97 lakhs, and for Pigeon pea it was Rs. 235.98 lakhs. Over a period of time transaction of all commodities under consideration has increased except Groundnut and Sunflower.

In case of Rice, value transaction has increased from Rs. 785.25 lakhs in the Ist period to Rs. 7088.27 lakh in the IVth period, indicating a substantial improvement during the period. Jaggery also showed an improvement in value transaction from Rs. 266.97 lakhs to Rs. 2466.98 lakhs. Value transaction of Wheat has been raised from Rs. 326.30 lakhs to Rs. 2237.97 lakhs during the same period. It was also seen that the position of Jowar and Maize too has increased in the recent period as compared to earlier period. Similarly, pulses have showed the same trend in recent period as compared to earlier periods.

Thus, in a relative term, overall change in value transaction of Jaggery has increased by 824.06 per cent during fourth period. Rice stood next to

Table 3
Progress of Value Transaction of Foodgrains

(Figure in Lakh Rupees)

Sl.		*Period*				*Percentage Change*			
No.	*Foodgrains*	*I*	*II*	*III*	*IV*	*1st*	*2nd*	*3rd*	*4th*
1.	Bajra	43.41	11.79	13.95	46.35	-72.84	18.36	232.20	6.78
2.	Black gram	41.57	59.21	149.24	187.78	42.43	152.06	25.83	351.72
3.	Capsicum	146.38	235.22	202.93	258.96	60.69	-13.73	27.61	76.91
4.	Gram	32.95	56.11	98.22	141.89	70.31	75.04	44.47	330.68
5.	Green gram	18.57	15.78	33.39	27.36	-15.00	111.57	-18.05	47.37
6.	Groundnut	106.37	61.81	206.86	21.31	-41.89	234.65	-89.70	-79.96
7.	Jowar	405.54	517.59	875.59	1584.72	27.63	69.16	80.99	290.76
8.	Maize	6.24	18.62	30.33	26.98	198.52	62.91	-11.05	332.58
9.	Pigeon pea	235.98	273.48	269.75	527.69	15.89	-1.36	95.62	123.62
10.	Rice	785.25	1546.65	3011.69	7088.27	96.96	94.72	135.36	802.67
11.	Sunflower	81.21	119.37	321.44	10.93	46.99	169.28	-96.60	-86.54
12.	Wheat	326.30	579.29	1509.02	2237.97	77.53	160.49	48.31	585.86
13.	Jaggery	266.97	1010.87	1367.06	2466.98	278.64	35.24	80.46	824.06

Note:
(1) Period: I =1983-84 to 1987-88, II=1988-89 to 1992-93, III=1993-94 to 1997-98, IV=1998-99 to 2002-03
(2) Percentage Change: 1st ={(II-I)/I}*100, 2nd={(III-II)/II}*100, 3rd={(IV-III)/III}*100, 4th={(IV-I)/I}*100
Source: As per Table 1.

Jaggery with 802.67 per cent. Wheat, Maize and Jowar have increased at a greater degree. Among the pulses, Black gram has increased with 351.72 per cent and Gram at a greater value transaction with 330.68 per cent. Meanwhile value transaction of Sunflower and Groundnut has recorded to decline by 86.54 and 79.96 per cent respectively.

Thus, value transaction of most of the commodities has increased during 1998-99 to 2002-03 as compared to 1983-84 to 1987-88, at varying rates.

COMPOUND GROWTH RATES IN THE VALUE TRANSACTION OF FOODGRAINS

Table 4 gives temporal annual compound growth rates in value transaction of food grains and other agricultural commodities for the entire period from 1983-84 to 2002-03. The entire period has been sub-divided in four periods.

Period-I

In the case of most of the major foodgrains and other commodities, this period was generally characterized as combination of positive as well as negative growth rates. Bajra was recorded highest positive growth rate among cereals by 36.13 per cent per annum. While other cereals namely; Jowar, Wheat and Rice showed a negative growth rates. Among pulses crops Black gram was registered greater performance with 10.12 per cent per annum. While Gram, Green gram and Pigeon pea were recorded a negative growth rates.

Table 4
Compound Growth Rates in Value Transaction of Foodgrains

Sl.		*Period of CGR*				
No.	*Foodgrains*	*I*	*II*	*III*	*IV*	*V*
1.	Bajra	36.13	-1.51	-10.93	-22.46	3.36
2.	Black gram	10.12	-7.04	28.54	-24.21	11.02
3.	Capsicum	-7.41	2.02	0.45	-19.02	2.32
4.	Gram	-2.57	-22.08	-19.69	19.55	9.02
5.	Green gram	-8.15	21.09	7.38	-14.30	3.86
6.	Groundnut	-23.17	12.39	4.87	-32.27	-7.61
7.	Jowar	-9.56	6.73	16.25	-17.42	8.77
8.	Maize	3.72	28.16	17.08	-12.78	10.59
9.	Pigeon pea	7.69	-0.07	2.95	8.27	5.94
10.	Rice	-4.84	15.74	13.11	5.15	14.91
11.	Sunflower	17.52	67.44	-16.65	-15.25	-12.56
12.	Wheat	-6.24	42.43	8.05	-0.13	14.42
13.	Jaggery	3.34	9.16	23.81	-4.25	14.42

Note: (1) CGR calculated as Antilog (b-1)*100
(2) Period: I = 1983-84 to 1987-88, II = 1988-89 to 1992-93, III = 1993-94 to 1997-98, IV = 1998-99 to 2002-03, V = 1983-84 to 2002-03

Source: As per Table 1.

Period-II

Jowar, Wheat and Rice contributed to a positive growth in value transactions during the second period. Among the cereals, performance of Wheat was relatively impressive with 42.43 per cent per annum, also recorded a significant growth rate in Rice by 15.74 per cent. Green gram showed a greater growth rate among the pulses with 21.09 per cent, while the Gram has declined to a greater extent by 22.08 per cent. Of special significance, the Sunflower registered a highest growth rate than other commodities with 67.44 per cent per annum.

Period-III

The third period was generally characterized by a positive growth rates in sale proceeds of major food grains and other agricultural commodities, except Barja, Gram and Sunflower. Among the cereals, performance of Maize, Jower and Rice were significant. A sale of Maize has increased by 17.08 per cent. Jower was the next product with 16.25 per cent per annum shares. Black gram among the pulses has a share with 28.54 per cent. It was observed that the value transaction of processed commodity i.e. Jaggery has increased by 23.81 per cent per annum and it was greater than earlier two period.

Period-IV

Among the cereals crops most of commodities performed a negative growth rates in the fourth period. Bajra was registered higher negative growth with 22.46 per cent. Most of pulses also registered a negative growth rate in value transaction during the same period. Gram has indicated a positive growth rate among the pulses in value transaction with 19.55 per cent. On the hand Ground has recorded a highest negative growth rate with 32.27 per cent during 1998-99 to 2002-03.

Period-V

Almost all cereal crops have recorded a positive and significant growth rates in total value transaction in the fifth period. Rice has registered highest growth rate compared to all other crops with 14.91 per cent per annum. Wheat and Jaggery were the next to Rice with a share of 14.42 per cent. Among the pulses, Black gram showed a better performance with 11.02 per cent. Meanwhile Sunflower and Groundnut have showed a negative performance during entire study period. This picture has been shown in Diagram 2.

During the period over all position of value transaction of food grains and other agricultural commodities showed an increasing trend at a significant level.

PRICE BEHAVIOUR OF FOODGRAINS

Table 5 shows progress of Prices of Foodgrains and agricultural commodities. It is observed from the Table 5 that Siddheshwar Market

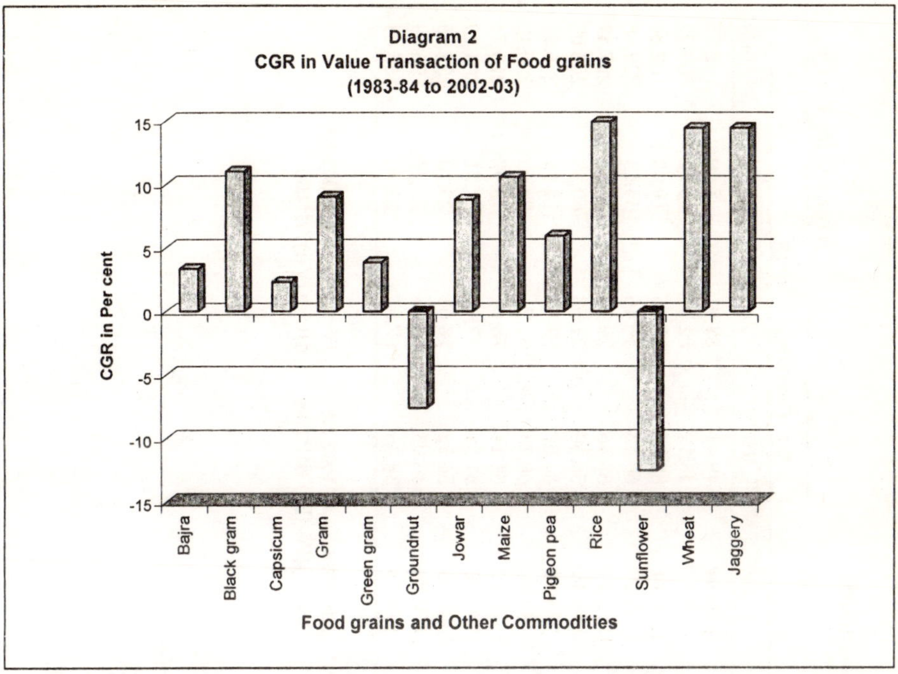

Yard, Solapur has been making progress in the prices of foodgrains and other commodities over a period of time. Therefore, it reflects the fact that agricultural producers prefer to sale their food grains in the market yard.

In the first period, Capsicum has recorded a highest price by Rs. 961.26 per quintal; Rs. 1811 per quintal increase is seen in the second period, further it has increased to Rs. 2121.83 per quintal in the third period, and it has still increased in the fourth period by Rs. 2526.74 per quintal. This price is greater than other commodity prices in all the sub-periods.

Among the cereals, Bajra recorded a highest price in the first period with Rs. 501.67 per quintal, in the second period price has reduced to Rs. 253.78, but during the third period it increased to Rs. 479.41 and Rs. 512.94 in fourth period. Overall change in Bajra has increased much little than other cereals. In the case of Rice, it has recorded Rs. 458.04 per quintal in the first period, further increased by Rs. 602.78 in the second period, again increased by Rs. 1012.12 in the third and still increased by Rs. 1393.78 in the fourth period. Jowar, Wheat and Maize have recorded an increasing trend continuously during the study period.

In case of pulses, Pigeon pea has recorded a highest price than others. It was Rs. 502.24 per quintal during first period; Rs. 809.30 increased it in the second period, Rs. 1445.99 in the third period and in the recent past it has increased by Rs. 1575.70 per quintal. Among the pulses, other pulses Black gram, Gram, and Green gram also achieved better price during the entire period of study.

Table 5
Progress of Prices of Foodgrains

(Figure in Rs. Per Qtl.)

Sl. No.	Foodgrains	Period I	II	III	IV	Percentage Change 1st	2nd	3rd	4th
1.	Bajra	501.67	253.78	479.41	512.94	-49.41	88.91	7.00	2.25
2.	Black gram	425.44	630.15	1148.93	1570.81	48.12	82.33	36.72	269.22
3.	Capsicum	961.26	1811.28	2121.83	2526.74	88.43	17.15	19.08	162.86
4.	Gram	427.86	712.08	1042.93	1409.29	66.43	46.46	35.13	229.68
5.	Green gram	440.88	742.73	1263.65	1752.11	68.46	70.14	38.65	297.41
6.	Groundnut	553.71	866.57	1053.58	1689.19	56.50	21.58	60.33	205.07
7.	Jowar	218.04	406.82	640.85	733.74	86.58	57.53	14.49	236.51
8.	Maize	161.27	259.28	393.42	484.48	60.78	51.74	23.15	200.42
9.	Pigeon pea	502.24	809.30	1445.99	1575.70	61.14	78.67	8.97	213.74
10.	Rice	458.04	602.78	1012.12	1393.78	31.59	67.93	37.71	204.29
11.	Sunflower	584.46	917.77	1084.99	1303.03	56.52	18.61	20.10	122.95
12.	Wheat	294.12	429.55	706.41	870.86	46.05	64.46	23.28	196.09
13.	Jaggery	331.92	460.91	773.72	879.73	38.86	67.87	13.70	165.04

Note:
(1) Period: I=1983-84 to 1987-88, II=1988-89 to 1992-93, III=1993-94 to 1997-98, IV=1998-99 to 2002-03
(2) Percentage Change: 1st={(II-I)/I}*100, 2nd={(III-II)/II}*100, 3rd = {(IV-III)/III}*100, 4th={(IV-I)/I}*100
Source: As per Table 1

The most prominent change observed in the price was of Green gram with 297.41 per cent between 1983-84 to 1987-88 and 1998-99 to 2002-03, followed by Black gram (269.22 per cent), Jowar (236.51 per cent). The prices of other food grains too, has increased by less than 230 per cent to more than 120 per cent except Bajra during the same period. Thus the overall performance of price of foodgrains in the Market Yard showed a satisfactory result during the study period.

COMPOUND GROWTH RATES IN THE PRICES OF FOODGRAINS

Table 6 exhibits the annual compound growth rates of Prices of Foodgains and other agricultural commodities during 1983-84 to 2002-03.

Period-I

The prices of almost all food grains and other commodities have increased during the first period. Prominent among that are cereals, maize have shown an increase by 9.89 per cent per annum per quintal, which is higher than other cereals. Wheat, Jower and Bajra also recorded a good performance.

The pulses, Pigeon pea has also shows a highest growth in price, not only highest among the pulses, but also in other crops with 14.83 per cent change. Groundnut was next to Pigeon pea with 13.01 per cent change. All commodities have enjoyed a positive and significant growth performance during the period.

Table 6
Compound Growth Rates in the Prices of Foodgrains

Sl. No.	*Foodgrains*	*CGR Period* I	*II*	*III*	*IV*	*V*
1.	Bajra	6.31	13.77	-1.84	-0.15	5.12
2.	Black gram	7.18	2.80	3.27	-6.23	8.91
3.	Capsicum	4.88	8.55	5.89	-3.20	6.44
4.	Gram	5.29	1.90	9.24	6.90	8.04
5.	Green gram	9.45	8.51	8.24	3.09	9.69
6.	Groundnut	13.01	14.66	8.93	18.90	7.53
7.	Jowar	7.66	11.69	12.97	-11.49	8.22
8.	Maize	9.89	11.66	12.20	0.78	7.82
9.	Pigeon pea	14.83	7.37	6.09	-3.80	8.43
10.	Rice	4.79	11.53	11.13	-4.04	8.06
11.	Sunflower	11.37	9.93	4.48	11.95	5.74
12.	Wheat	7.75	12.14	10.53	-0.68	7.82
13.	Jaggery	3.35	12.00	17.77	3.39	7.20

Note: (1) CGR calculated as Antilog (b-1)*100
(2) Period: I = 1983-84 to 1987-88, II = 1988-89 to 1992-93, III = 1993-94 to 1997-98, IV = 1998-99 to 2002-03, V = 1983-84 to 2002-03

Source: As per Table 1.

Period-II

The second period also showed a positive trend. The same story of the first period has been repeated in the second period since each commodity has enjoyed positive and significance growth rate in prices. The story of cereals in the second period was interested; Rice, Wheat, Jowar, Maize and Bajra were recorded a better performance than earlier period. The growth rates of cereal prices were registered in between 11 per cent to 14 per cent per annum per quintal during the period.

Period-III

Except Bajra, growth rate of prices of all commodities in the third period showed a positive as well as significant trend. Processed goods namely Jaggery has recorded a highest growth rate in the price per quintal with 17.77 per cent during the period. Jowar has showed a greater growth rate in price among the cereals; the growth rates of Rice, Wheat and Bajra including Jowar prices have registered a growth between 10 to 13 per cent per annum.

Period-IV

In the fourth period, the growth rate of cereal prices as well as pulses recorded ups and downs. Compared to earlier three periods this period has not performed better. Groundnut and sunflower were significant. Except Maize with marginal growth rate remaining cereals shows a negative growth in the prices. Among the pulses, Gram and Green gram recorded a positive growth rates.

Period-V

Diagram 3 shows annual compound growth rate in the prices of food grains and other agricultural commodities during the study period. During the period under study, all commodities have registered a positive trend. It means that farmers are getting remunerative prices to their products during 1983-84 to 2002-03. Not only cereals but also pulses and other agricultural commodities have recorded a better growth rates in price. The ranges of growth rates of all commodities are between 5 per cent and 10 per cent per annum per quintal.

VARIATION IN ARRIVALS

The quantitative techniques like, relative range, standard deviation, coefficient of variation and skewness were applied for analyzing the overall arrival of agricultural commodities in the market yard.

Range: The range of a set of numbers is the difference between the maximum and minimum values. It indicates the limits within which the values fall. Relative range or the coefficient of range is defined by the ratio:

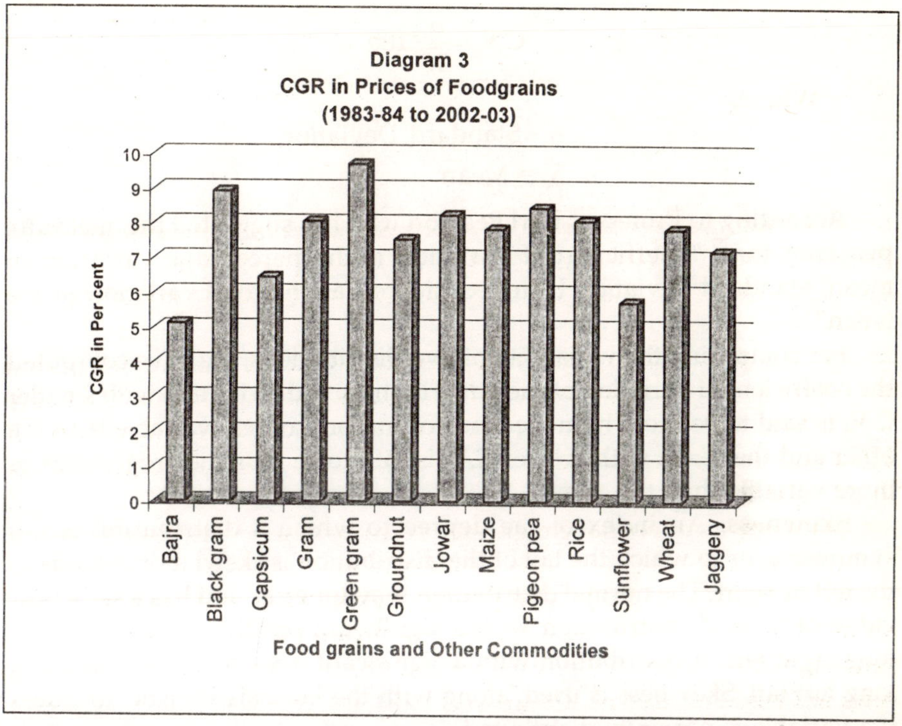

$$RR = \frac{X_{max} - X_{min}}{X_{max} + X_{min}}$$

Standard deviation: Standard deviation is only an absolute measure of dispersion, depending upon the units of measurement. The relative measure of dispersion based on standard deviation is called the coefficient of standard deviation and is given by:

Coefficient of Standard Deviation= $\sigma / \bar{X}$

This is a pure number independent of the units of measurement and thus, is suitable for comparing the variability, homogeneity or uniformity of two or more distributions.

Standard deviation is by far the best measure of dispersion, for comparing the homogeneity or heterogeneity of two or more distributions we generally compute the coefficient of standard deviation unless asked otherwise. Standard deviation is calculated as:

$$S.D. = \sqrt{\frac{\sum X^2}{N} - \left(\frac{\sum X}{N}\right)^2}$$

100 times the coefficient of dispersion based on standard deviation is called the coefficient of variation, abbreviated as C.V. Thus,

$$C.V. = \frac{\sigma}{\overline{X}} * 100$$

Where,

σ = Standard Deviation

$\overline{X}$ = Mean

According to Professor Karl Pearson who has suggested this measure, proclaim that, "coefficient of variation is the percentage variation in mean, standard deviation being considered as the total variation in the mean".

For comparing the variability of two distributions, we have computed the coefficient of variation of each distribution. A distribution with smaller C.V. is said to be more homogeneous or uniform or less variable than the other and the series with greater C.V. is said to be more heterogeneous or more variable than the other.

Skewness: An index of the degree to which a distribution is not symmetric, or to which the tail of the distribution is skewed or extends to the left or right. The normal distribution is symmetric, and has a skewness value of zero. A distribution with a significant positive skewness has a long right tail. A distribution with a significant negative skewness has a long left tail. Skewness is used, along with the kurtosis statistic, to assess if a variable is normally distributed.

Skewness refers to lack of symmetry in a distribution. In a symmetrical distribution, the mean, median and mode coincide. In a positively skew distribution the longer tail is on the right side and the mean is on the right of the median. In a negatively skew distribution the longer tail is on the left and the mean is on the left of the median. In a skew distribution the distance between the mean and median is nearly one-third of that between the mean and mode.

A measure of skewness gives a numerical expression for and the direction of asymmetry in a distribution. It gives information about the shape of the distribution and the degree of variation on either side of the central value. We consider Pearson's Coefficient of Skewness.

$$PSk = \frac{\overline{X} - Mo}{s}$$

Variation in the arrival of Food grains, Fruits and Vegetables are discussed in next part by using dispersion techniques.

VARIATION IN THE ARRIVALS OF FOODGRAINS

In Table 7, a variation in arrival of foodgrains and other agricultural commodities has been analyzed. For this purpose some tools of dispersion are used like range, coefficient of range, standard deviation, coefficient of variation and skewness. Minimum and maximum quantity of arrivals of foodgrains and other commodities are measured in Table 7 for the entire period under study. This is nothing but two extreme values.

It is observed different variability among the foodgrains and other commodity. Sunflower's coefficient of range in arrival is highest than other commodities with 1. In case of cereals, higher variability is registered in arrivals of Bajra, Rice and Maize than Wheat and Jowar. Jowar recorded a lowest range coefficient not only in the cereals but also in the other commodities. Among the pulses, Green gram has recorded a higher variability with 0.85 during the same period, followed by Black gram with 0.81. The distribution of arrival of Gram has recorded a lower variability than other pulses. Groundnut has also registered a high relative range.

Standard deviation of arrival of foodgrains is measured for five periods. First four periods are sub-period of the entire period and each period carrying five year and fifth period is taken as the entire period for calculation of standard deviation. Standard deviation shows an absolute variability. On the other hand coefficient of variation shows a relative variability.

Therefore, it is possible to study a comparative variability among the food grains and other commodities. The entire period is divided for analysis of coefficient of variation like standard deviation. Coefficient of variation in arrival of foodgrains and other agricultural commodities for the period from 1983-84 to 2002-03 is shown in Diagram 4.

Among the cereals, Jowar has registered a lowest coefficient of variation by 29.75 per cent during the entire period. It is not only a lowest

Diagram 4
C.V. in the Arrival of Food grains
(1983-84 to 2002-03)

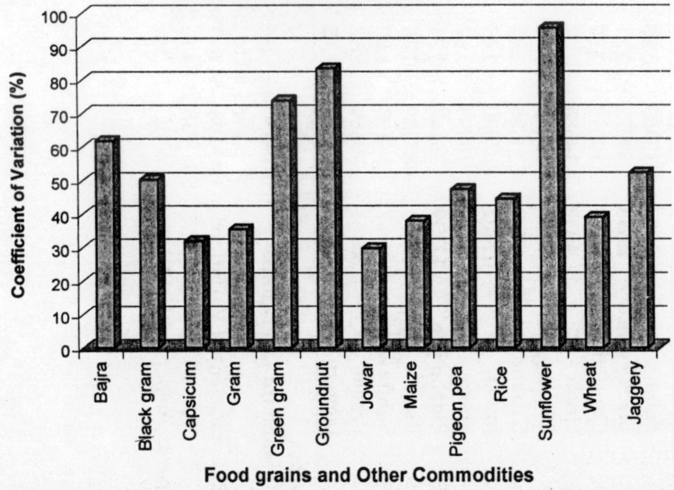

Table 7
Variations in Arrival of Foodgrains

Sl.		Range			Standard Deviation					Coefficient of Variation					
No.	*Foodgrains*	*Min.*	*Max.*	*RR*	*I*	*II*	*III*	*IV*	*V*	*1st*	*2nd*	*3rd*	*4th*	*5th*	*Skew*
1.	Bajra	1887	17389	0.80	4555	1863	1364	4229	4217	45.98	37.76	37.60	48.07	61.88	1.14
2.	Black gram	2656	24972	0.81	5585	2533	6846	5669	5666	56.16	27.04	49.98	47.22	50.35	0.81
3.	Capsicum	6480	19619	0.50	3046	3971	2503	2797	4061	19.10	27.34	24.46	27.75	31.98	0.10
4.	Gram	4032	14688	0.57	1815	2829	3992	2887	3160	23.43	35.46	40.34	28.88	35.49	0.36
5.	Green gram	827	10509	0.85	3143	468	559	742	2017	68.14	22.21	21.20	47.52	73.89	3.06
6.	Groundnut	359	30635	0.98	10415	2459	6380	1064	10415	49.49	33.53	31.83	70.76	83.44	0.67
7.	Jowar	109802	287520	0.45	58275	25040	25007	21957	50026	30.39	19.18	18.16	10.33	29.75	0.74
8.	Maize	2609	10993	0.62	1622	2023	1895	1449	2279	41.52	30.09	24.24	25.87	37.91	0.45
9.	Pigeon pea	12139	76167	0.73	21618	4379	4091	10821	15758	47.07	12.75	21.81	31.66	47.31	0.95
10.	Rice	105514	687589	0.73	49307	30848	17333	123052	138544	26.76	12.03	5.83	24.23	44.48	1.39
11.	Sunflower	87	54493	1.00	4741	10066	14731	862	17033	32.36	79.92	48.24	97.73	95.68	1.39
12.	Wheat	76084	278569	0.57	21821	49078	46468	7807	69474	19.28	38.45	21.48	3.06	39.00	0.02
13.	Jaggery	67617	407063	0.72	11447	108952	37126	66322	100938	14.19	46.16	21.67	23.46	52.38	0.74

Note:

(1) Standard Deviation: I=1983-84 to 1987-88, II=1988-89 to 1992-93, III=1993-94 to 1997-98, IV=1998-99 to 2002-03, V = 1983-84 to 2002-03

(2) Coefficient of Variation: 1st=1983-84 to 1987-88, 2nd=1988-89 to 1992-93, 3rd=1993-94 to 1997-98, 4th=1998-99 to 2002-03, 5th = 1983-84 to 2002-03

Source: As per Table 1

variability among cereals and pulses but also in the other commodities. Maize is a next to Jowar with 37.91 per cent. Rice and Wheat have recorded a lower coefficient of variation. Bajra showed a higher coefficient of variation of 61.88 per cent than other cereals. In the case of pulses, Gram has registered a lowest coefficient of variation of 35.49 per cent. Pigeon pea is the next to Gram with 47.31 per cent of share. Black gram has recorded a lower coefficient of variation. Green gram showed a higher coefficient of variation among pulses by 73.89 per cent.

Capsicum has registered a lower coefficient of variation with 31.98 per cent. In the case of Groundnut, it appears a higher coefficient of variation with 83.44 per cent share. Sunflower showed a highest coefficient of variation with 95.68 per cent where is highest during the entire period.

While 'dispersion' studies the degree of variation in the given distribution, skewness attempts at studying the direction of variation. Extreme variations toward higher values of the variables give a positively skewed distribution; while in a negatively skewed distribution; the extreme variations are towards the lower values of the variable.

Skew ness of arrival of foodgrains and other commodities is shown in Table 7. Almost all (commodities) arrivals distribution showed a positive skewed for the entire period. Distribution in the arrival of Green gram showed a very high skewed of 3.06; it implies that the curve of distribution of arrival has a very longer tail towards the right. Bajra, Rice and Sunflower are forecasted a high positive skewed. Many commodities seemed moderately positive skewed. On the other hand Wheat and Capsicum has observed a positive but very less skewed like as 0.02 and 0.10 respectively. We can say in the case of Wheat, the distribution in the arrival is symmetric during the study period.

VARIATION IN THE VALUE TRANSACTION OF FOODGRAINS

The variation in Value Transaction of foodgrains and other agricultural commodities is exhibited in Table 8. Some tools of dispersions like minimum and maximum value are used. The powerful tools such as coefficient of range, standard deviation, coefficient of variation and skewness are also applied.

There is variability among the foodgrains and other commodities in the value of transactions during the period from 1983-84 to 2002-03. Sunflower's coefficient of range in sales is higher than other commodities (with 1) followed by Groundnut with a relative range of 0.94. Processed produce like Jaggery showed a relative range of 0.87. The highest variability has been registered in the sale of Bajra by 0.93. Wheat, Jowar, Maize and Rice have also showed a higher variability. Among the pulses, Black gram has a record of highest variability with 0.93 during the same period.

Table 8
Variations in Value Transaction of Foodgrains

No.	Foodgrains	Range			Standard Deviation					Coefficient of Variation					Skew
		Min.	Max.	RR	I	II	III	IV	V	1st	2nd	3rd	4th	5th	
1.	Bajra	546305	14952557	0.93	5369021	343081	440669	2560078	3391294	123.69	29.10	31.58	55.24	117.45	2.67
2.	Black gram	1270847	35085438	0.93	2507594	1767644	7465986	9163592	8629029	60.32	29.85	50.03	48.80	78.81	1.35
3.	Capsicum	10887456	45477648	0.61	3212797	3943802	1835183	10375678	7214132	21.95	16.77	9.04	40.07	34.21	1.83
4.	Gram	2005281	22048855	0.83	756604	1930027	3780740	4785669	5262109	22.96	34.40	38.49	33.73	63.94	1.06
5.	Green gram	838274	5137848	0.72	920342	433913	882715	1273482	1161850	49.57	27.49	26.44	46.54	48.87	0.93
6.	Groundnut	929643	27988483	0.94	4165870	2293815	5885415	1228470	7903118	39.16	37.11	28.45	57.65	79.76	0.99
7.	Jowar	32259420	236676920	0.76	8331271	9906415	25547449	46730596	53591642	20.54	19.14	29.18	29.49	63.36	1.48
8.	Maize	317262	4559870	0.87	247276	1068686	963378	691173	1231354	39.65	57.40	31.76	25.76	59.95	0.42
9.	Pigeon pea	7312645	66385543	0.80	16261180	4747863	6287631	14387153	16435692	68.91	17.36	23.31	27.26	50.30	0.91
10.	Rice	66370790	952726250	0.87	7699193	32551646	54341106	187177001	262657056	9.80	21.05	18.04	26.41	84.51	1.32
11.	Sunflower	105431	56858192	1.00	2228420	9656857	14105467	950452	14412452	27.44	80.90	43.88	86.97	108.17	1.68
12.	Wheat	25414157	230778030	0.80	3961384	30477350	29294507	5696998	78525028	12.14	52.61	19.41	2.56	67.74	0.22
13.	Jaggery	21622086	322922632	0.87	3571126	34637439	59219398	49563736	89899064	13.38	34.26	43.32	20.09	70.35	0.67

Note:

(1) Standard Deviation: I =1983-84 to 1987-88, II=1988-89 to 1992-93, III= 1993-94 to 1997-98, IV=1998-99 to 2002-03
V=1983-84 to 2002-03

(2) Coefficient of Variation: 1st=1983-84 to 1987-88, 2nd=1988-89 to 1992-93, 3rd=1993-94 to 1997-98, 4th=1998-99 to 2002-03
5th=1983-84 to 2002-03

Source: As per Table 1.

Gram is next to Black gram with 0.83. Remaining pulses have also reflected variability. It means that a very high-level variability is observed in the sales of major foodgrains and other commodities. Coefficient of variation in value transaction of foodgrains and other agricultural commodities is shown in the Diagram 5 for the period from 1983-84 to 2002-03.

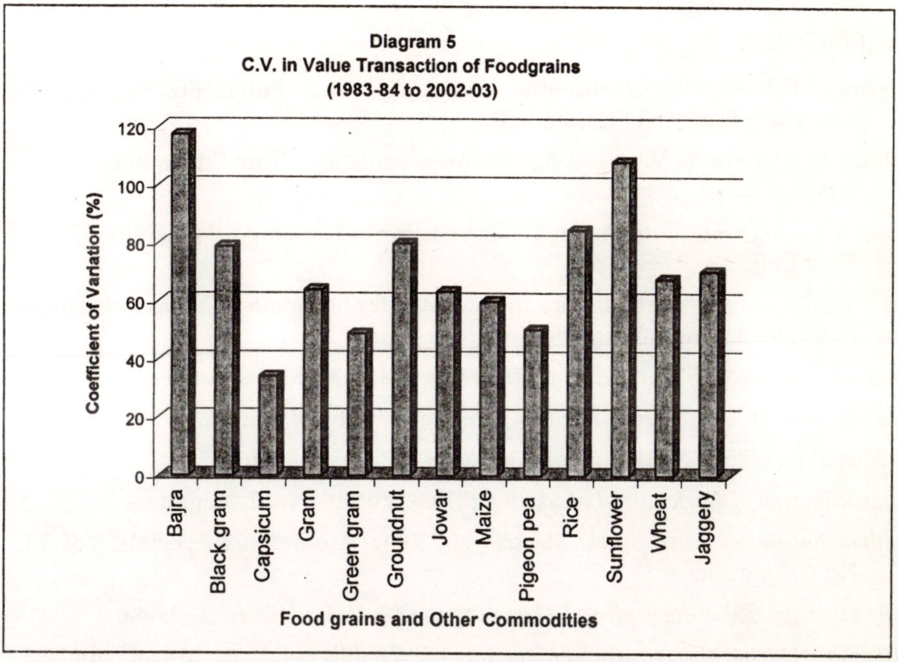

The coefficient of variations in sales of food grains and other commodities is calculated for the same period. Among the cereals, Maize has registered the lowest coefficient of variation by 59.95 per cent. Jowar is next to Maize with 63.36 per cent. Rice and Wheat have also recorded a higher coefficient of variation in value transactions. Bajra has showed the highest coefficient of variation of 117.45 per cent. It is highest in sales among cereals, pulses and other commodities. Green gram registered lowest coefficient of variation of 48.87 per cent. Pigeon pea is next to Green gram with 50.30 per cent. Remaining pulses have showed a higher coefficient of variation. Capsicum has registered lowest coefficient of variation of 34.21 per cent. Groundnuts also experience a higher coefficient of variation. Sunflower has observed a second position in the coefficient of variation with 108.17 per cent.

Skewness of foodgrains and other commodities in value transaction is shown in the same table. The sale distribution commodities showed a positive skewness for the entire period. Distribution in the sales of Bajra showed a very high skewed with 2.67; it implies that the distribution curve of sales has a very longer tail towards the right. Jowar and Rice are also positively skewed. Maize is moderately skewed. On the other hand Wheat experience a positive skewness of 0.22 among the cereals; it implies that the curve of distribution of sales has less long tail towards the right. Black gram has higher skewness of 1.35. Remaining pulses are also highly skewed in sales. Capsicum ranks the second position in the skew ness with 1.83.

REFERENCE

Agarwal D.R. (2003), "Quantitative Methods", Vrinda Publicatios Pvt. Ltd., 3rd Revised & Enlarged Edition, Delhi.

Bhatia D.K. & Gupta Vijay (1986), "Business Statistics", Vani Educational Books, New Delhi.

Gupta S.C. (1996), "Fundamentals of Statistics", Himalaya Publishing House, New Delhi.

Monga G.S. (2000), "Mathematics and Statistics for Economics", Vikas Pub. House Pvt. Ltd., Second Revised Edition, New Delhi.

Prasad A.S. (1985), "Agricultural Marketing in India", Mittal Publications, Delhi.

Reddy A.V. (1991), "Agricultural Marketing", Printwell, Jaipur.

Reddy P.I. (1995), "Marketing of Vegetables", Printwell, Jaipur.

Indian Journal of Agricultural Marketing (2002), Vol. 16, No. 2, Nagpur.

Indian Journal of Agricultural Marketing (2000), (Conference Special), Vol. 14, No. 3, Nagpur.

The Bihar Journal of Agricultural Marketing (2000), Vol. VIII, No. 1, Patna.

The Bihar Journal of Agricultural Marketing (1997), (Silver Jubilee Special Number), Vol. V, No. 3, Patna.

The Bihar Journal of Agricultural Marketing (1997), (Bansil P. C., Article on, 'Regulated Market System in Meeting Urban Food'), (Silver Jubilee Special Number), Vol. V, No. 3, Patna.

5

ANALYSIS AND INTERPRETATION OF MARKETING ACTIVITIES OF A.P.M.C. SOLAPUR: FRUITS

This chapter explains the analysis and interpretation of marketing activities of Agricultural Produce Market Committee, Solapur in terms of growth in arrival, value transaction and price behaviour of fruits and also in terms of variation and other economic variables performed during 1983-84 to 2002-03.

PROGRESS OF ARRIVAL OF MAJOR FRUITS

The physical performance indicator in the form of arrivals of important fruits in Regulated Markets for the period 1983-84 to 2002-03 is exhibited in Table 1. The table shows an increasing trend in the arrival of major fruits over years.

Quantity of Apple, Mango, Orange, Papaya, Pomegranate and Sapota is measured in terms of dozen (i.e. 12 number). Whereas Banana, Ber, Custard Apple, Guava, and Lemon is measured in quintals. The quantity of Grapes and Watermelon is measured in number of boxes and in number respectively.

In the case of Apple, Banana, Grapes, Guava, Mango, Papaya and Watermelon there is ups and down in the arrivals. Ber, Orange, Pomegranate and Sapota have shown tremendous improvements during the study period, but a declining trend is observed in the case of Custard Apple. In relative terms, arrival of Apple has increased by 34.49 per cent during first period, and declined by 20.49 per cent during second period and increased by 98.58 per cent in the third period. The overall change was recorded at 112.35 per cent. Arrival of Grapes has increased to 135.42 per cent during first period, but decline to 22.60 per cent in the second period and increased by 80.28 per cent in the third period and overall positive change recorded by 228.51 per cent.

Table 1
Progress of Arrival of Fruits

Sl.			Period				Percentage Change			
No.	Fruits	Quantity	I	II	III	IV	1st	2nd	3rd	4th
1.	Apple	Dozen	282526	379961	302117	599936	34.49	-20.49	98.58	112.35
2.	Banana	Quintal	757983	27116	157690	40645	-96.42	481.54	-74.22	-94.64
3.	Ber	Kilogram	207969	692509	2863394	4138129	232.99	313.48	44.52	1889.78
4.	Custard apple	Quintal	61922	3764	2762	1733	-93.92	-26.64	-37.25	-97.20
5.	Grapes	Boxes	41574	97876	75759	136576	135.42	-22.60	80.28	228.51
6.	Guava	Kilogram	464289	410852	458822	479677	-11.51	11.68	4.54	3.31
7.	Lemon	Kilogram	1358454	2554194	1136515	3270722	14.41	-26.87	187.78	140.77
8.	Mango	Dozen	412682	184973	87296	254266	-55.18	-52.81	191.27	-38.39
9.	Orange	Dozen	7049	24351	50609	57598	245.45	107.83	13.81	717.11
10.	Papaya	Dozen	402	1049	13001	10472	160.94	1139.39	-19.46	2504.88
11.	Pomegranate	Dozen	62218	221401	292465	927108	255.85	31.10	217.00	1390.10
12.	Sapota	Dozen	5482	39430	123785	549388	619.27	213.93	343.82	9921.68
13.	Watermelon	Number	686551	729533	481778	658370	6.26	-33.96	36.65	-4.10

Note:
(1) Period: I =1983-84 to 1987-88, II =1988-89 to 1992-93, III=1993-94 to 1997-98, IV=1998-99 to 2002-03
(2) Percentage Change: 1st={(II-I)/I}*100, 2nd={(III-II)/II}*100, 3rd={(IV-III)/III}*100, 4th={(IV-I)/I}*100
Source: Processed data on the basis of Annual Report of APMC, Solapur, Period from 1983-84 to 2002-03.

Ber, Pomegranate, Papaya and Sapota's performance was amazing during the study period. The arrival of the Ber has raised to 232.99 per cent during first period, which further has raised to 313.48 per cent during second period. A marginally rise by 44.52 per cent was recorded in the third period. Arrival of Pomegranate has increased to 255.85 per cent during first period, which has increased marginally by 31.10 per cent during the second period and a rapid rise was recorded at 217 per cent during the third period. Papaya has recorded 160.94 per cent growth during first period, which has remarkably increased to 1139.39 per cent during the second period, and marginally declined by 19.46 per cent during third period. In the case of Sapota, there is a recorded high positive change by 619.27 per cent during the first period. The arrival has increased by 213.93 per cent during the second phase, which has increased to 343.82 per cent during the third period.

The overall change in the arrival of Pomegranate, Ber, Papaya and Sapota was recorded by 1390.10 per cent, 1889.78 per cent, 2504.88 per cent and 9921.68 per cent during the period referred above respectively. But in the case of Banana, Custard Apple, Mango, and Watermelon negative growth rates were observed during the period from 1983-84 to 2002-03.

COMPOUND GROWTH RATES IN ARRIVALS OF FRUITS

Point to point annual compound growth rate was calculated for the analysis of growth of arrival of agricultural commodity in the market yard for twenty year. This period is further divided into four sub-periods with a unit of five years.

Table 2 exhibits the annual compound growth rates in arrival of major Fruits. It is observed from the Table 2 that, the performance of Sapota and Papaya were relatively impressive during the study period. Arrival of Sapota has increased by 36.24 per cent and arrival of Papaya has increased by 32.29 per cent during 1983-84 to 2002-03. Ber has also recorded a significant performance in arrivals with 24.31 per cent growth rate, followed by Pomegranate (15.84 per cent), Orange (11.00 per cent). Grapes, Lemon and Apple have registered a positive trend during the same period by 6.65 per cent, 4.01 per cent and 3.65 per cent respectively.

Some fruits were recorded a negative growth rates during entire study period. Arrival of Custard apple has reduced by 17.80 per cent per annum. It is much higher rate than other fruits. Banana is one of the most important fruits in the human diet, but it has also recorded a negative growth rate in arrival with 10.09 per cent. The main reason behind this negative growth is scarcity of water in the producing area particularly in North and South Solapur tehsils. Arrival of Mango has reduced by 6.68 per cent during same period and Guava has marginally reduced with 0.68 per cent.

Table 2
Compound Growth Rates in Arrival of Fruits

Sl. No.	*Fruits*	*Period of CGR* I	II	III	IV	V
1.	Apple	53.84	-5.01	10.71	22.49	3.65
2.	Banana	-59.54	20.19	55.31	-17.75	-10.09
3.	Ber	25.75	64.50	22.19	9.12	24.31
4.	Custard apple	-52.13	-36.46	50.86	-16.08	-17.80
5.	Grapes	-10.85	16.82	1.09	31.83	6.65
6.	Guava	-0.44	-25.31	9.40	-20.49	-0.68
7.	Lemon	0.75	-23.02	-8.67	4.59	4.01
8.	Mango	2.87	-31.46	-46.42	-21.75	-6.68
9.	Orange	279.33	-5.91	10.42	114.15	11.00
10.	Papaya	100.24	32.34	98.84	-6.90	32.29
11.	Pomegranate	221.00	-2.13	7.35	61.03	15.84
12.	Sapota	103.16	69.24	-11.96	103.43	36.24
13.	Watermelon	-1.93	-4.07	-7.95	15.74	-1.24

Note: (1) CGR calculated as Antilog (b-1)*100.
(2) Period: I = 1983-84 to 1987-88, II = 1988-89 to 1992-93, III = 1993-94 to 1997-98, IV = 1998-99 to 2002-03, V = 1983-84 to 2002-03.

Source: As per Table 1.

The annual compound growth rate of arrival of Food grains and other commodity for entire period is shown in Diagram 1.

Sub period wise position as indicated in the Period-I to IV, shows that only Ber has recorded a positive growth continuously during the periods, on the other hand, remaining fruits were registered ups and downs in their growth rates of arrival.

Diagram 1
CGR in Arrival of Fruits
(1983-84 to 2002-03)

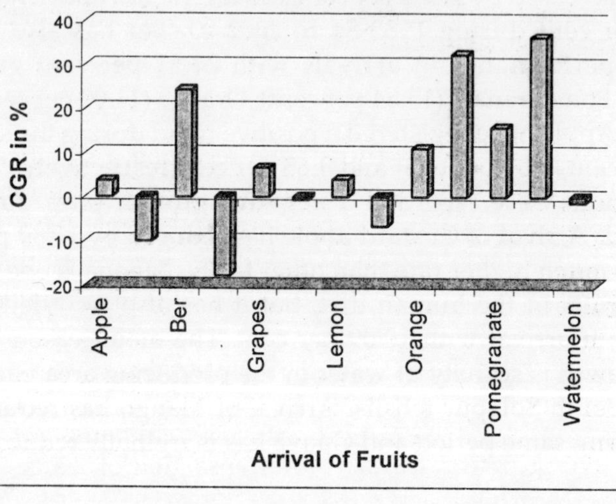

PROGRESS OF FRUITS IN VALUE TRANSACTION OF FRUITS

It is observed from Table 3 that, Agriculture Produce Market Committee, Solapur is making a progress in value transaction of Fruits over a period of time. Therefore, it reflects that agricultural producers in this region prefer to sale agricultural commodities in the market yard, because it ensures the reasonable price to their products.

The value transaction of Banana was recorded a first rank with Rs. 46.11 lakhs during 1983-84 to 1987-88 (I period). Lemon was next to Banana by Rs. 33.88 lakhs. But this picture has slightly changed in the 1988-89 to 1992-93 (II period), Lemon was recorded its position as first with Rs. 39.22 lakhs in value transaction; it was also observed that, value is higher than earlier period. Banana was next to Lemon by Rs. 36.23 lakhs, it showed a declining trend during this period. But in the III period, Banana achieved the first position with Rs. 106.33 lakhs in value transaction. Pomegranate stands next to Banana. In the recent period (1998-99 to 2002-03) except Banana, almost all fruits have recorded an increasing trend in the value transaction. Pomegranate has recorded the first rank among the fruits with Rs. 192.25 lakhs. Apple has achieved second rank in value transaction among all fruits by Rs. 160.46 lakhs.

In the relative terms, Sapota stood first among all fruits. Ber increased by 3752.69 per cent during fourth period. Papaya is next to Ber with 3465.93 per cent. Pomegranate, Orange, Grapes and Apple too have increased in a great extent. While value transaction of Mango recorded to decline by 11.53 per cent. The overall performance of fruits in value transaction in Market Yard shows a satisfactory level during 1983-84 and 2002-03.

COMPOUND GROWTH RATES IN THE VALUE TRANSACTION OF FRUITS

Table 4 gives annual compound growth rates in value transaction of fruits for entire period 1983-84 to 2002-03.

Period-I

During the first period, some fruits have recorded a significant growth rates and some fruits have registered a negligible growth rates in value transaction. Orange, Papaya, Pomegranate and Apple have recorded a grater amount of growth rates, which is due to the reason that only two years aggregates were considered for calculation of compound growth rates.

Period-II

This period was generally characterized as a combination of positive as well as negative growth rates in value transaction of fruits. Sapota has

Table 3
Progress of Value Transaction of Fruits

(Figures in Lakh Rupees)

Sl.			*Period*				*Percentage Change*			
No.	*Fruits*	*Quantity*	*I*	*II*	*III*	*IV*	*1st*	*2nd*	*3rd*	*4th*
1.	Apple	Dozen	22.25	34.53	43.33	160.46	55.18	25.47	270.32	621.04
2.	Banana	Quintal	46.11	36.23	106.33	104.43	-21.43	193.45	-1.78	126.47
3.	Ber	Kilogram	3.50	24.98	70.35	134.87	613.52	181.67	91.70	3752.69
4.	Custard apple	Quintal	0.89	2.32	2.66	3.48	158.87	14.88	30.60	288.38
5.	Grapes	Boxes	7.70	25.55	30.83	71.48	232.01	20.65	131.85	828.74
6.	Guava	Kilogram	5.58	5.85	6.37	12.89	4.86	8.79	102.43	130.94
7.	Lemon	Kilogram	33.88	39.22	61.75	156.36	15.76	57.45	153.21	361.53
8.	Mango	Dozen	25.15	11.82	7.33	22.25	-53.01	-37.99	203.56	-11.53
9.	Orange	Dozen	0.20	0.83	3.82	6.56	308.01	361.44	71.45	3128.02
10.	Papaya	Dozen	0.03	0.04	0.43	1.12	42.71	862.46	159.62	3465.93
11.	Pomegranate	Dozen	7.20	29.47	73.01	192.25	309.54	147.68	163.33	2571.19
12.	Sapota	Dozen	0.12	1.07	5.15	27.17	818.49	383.62	427.05	23311.31
13.	Watermelon	Number	17.94	26.02	25.56	46.70	45.06	-1.76	82.67	160.32

Note:
(1) Period: I=1983-84 to 1987-88, II=1988-89 to 1992-93, III=1993-94 to 1997-98, IV=1998-99 to 2002-03
(2) Percentage Change: 1st={(II-I)/I}*100, 2nd={(III-II)/II}*100, 3rd={(IV-III)/III}*100, 4th={(IV-I)/I}*100
Source: As per Table 1.

registered a highest growth rate with 87.21 per cent. Ber was the next product with 76.16 per cent of share. Mango has declined by 28.63 per cent per annum during the period.

Period-III

The third period was better than earlier two periods. Most of the fruits were recorded positive growth rates in their value transaction except Mango and Guava. Papaya has registered highest growth rate by 93.03 per cent. Papaya was significant in this period compared to earlier period.

Table 4
Compound Growth Rates in Value Transaction of Fruits

Sl. No.	*Fruits*	*CGR Period* I	II	III	IV	V
1.	Apple	52.02	-2.52	23.97	36.06	13.75
2.	Banana	38.87	25.36	6.91	-3.29	8.64
3.	Ber	47.79	76.16	4.35	10.22	24.84
4.	Custard apple	15.09	-21.71	61.20	-4.50	9.57
5.	Grapes	-2.49	16.00	14.14	27.65	13.99
6.	Guava	7.18	-19.35	-11.81	-13.98	4.20
7.	Lemon	2.72	-4.86	12.83	3.68	10.20
8.	Mango	15.77	-28.63	-33.76	8.02	-2.02
9.	Orange	345.31	8.14	31.42	141.99	23.26
10.	Papaya	327.31	2.24	93.03	65.71	35.58
11.	Pomegranate	303.86	11.05	17.52	48.19	22.28
12.	Sapota	-26.70	87.21	6.84	91.67	2.63
13.	Watermelon	13.46	-3.60	10.73	10.07	6.12

Note: (1) CGR calculated as Antilog (b-1)*100
(2) Period: I=1983-84 to 1987-88, II=1988-89 to 1992-93, III=1993-94 to 1997-98, IV=1998-99 to 2002-03, V=1983-84 to 2002-03.

Source: As per Table 1.

Period-IV

Orange has indicated a highest growth rate among the fruits during the period. This period was also better like third period in value transaction of fruits. Most of the fruits showed a positive trend. Sapota has also showed good performance next to Orange with 91.67 per cent.

Period-V

Diagram 2 shows annual compound growth rate in the value transaction of fruits during the entire period. Surprising, over all performance of fruits in value transaction is better than foodgrains and other commodities.

Almost all fruits showed a positive trend except Mango marginally by 2.02 per cent. Papaya has showed a highest growth rate among all fruits with 35.58 per cent. Pomegranate, Ber and Orange were also much more significant.

Diagram 2
CGR in Value Transaction of Fruits
(1983-84 to 2002-03)

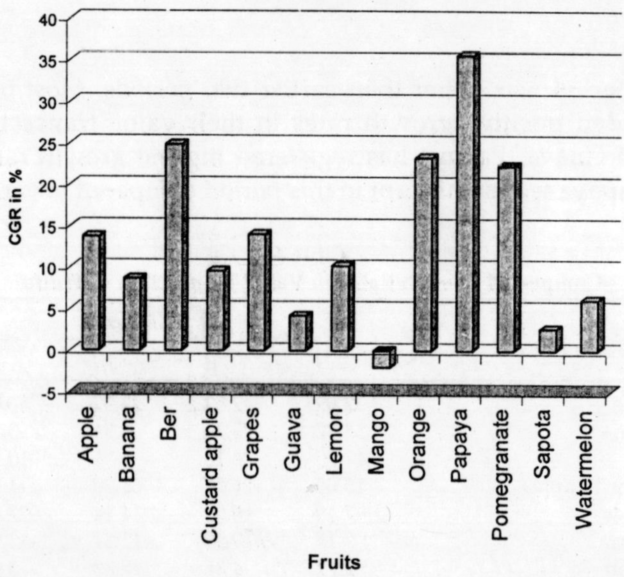

PRICE BEHAVIOUR OF FRUITS

The Table 5 accounts for the progress of Fruits in the prices. The Fruitswise position in the first period showed that price of Banana has attained to the level of Rs. 56.91 per quintal. It has increased by Rs. 134.33 in the second period by Rs. 144.57 in the third period and by Rs. 272.96 per quintal during the fourth period. Quantity of Custard apple also measured in the quintal form. It has recorded Rs. 10.29 per quintal in the first period; with an increase by Rs. 214.43 in the fourth period.

Quantity of Apple, Mango, Papaya, Pomegranate and Sapota are measured in the dozen forms. Among these, Pomegranate has recorded highest price with Rs. 10.20 per dozen, next to Apple with Rs. 8.05.

Pomegranate again has achieved the first position with Rs. 13.42, next to Apple with Rs. 9.11. The story repeated are during the third period, it has further increased by Rs. 24.58 in Pomegranate followed by Apple with Rs. 14.03 per dozen. But in the fourth period, Apple achieved first position in price with 25.64 per dozen, followed by Pomegranate with Rs. 22.27.

The price of Grapes has increased continuously during the entire period of study. It has recorded at Rs. 19.51 per box, further it has increased by Rs. 26.27 per box in the second period; again it has increased by Rs. 39.12 in the third period, and Rs. 52.68 per box in the recent past. There is a positive trend in the price of Grapes.

Table 5
Progress in Prices of Fruits

(Figures in Rs.)

Sl.			*Period*				*Percentage Change*			
No.	*Fruits*	*Quantity*	*I*	*II*	*III*	*IV*	*1st*	*2nd*	*3rd*	*4th*
1.	Apple	Dozen	8.05	9.11	14.03	25.64	13.24	53.97	82.75	218.65
2.	Banana	Quintal	56.91	134.33	144.57	272.96	136.02	7.63	88.81	379.61
3.	Ber	Kilogram	1.67	3.56	2.75	3.25	113.61	-22.86	18.22	94.78
4.	Custard apple	Quintal	10.29	76.65	94.72	214.43	645.06	23.58	126.39	1984.35
5.	Grapes	Boxes	19.51	26.27	39.12	52.68	34.64	48.93	34.66	170.03
6.	Guava	Kilogram	1.20	1.49	1.67	2.80	24.12	11.97	67.43	132.69
7.	Lemon	Kilogram	2.49	2.92	5.89	4.87	17.27	101.36	-17.22	95.47
8.	Mango	Dozen	5.73	6.56	11.77	10.27	14.38	79.48	-12.75	79.12
9.	Orange	Dozen	2.55	3.85	7.42	10.82	50.66	92.92	45.75	323.62
10.	Papaya	Dozen	6.05	6.04	3.86	12.25	-0.20	-36.13	217.57	102.43
11.	Pomegranate	Dozen	10.20	13.42	24.58	22.27	31.54	83.26	-9.39	118.38
12.	Sapota	Dozen	1.85	2.51	4.45	5.28	35.92	77.71	18.46	183.14
13.	Watermelon	Number	2.59	3.59	5.55	7.45	38.65	54.63	34.13	187.57

Note:
(1) Period: I=1983-84 to 1987-88, II=1988-89 to 1992-93, III=1993-94 to 1997-98, IV=1998-99 to 2002-03
(2) Percentage Change: 1st={(II-I)/I}*100, 2nd={(III-II)/II}*100, 3rd={(IV-III)/III}*100, 4th={(IV-I)/I}*100
Source: As per Table 1

In the case of Ber and Lemon there are ups and downs situation in the price during sub-periods. Watermelon showed an increasing trend in the price during same period.

In relative terms, overall change has reflected in the price of Custard apple with the first rank among all fruits with 1984.35 per cent of change. Banana with 379.61 per cent, Orange is next to Banana with 323.62 per cent, followed by Apple with 218.65 per cent. Pomegranate, Guava, Grapes, Papaya, Sapota, Watermelon and Apple too have increased from 100 to 200 per cent. Remaining fruits have increased between 75 to 99 per cent during 1983-84 and 2002-03. Thus overall performance of fruits in prices in the Siddheshwar Market Yard shows satisfactory picture during the entire period of the study.

COMPOUND GROWTH RATES IN THE PRICES OF FRUITS

The compound growth rate in the prices of fruits is shown in the Table 6.

Period-I

Remarkable growth rates in prices are seen in Banana, Custard apple and Papaya. Banana achieved a first rank among all the fruits. Pomegranate and Sapota were also significant achiever during the first period. A general characteristic of this period was that most of the Fruits have showed a positive trend. While only Apple has experienced the reduced growth rate of 1.18 per cent.

Period-II

An increasing trend in the prices of fruits has continued in the second period. However, some changes have been observed in the same period, particularly in Apple, it shows a better performance than earlier period. On the other hand this period has created an unfavorable atmosphere in the case of Papaya and Grapes. Papaya recorded a significant growth rate in the first period, but lost its rank and registered a highest negative growth rate of 22.74 per cent in the second period.

Period-III

The third period almost shows a combination of positive and negative performance of growth rates in fruits prices. Lemon, Mango, Sapota and Watermelon shows a better performance. On the other hand Banana has recorded highest negative growth rate of 31.16 per cent, followed by Guava with 19.39 per cent. These two fruits have achieved a better position in the earlier two periods.

Period-IV

In the fourth period Papaya has observed a highest growth rate in price among the fruits with 77.99 per cent. Mango stood next to Papaya with

38.06 per cent per annum. While Lemon, Pomegranate, Sapota, Watermelon and Grapes showed a negative growth rates. Among these five fruits, first four have observed better performance in the earlier three periods.

Table 6
Compound Growth Rates in the Prices of Fruits

Sl. No.	*Fruits*	*Period of CGR* I	II	III	IV	V
1.	Apple	-1.18	2.62	11.99	11.07	8.99
2.	Banana	243.25	4.30	-31.16	17.58	20.83
3.	Ber	17.53	7.09	-14.60	1.01	1.67
4.	Custard apple	140.40	24.07	6.85	16.58	33.52
5.	Grapes	9.37	-0.70	12.91	-3.17	6.88
6.	Guava	7.66	7.99	-19.39	8.18	4.18
7.	Lemon	1.95	23.59	23.55	-0.85	5.94
8.	Mango	12.54	4.13	23.64	38.06	5.00
9.	Orange	17.39	14.93	19.02	13.00	11.53
10.	Papaya	113.40	-22.74	-2.92	77.99	3.94
11.	Pomegranate	25.81	13.47	9.78	-7.97	6.21
12.	Sapota	56.24	10.62	21.35	-5.78	8.56
13.	Watermelon	15.69	0.50	20.29	-4.90	7.45

Note: (1) CGR calculated as Antilog (b-1)*100
(2) Period: I=1983-84 to 1987-88, II=1988-89 to 1992-93, III=1993-94 to 1997-98, IV=1998-99 to 2002-03, V=1983-84 to 2002-03.
Source: As per Table 1.

Period-V

Diagram 3 shows annual compound growth rate of prices of fruits during the entire period under study. All major fruits, during 1983-84 to 2002-03, observed a positive performance. Fruits have experienced increasing growth rates in the prices. Custard apple has recorded a highest growth rate in prices among the fruits with 33.52 per cent. Banana is next to Custard apple with 20.83 per cent. Banana is one of the important nutrient fruit in human life. Increasing trend in the price of Banana creates favorable atmosphere among the farmers.

VARIATION IN ARRIVAL OF FRUITS

The quantitative techniques like, relative range, standard deviation, coefficient of variation and skewness were applied for analyzing the overall arrival of agricultural commodities in the market yard.

A variation in arrival of Fruits has been analyzed in Table 7. It has been observed variability in the arrival of Fruits. Coefficient of range of arrival of Sapota is highest among the fruits. Custard apple, Orange, Papaya and Pomegranate have also registered the same variability with 0.99 coefficients. Banana and Mango have recorded the same variability in arrival with 0.98 coefficients. Watermelon has showed a lowest relative

Diagram 3
CGR in Prices of Fruits
(1983-84 to 2002-03)

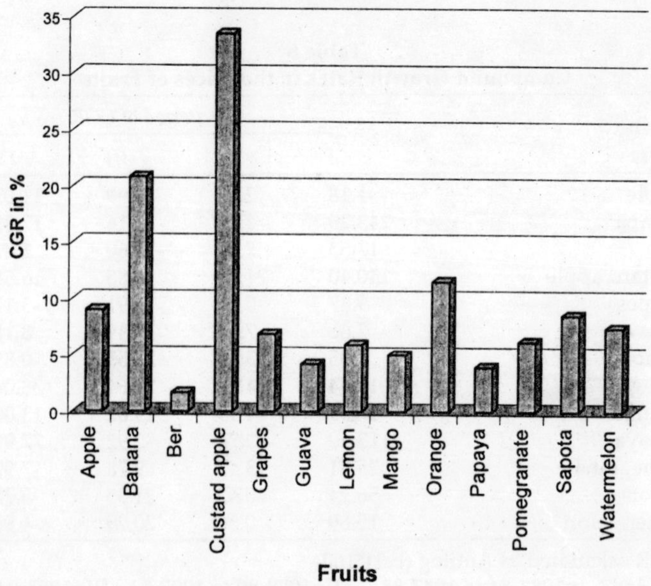

range of 0.48. Standard deviation for the entire period is calculated in Table 7.

Watermelon registered lowest coefficient of variation by 26.95 per cent among the fruits during 1983-84 to 2002-03. Guava is the next to Watermelon with 37.91 per cent variation, followed by Apple with 46.33 per cent of variations. Grapes and Lemon have also recorded a lower coefficient of variation. Custard apple has showed the highest coefficient of variation by 193.51 per cent. Banana, Papaya, Pomegranate and Sapota have also registered the highest coefficient of variation. Ber and Orange have also recorded a high degree of coefficient of variation. A coefficient of variation in arrival of fruits is shown in Diagram 4.

Skewness of fruits arrivals is shown in the last column of Table 7. Distribution of arrival of Fruits, among all fruits showed a positive skewness for the entire period except Watermelon. Distribution in the arrival of Watermelon shows slightly negative skewness with 0.08. It implies that the curve of distribution of arrival of Watermelon has less long tail towards the left. On the other hand, Papaya showed a very high skewed with 2.99; it implies that the curve of distribution of arrival has very longer tail towards the right. Custard apple, Apple, Banana, Lemon, Orange, Pomegranate and Sapota have also showed a high positive skewed between 1 and 2.5. Many commodities like Mango, Grapes have

Table 7
Variations in Arrival of Fruits

Sl.			Range			Standard Deviation					Coefficient of Variation					
No.	Fruits	Quantity	Min.	Max.	RR	I	II	III	IV	V	1st	2nd	3rd	4th	5th	Skew
1.	Apple	Dozen	146926	880700	0.71	95907	29913	51239	185745	168111	33.95	7.87	16.96	30.96	46.33	1.40
2.	Banana	Quintal	14333	1316242	0.98	579986	8325	196305	12231	428703	76.52	30.70	124.49	30.09	174.37	1.95
3.	Ber	Kilogram	184249	5117180	0.93	23720	519186	1131809	908942	1749555	11.41	74.97	39.53	21.97	89.98	0.35
4.	Custard apple	Quintal	472	129661	0.99	44453	2298	1270	426	33952	71.79	61.05	45.99	24.59	193.51	2.45
5.	Grapes	Boxes	23807	182300	0.77	9480	20984	22894	49230	45388	22.80	21.44	30.22	36.05	51.61	0.93
6.	Guava	Kilogram	175380	816251	0.65	23469	155151	222798	146633	156853	5.05	37.76	48.56	30.57	34.59	0.08
7.	Lemon	Kilogram	834238	4365085	0.68	206284	598231	255640	758354	986903	15.19	38.49	22.49	23.19	53.93	1.27
8.	Mango	Dozen	7235	590521	0.98	104111	85801	62428	107877	149998	25.23	46.39	71.51	42.43	63.88	0.63
9.	Orange	Dozen	715	138690	0.99	4479	21069	16912	45197	33702	63.54	86.52	33.42	78.47	98.55	1.39
10.	Papaya	Dozen	154	45770	0.99	312	1324	16583	3846	10556	77.60	126.22	127.55	36.73	170.52	2.99
11.	Pomegranate	Dozen	12414	1734250	0.99	48477	32283	31182	509184	425587	77.91	17.58	10.66	54.92	115.16	2.11
12.	Sapota	Dozen	1859	1173842	1.00	2581	40114	56049	383685	301998	47.07	101.73	45.28	69.84	168.74	2.32
13.	Watermelon	Number	333925	961004	0.48	117264	124157	116605	200876	172239	17.08	17.02	24.20	30.51	26.95	-0.08

Note:

(1) Standard Deviation: I=1983-84 to 1987-88, II=1988-89 to 1992-93, III=1993-94 to 1997-98, IV=1998-99 to 2002-03, V=1983-84 to 2002-03

(2) Coefficient of Variation: 1st=1983-84 to 1987-88, 2nd=1988-89 to 1992-93, 3rd=1993-94 to 1997-98, 4th=1998-99 to 2002-03, 5th=1983-84 to 2002-03

Source: As per Table 1.

Diagram 4
C.V. in Arrival of Fruits
(1983-84 to 2002-03)

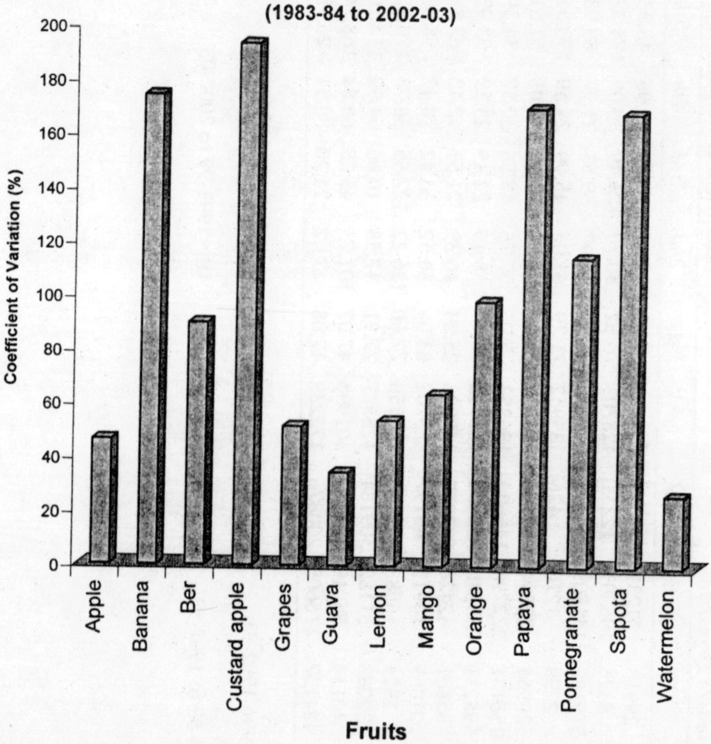

moderately positive skewed. Distribution in the arrival of Guava showed slightly positive skewed with 0.08; it implies that the curve of distribution of arrival of Guava has little long tail towards the right.

VARIATION IN THE VALUE TRANSACTION OF FRUITS

The variation in the sale of Fruits is analyzed in Table 8. It is observed from the variability of the Fruits that Orange, Papaya and Sapota have recorded the highest coefficient of range in sales with 1 for the entire period. A value transaction in Pomegranate shows a high range coefficient among the fruits with 0.99. Ber has also registered a higher variability of 0.97. On the contrary Guava has showed the lowest relative range among the fruits with 0.61. Remaining Fruits have also showed a higher relative range during the period under study. The standard deviation is considered for the entire period as shown in the Table. Coefficient of variation in value transaction of fruits is shown in Diagram 5.

Watermelon has registered the lowest coefficient of variation of 42.41 per cent during the period from 1983-84 to 2002-03. Guava stands next with 47.04 per cent, followed by Banana with 51.60 per cent. Custard apple,

Table 8
Variations in Value Transaction of Fruits

Sl. No.	Fruits	Quantity	Range Min.	Range Max.	RR	Standard Deviation I	II	III	IV	V	Coefficient of Variation 1st	2nd	3rd	4th	5th	Skew
1.	Apple	Dozen	1283864	26481220	0.91	701538	229834	1377572	6853572	6757955	31.52	6.66	31.79	42.71	107.41	1.88
2.	Banana	Quintal	1961822	13431053	0.75	2654146	1108532	1937557	1854282	3781438	57.56	30.59	18.22	17.76	51.60	0.07
3.	Ber	Kilogram	282537	18283765	0.97	67520	1786436	875015	3448660	5307263	19.29	71.52	12.44	25.57	91.66	0.67
4.	Custard apple	Quintal	35174	446100	0.85	63517	99807	130716	59758	133100	70.98	43.08	49.12	16.96	56.59	0.10
5.	Grapes	Boxes	670701	10655341	0.88	53482	515827	1520211	2591119	2787207	6.95	20.19	49.31	36.25	82.24	1.35
6.	Guava	Kilogram	376491	1536975	0.61	73177	178625	198702	279879	361029	13.11	30.51	31.20	21.71	47.04	1.08
7.	Lemon	Kilogram	2347206	18619460	0.78	713596	314552	1143503	2370910	5123678	21.06	8.02	18.52	15.16	70.38	1.23
8.	Mango	Dozen	155675	5339672	0.94	1449593	516474	417285	498820	1110189	57.63	43.69	56.92	22.41	66.72	1.75
9.	Orange	Dozen	1298	1580000	1.00	13854	71999	166851	513147	381193	68.20	86.87	43.62	78.25	134.54	2.12
10.	Papaya	Dozen	435	180955	1.00	3409	3773	45381	54169	58140	108.77	84.36	105.42	48.47	144.31	1.18
11.	Pomegranate	Dozen	96675	34928430	0.99	626491	640443	1876036	9672305	8838026	87.05	21.73	25.70	50.31	118.21	1.88
12.	Sapota	Dozen	1995	4970750	1.00	7433	114774	213737	1625436	1419093	64.05	107.68	41.46	59.82	169.65	1.94
13.	Watermelon	Number	1236223	5606511	0.64	604230	332446	564550	846255	1232126	33.68	12.78	22.09	18.12	42.41	0.88

Note:

(1) Standard Deviation: I=1983-84 to 1987-88, II=1988-89 to 1992-93, III=1993-94 to 1997-98, IV=1998-99 to 2002-03
V =1983-84 to 2002-03

(2) Coefficient of Variation: 1st = 1983-84 to 1987-88, 2nd=1988-89 to 1992-93, 3rd=1993-94 to 1997-98, 4th=1998-99 to 2002-03
5th =1983-84 to 2002-03

Source: As per Table 1.

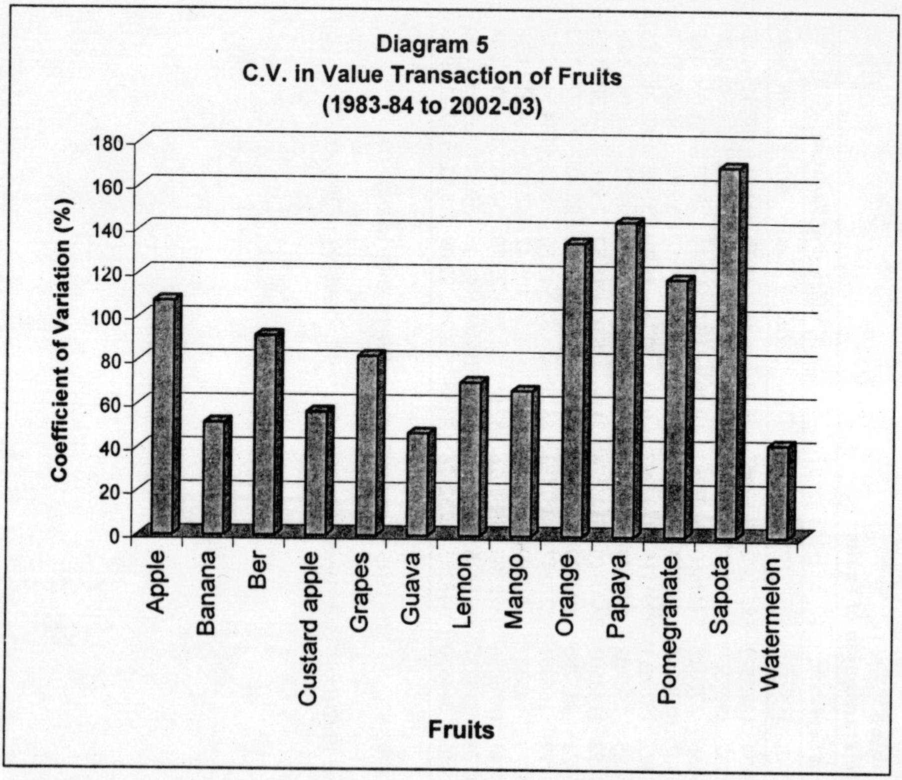

Mango and Lemon have recorded a lower coefficient of variation. Sapota showed the highest coefficient of variation of 169.65 per cent. Apple, Orange, Papaya and Pomegranate have registered high coefficient of variation i.e., of more than 100 per cent. Ber has also recorded a high degree of variation with 91.66 per cent.

Skewness of sale of fruits is explained in Table 8. It accounts for the information about the shape of the distribution and the degree of variation on either side of the central value. Distribution of sale of Fruits is positively skewed for the entire period except Custard apple. Distribution in the sale of Custard apple shows slightly negative skewed with 0.10; it implies that the curve of distribution of sale of Custard apple has less long tail towards the left. On the other hand, Orange shows a very high skewed with 2.12; which implies that the curve of distribution of sale has a very longer tail towards the right. Apple, Grapes, Guava, Lemon, Mango, Papaya, Pomegranate and Sapota have also shows a high positive skewed between 1 and 2. Many other commodities like Ber and Watermelon are also moderately skewed. Distribution in the sale of Banana is slightly positive skewed with 0.07; which implies that the curve of distribution of sale of Banana has little long tail towards the right.

REFERENCE

Bhatia D.K. and Gupta Vijay (1986), "Business Statistics", Vani Educational Books, New Delhi.

Gupta S.C. (1996), "Fundamentals of Statistics", Himalaya Publishing House, New Delhi.

Monga G.S. (2000), "Mathematics and Statistics for Economics", Vikas Pub. House Pvt. Ltd., Second Revised Edition, New Delhi.

Prasad A.S. (1985), "Agricultural Marketing in India", Mittal Publications, Delhi.

Reddy A.V. (1991), "Agricultural Marketing", Printwell, Jaipur.

Reddy P.I. (1995), "Marketing of Vegetables", Printwell, Jaipur.

Indian Journal of Agricultural Marketing (2002), Vol. 16, No. 2, Nagpur.

Indian Journal of Agricultural Marketing (2000), (Conference Special), Vol. 14, No. 3, Nagpur.

The Bihar Journal of Agricultural Marketing (2000), Vol. VIII, No. 1, Patna.

The Bihar Journal of Agricultural Marketing (1997), (Silver Jubilee Special Number), Vol. V, No. 3, Patna.

6

ANALYSIS AND INTERPRETATION OF MARKETING ACTIVITIES OF A.P.M.C. SOLAPUR: VEGETABLES

This chapter deals with the analysis and interpretation of marketing activities of Agricultural Produce Market Committee, Solapur in terms of growth in arrival, value transaction and price behaviour of vegetables and also in terms of variation and other economic variables performed during 1983-84 to 2002-03.

PROGRESS OF ARRIVALS OF MAJOR VEGETABLES

It is observed from the Table 1 that Agricultural Produce Market Committee, Solapur has been making progress in the arrivals of vegetables over a period of time. It reflects the fact that the producers in this region prefer to sale vegetables in the market yard only because of the fact that the market provides basic infrastructural facilities to the products as well as it is convenient to sell the products in many ways in the market yard.

Onion occupies major share among the vegetables in the market. During the first period by 3177 hundred quintals of Onion was arrived. It has increased in the second period by 4827 hundred quintals, further continued to increase by to 10446 hundred quintals in the third period and 15425 hundred quintals in the fourth period.

Most of the vegetables showed a better position in arrival namely; Tomato, Potato, Brinjal, Coriander Leaves, Fenugreek, and Green Chilies. But Chuka, Garlic and Hemp recorded a negative performance during the study period.

Remarkable overall change in the case of Potato was recorded at 509.75 per cent, followed by Onion with 385.50 per cent. Tomato was next to the Onion with 377.48 per cent. Spinach has also achieved a better position by 258.58 per cent. Cabbage, Carrot, Cucumber, Gourd, Green Chilies have

Table 1
Progress of Arrival of Vegetables

Sl. No.	Vegetables	Quantity	Period I	II	III	IV	Percentage Change 1st	2nd	3rd	4th
1.	Bitter gourd	Kilogram	150760	163010	186374	248833	8.12	14.33	33.51	65.05
2.	Brinjal	Kilogram	2217529	2556288	2168345	3177223	15.28	-15.18	46.53	43.28
3.	Cabbage	Kilogram	544481	72258	1107449	1507693	32.71	53.26	36.14	176.90
4.	Carrot	Kilogram	506659	702148	867038	1207173	38.58	23.48	39.23	138.26
5.	Cauliflower	Number	516544	643924	899591	911168	24.66	39.40	1.29	76.40
6.	Chuka	Bundle	573839	728419	421542	464457	26.94	-42.13	10.18	-19.06
7.	Coriander Leaves	Bundle	2733553	3033208	3227856	4174202	10.96	6.42	29.32	52.70
8.	Cucumber	Kilogram	329711	445596	532709	889761	35.15	19.55	67.03	169.86
9.	Dodaka	Kilogram	320714	363134	404858	469187	13.23	11.49	15.89	46.29
10.	Fenugreek	Bundle	2592517	3077745	2129385	3038015	18.72	-30.81	42.67	17.18
11.	Garlic	Quintal	34305	5981	10363	14876	-82.57	73.28	43.55	-56.64
12.	Gourd	Number	90905	167527	218071	258597	84.29	30.17	18.58	184.47
13.	Green Chilies	Kilogram	1014945	1595120	1551524	2061441	57.16	-2.73	32.87	103.11
14.	Hemp	Bundle	128516	104277	120894	112591	-18.86	15.93	-6.87	-12.39
15.	Lady's finger	Kilogram	392580	540910	442899	586413	37.78	-18.12	32.40	49.37
16.	Onion	Quintal	317711	482687	1044613	1542499	51.93	116.42	47.66	385.50
17.	Potato	Kilogram	3091201	3495453	7888498	18848546	13.08	125.68	138.94	509.75
18.	Shepu	Bundle	1084442	1415059	1366544	1567705	30.49	-3.43	14.72	44.56
19.	Spinach	Bundle	345253	921380	930470	1238027	166.87	0.99	33.05	258.58
20.	Sweet Potato	Kilogram	334272	265241	203187	469331	-20.65	-23.39	130.98	40.40
21.	Tomato	Kilogram	3949518	5442228	9061880	18858284	37.79	66.51	108.11	377.48
22.	Vetch	Kilogram	315655	313018	427230	4463695	-0.83	36.49	3.85	40.56

Note:
(1) Period: I=1983-84 to 1987-88, II=1988-89 to 1992-93, III=1993-94 to 1997-98, IV=1998-99 to 2002-03
(2) Percentage Change: 1st = {(II-I)/I}*100, 2nd={(III-II)/II}*100, 3rd={(IV-III)/III}*100, 4th={(IV-I)/I}*100
Source: Processed data on the basis of Annual Report of APMC, Solapur, Period from 1983-84 to 2002-03.

also showed better performance in arrival between 100 per cent and 200 per cent during the 1983-84 to 2002-03.

ANNUAL COMPOUND GROWTH RATES IN ARRIVALS OF VEGETABLES

Point to point annual compound growth rate was calculated for the analysis of growth of arrival of agricultural commodity in the market yard for twenty year. This period is further divided into four sub-periods with a unit of five years.

Table 2 accounts for the annual compound growth rates of arrival of vegetables during 1983-84 to 2002-03. It is observed that, a remarkable better performance of arrival of vegetable in the market yard during the entire study period. In the case of arrival of vegetables, 18 vegetables out of 22, showed a positive growth rates except Sweet Potato, Fenugreek and Chuka and Hemp. Arrival of potato has recorded highest growth rate among the vegetable crops. Potato increased by 12.59 per cent per annum during the entire period of 20 years. Growth rates of Potato in the divided periods also satisfactory, except a marginal negative growth rate of 0.89 per cent during the second period.

Table 2
Compound Growth Rates in Arrival of Vegetables

Sl.		*CGR Period*				
No.	*Vegetables*	*I*	*II*	*III*	*IV*	*V*
1.	Bitter gourd	16.48	-1.36	0.34	4.12	3.59
2.	Brinjal	3.68	4.07	-2.62	22.96	1.77
3.	Cabbage	-4.67	-2.27	0.16	16.37	6.77
4.	Carrot	1.96	17.66	-4.01	11.67	5.77
5.	Cauliflower	22.75	-0.32	-10.81	25.14	4.69
6.	Chuka	-7.15	-11.29	9.58	3.17	-2.13
7.	Coriander Leaves	1.38	-4.21	1.17	11.36	2.60
8.	Cucumber	3.65	-1.56	0.06	17.26	6.26
9.	Dodake	5.99	8.33	0.33	8.55	2.66
10.	Fenugreek	2.88	0.25	-41.33	9.15	-1.84
11.	Garlic	-62.51	9.43	23.48	-17.98	1.06
12.	Gourd	10.76	34.16	7.12	28.99	7.54
13.	Green Chilies	14.98	-3.87	5.00	4.57	4.43
14.	Hemp	9.18	1.78	12.29	4.60	-0.25
15.	Lady's finger	16.47	-10.36	2.74	8.31	2.25
16.	Onion	4.39	13.59	9.67	16.66	11.47
17.	Potato	9.59	-0.89	14.31	23.02	12.59
18.	Shepu	6.19	-11.12	-6.98	20.45	1.91
19.	Spinach	28.19	0.92	1.11	20.95	8.43
20.	Sweet Potato	-3.37	-20.96	-9.10	67.26	-1.36
21	Tomato	9.02	4.49	16.07	4.47	10.79
22	Vetch	12.56	9.46	1.93	9.46	3.01

Note: (1) CGR calculated as Antilog (b-1)*100
(2) Period: I=1983-84 to 1987-88, II=1988-89 to 1992-93, III=1993-94 to 1997-98, IV=1998-99 to 2002-03, V=1983-84 to 2002-03.

Source: As per Table 1.

Onion is less perishable vegetable than other. It has registered a remarkable growth rate of 11.47 per cent during the study period. Arrival of tomato has increased by 10.79 per cent per annum during the same period. The three vegetables namely Potato, Tomato and Onion have registered two-digit growth rate. After that above mentioned three vegetables Spinach achieved a better growth rate than other with 8.43 per cent, followed by Gourd (7.54 per cent), Cabbage (6.77 per cent), Cucumber (6.26 per cent), Carrot (5.77 per cent), Cauliflower (4.69 per cent), Green chilies (4.43 per cent), Bitter gourd (3.59 per cent), Vetch (3.01 per cent), Dodake (2.66per cent), Coriander leaves (2.60 per cent), Lady's finger (2.25 per cent), Shepu (1.91per cent), Brinjal (1.77 per cent) and marginally increased with 1.06 per cent growth rate of Garlic.

Diagram 1 shows the annual compound growth rate of arrival of vegetables during 1983-84 to 2002-03 period. It is observed that in the sub divided period of Period-IV shows a positive growth rates except one. vegetable. Many vegetables enjoyed a larger growth rate in the period-IV. Dodaka, Gourd, Hemp, Onion, Spinach, Tomato and Vetch are continuously showing a positive trend in the each sub divided period from Period-I to IV. Thus we can conclude that, growth of vegetables in recent period and future is better and bright in the market yard.

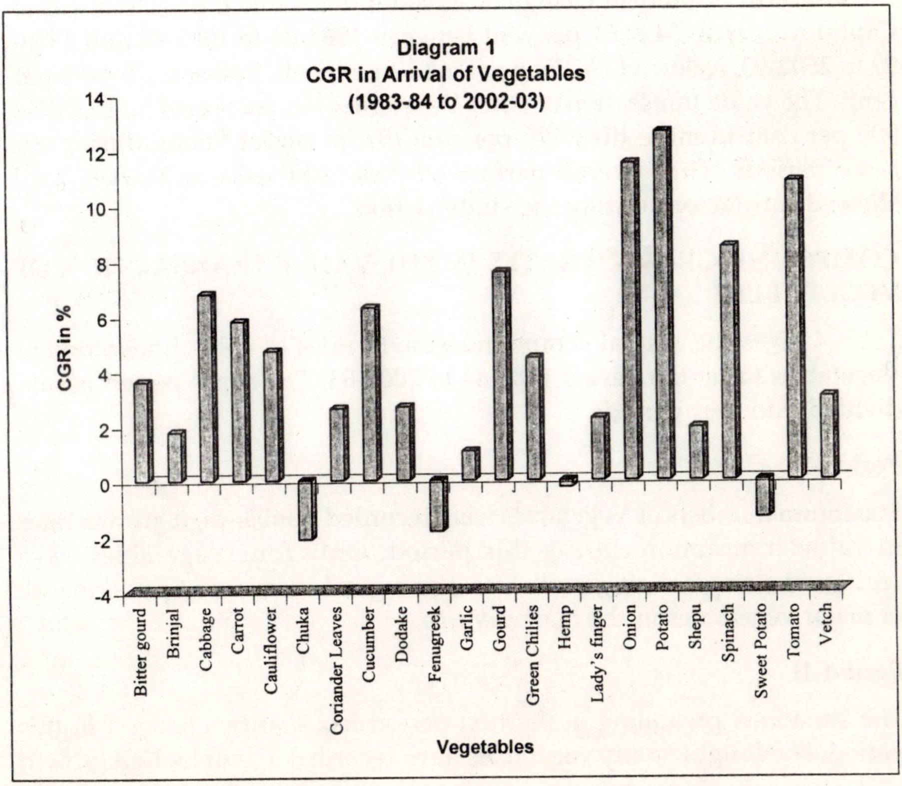

PROGRESS IN VALUE TRANSACTION OF VEGETABLES

It is observed from the Table 3 reflect a progress in the value transaction of Vegetables over a period of time. Which is also an indicative fact why the farmers prefer to sale their products in the market.

The value transaction of Onion was at the first rank with Rs. 369.40 lakh during 1983-84 to 1987-88 (I period). Tomato was next to Onion by Rs. 64.52 lakh, followed by Potato with Rs. 60.75 lakh. The picture was better in the second period (1988-89 to 1992-93) than the first period, because all vegetables were at an increasing trend. Again the Onion has been recorded its prime position with Rs. 720.81 lakh in the value transaction; it was also observed this value is higher than earlier period. Tomato was next to Onion with Rs. 118.43 lakh, followed by Potato with Rs. 82.23 lakh. In the third period, the story was repeated again in the case of Onion, it was recorded Rs. 2576.29 lakh value transaction with first rank. Second position has been achieved by Potato with Rs. 309.54 lakh share. While Tomato was losing its second position and got third rank with Rs. 299.37 lakhs. The picture in third period was repeated in the fourth period in the case of three vegetables referred above. Onion recorded value transaction of Rs. 3454.49 lakhs during 1998-99 to 2002-03.

The most prominent change observed in the value transaction was of Cauliflower with 3420.61 per cent between 1983-84 to 1987-88 and 1998-99 to 2002-03, followed by Potato (1164.12 per cent), Spinach (1099.91 per cent). The value transaction of other Vegetables too, increased by less than 900 per cent to more than 170 per cent except Sweet Potato during the same periods. Thus overall performance of Siddheshwar Market Yard showed satisfactory during the study period.

COMPOUND GROWTH RATES IN THE VALUE TRANSACTION OF VEGETABLES

Table 4 gives the annual compound growth rates in value transaction of Vegetables for entire period 1983-84 to 2002-03. The entire period is sub-divided into four periods.

Period-I

Maximum numbers of Vegetables were recorded double-digit growth rates in value transaction during this period. Only four Vegetables have registered a single digit growth rate. It is a good indicator of performance of major vegetables in the market yard.

Period-II

The situations prevailing in the first period has slightly changed in this period. No dought, many vegetables have recorded a double-digit growth

Table 3
Progress of Value Transaction of Vegetables

(Figures in Lakh Rupees)

Sl.			Period				Percentage Change			
No.	Vegetables	Quantity	I	II	III	IV	1st	2nd	3rd	4th
1.	Bitter gourd	Kilogram	2.26	3.86	7.77	12.74	71.17	101.11	64.05	464.73
2.	Brinjal	Kilogram	31.30	47.63	68.95	96.99	52.18	44.75	40.67	209.88
3.	Cabbage	Kilogram	6.02	10.56	21.31	34.58	75.37	101.82	62.23	474.20
4.	Carrot	Kilogram	3.73	10.22	15.22	25.24	174.27	48.89	65.85	577.26
5.	Cauliflower	Number	1.61	4.77	7.99	56.78	196.05	67.40	610.37	3420.61
6.	Chuka	Bundle	1.58	3.49	3.40	4.27	121.59	-2.77	25.70	170.84
7.	Coriander Leaves	Bundle	15.58	27.87	53.65	67.70	78.90	92.51	26.20	334.63
8.	Cucumber	Kilogram	4.91	9.03	15.06	33.30	84.04	66.73	121.13	578.50
9.	Dodaka	Kilogram	6.80	11.62	19.72	27.41	70.83	69.68	38.98	302.88
10.	Fenugreek	Bundle	8.30	19.11	18.85	37.56	130.37	-1.41	99.31	352.69
11.	Garlic	Quintal	19.89	34.38	113.45	191.12	72.80	230.02	68.46	860.73
12.	Gourd	Number	0.65	1.53	2.19	3.18	136.15	42.41	45.47	389.24
13.	Green Chilies	Kilogram	22.93	59.20	92.96	131.54	158.17	57.02	41.51	473.62
14.	Hemp	Bundle	0.25	0.36	0.57	0.74	39.76	61.67	29.29	192.14
15.	Lady's finger	Kilogram	9.30	17.92	26.04	41.65	92.66	45.33	59.92	347.77
16.	Onion	Quintal	369.40	720.81	2576.29	3454.49	95.13	257.42	34.09	835.17
17.	Potato	Kilogram	60.75	82.23	309.54	767.93	35.37	276.42	148.08	1164.12
18.	Shepu	Bundle	2.94	7.31	11.61	18.77	148.27	58.88	61.63	537.55
19.	Spinach	Bundle	1.01	4.57	6.94	12.10	352.85	51.95	74.38	1099.91
20.	Sweet Potato	Kilogram	3.12	3.26	4.38	5.40	4.57	34.45	23.30	73.34
21.	Tomato	Kilogram	64.52	118.43	299.37	549.28	83.55	152.77	83.48	751.29
22.	Vetch	Kilogram	6.48	12.61	23.19	29.87	94.62	83.89	28.77	360.86

Note:
(1) Period: I=1983-84 to 1987-88, II=1988-89 to 1992-93, III=1993-94 to 1997-98, IV=1998-99 to 2002-03
(2) Percentage Change: 1st={(II-I)/I}*100, 2nd={(III-II)/II}*100, 3rd={(IV-III)/III}*100, 4th={(IV-I)/I}*100
Source: As per Table 1.

rates in value transaction, but unable to maintain a positive growth rates in all vegetables. Cauliflower and Sweet Potato registered a negative growth rates.

Table 4
Compound Growth Rates in Value Transaction of Vegetables

Sl.		*CGR Period*				
No.	*Vegetables*	*I*	*II*	*III*	*IV*	*V*
1.	Bitter gourd	16.18	6.81	10.54	13.29	12.50
2.	Brinjal	11.77	4.02	14.99	0.60	7.84
3.	Cabbage	5.56	10.70	9.69	14.13	12.37
4.	Carrot	13.29	31.74	11.30	10.07	13.38
5.	Cauliflower	24.09	-1.02	10.16	113.74	18.92
6.	Chuka	8.98	9.03	5.02	8.78	6.47
7.	Coriander Leaves	22.92	15.83	19.99	-2.61	10.86
8.	Cucumber	14.07	10.44	7.20	19.28	13.17
9.	Dodake	10.59	19.27	10.96	13.19	10.13
10.	Fenugreek	15.88	15.08	-38.78	13.43	7.10
11.	Garlic	73.52	25.01	11.48	-5.93	19.55
12.	Gourd	11.87	35.71	4.35	38.50	10.95
13.	Green Chilies	30.02	6.30	17.15	10.97	12.64
14.	Hemp	16.55	29.71	13.09	10.01	8.26
15.	Lady's finger	25.89	1.02	11.62	14.44	10.57
16.	Onion	13.90	22.26	13.88	13.87	17.17
17.	Potato	17.34	10.27	25.69	15.75	19.22
18.	Shepu	0.35	7.21	5.53	23.48	13.93
19.	Spinach	41.19	19.27	14.48	22.00	18.14
20.	Sweet Potato	5.48	-8.32	6.60	21.63	3.93
21.	Tomato	20.72	10.65	33.32	11.04	15.97
22.	Vetch	16.81	22.08	11.49	16.81	11.37

Note: (1) CGR calculated as Antilog (b-1)*100
(2) Period: I=1983-84 to 1987-88, II=1988-89 to 1992-93, III=1993-94 to 1997-98, IV=1998-99 to 2002-03, V=1983-84 to 2002-03

Source: As per Table 1.

Period-III

The third period was also better unlike earlier two periods. Almost all vegetables have recorded a positive growth rates in value transaction except Fenugreek. Fenugreek has reduced a higher-level growth rate in value transaction per annum with 38.78 per cent. On the other hand many vegetables showed not only double-digit growth rates but also significant in the growth rates of value transaction. More than 60 per cent vegetables have registered a growth rate within the range of 10 to 20 per cent per annum.

Period-IV

In the recent past, Cauliflower has showed highest positive growth rate among the vegetables. On the other hand Coriander leaves and Garlic have indicated a negative growth rates. Both vegetables have recorded not only positive but also significant during the past three periods. Brinjal was positive but registered least growth rate with 0.60 per cent during this period in the market yard.

Period-V

Diagram 2 shows an annual compound growth rate in the value transaction of vegetables during the entire period. Entire period of the analysis showed a remarkable performance of vegetables in value transaction. Garlic has recorded a highest growth rate among all vegetables during the study period with 19.55 per cent share per annum in Value transaction. On the other hand Sweet Potato has registered a lowest growth rate with 3.93 per cent. Growth rates of Brinjal, Chuka, Fenugreek and Hemp have within the range of 6 to 9per cent. Remaining vegetables have recorded greater performance, which is between 10 and 20 per cent during 1983-84 to 2002-03.

Diagram 2
CGR in Value Transaction of Vegetables
(1983-84 to 2002-03)

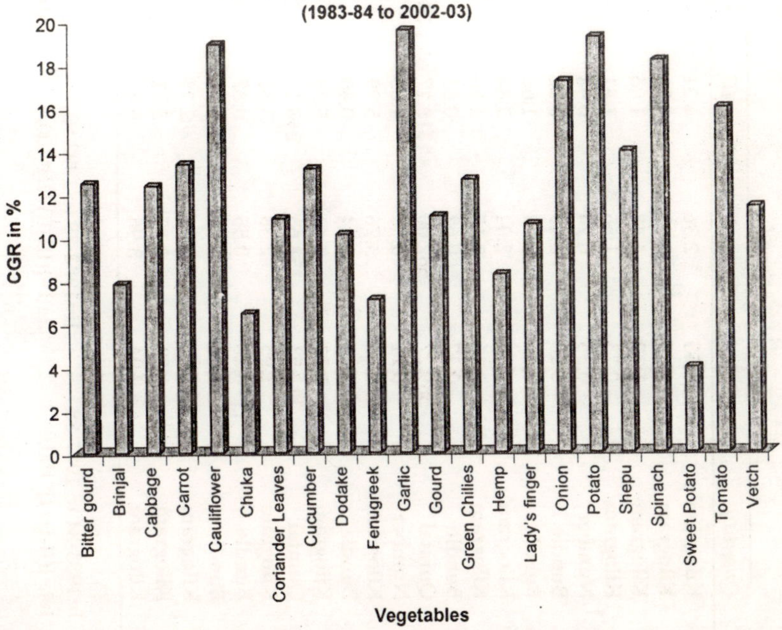

PRICE BEHAVIOUR OF VEGETABLES

It is observed from the Table 5 that, price of Garlic has remained at Rs. 589.27 per quintal, and declined by Rs. 562 in the second period. It has gone up by Rs. 1318.27 during the third period. It has further increased by Rs. 1395.54 in the fourth period. In the case of Onion, a record price of

Table 5
Progress in Prices of Vegetables

(Figures in Rs.)

Sl. No.	Vegetables	Quantity	Period I	Period II	Period III	Period IV	Percentage Change 1st	Percentage Change 2nd	Percentage Change 3rd	Percentage Change 4th
1.	Bitter gourd	Kilogram	1.55	2.36	4.21	5.11	52.61	78.08	21.53	230.26
2.	Brinjal	Kilogram	1.40	1.93	3.51	3.81	37.54	66.14	18.85	171.57
3.	Cabbage	Kilogram	1.12	1.48	1.96	2.32	32.25	32.35	18.37	107.18
4.	Carrot	Kilogram	0.73	1.56	1.81	2.14	112.61	16.07	18.17	191.58
5.	Cauliflower	Number	0.35	0.74	0.94	4.86	111.98	26.34	418.46	1288.51
6.	Chuka	Bundle	0.28	0.49	0.82	0.92	72.06	69.06	12.63	227.64
7.	Coriander Leaves	Bundle	0.57	0.94	1.66	1.89	64.79	76.79	14.25	232.85
8.	Cucumber	Kilogram	1.49	2.04	2.84	3.78	37.44	39.17	32.82	154.06
9.	Dodaka	Kilogram	2.11	3.15	4.86	5.93	49.54	54.22	21.96	181.27
10.	Fenugreek	Bundle	0.32	0.62	0.83	1.24	95.83	32.62	49.90	288.82
11.	Garlic	Quintal	589.27	562.00	1318.27	1395.54	-4.63	134.57	5.86	136.83
12.	Gourd	Number	0.71	0.95	1.03	1.19	32.95	8.36	16.08	67.23
13.	Green Chilies	Kilogram	2.19	3.76	5.99	6.37	71.79	59.44	6.26	191.06
14.	Hemp	Bundle	0.20	0.34	0.49	0.66	73.39	44.02	35.13	237.47
15.	Lady's finger	Kilogram	2.33	3.43	5.88	7.09	46.93	71.41	20.64	203.83
16.	Onion	Quintal	112.53	153.63	248.17	229.52	36.52	61.54	-7.52	103.97
17.	Potato	Kilogram	1.95	2.38	3.81	4.50	22.01	60.09	18.08	130.65
18.	Shepu	Bundle	0.26	0.55	0.87	1.19	106.71	59.52	36.73	350.88
19.	Spinach	Bundle	0.28	0.49	0.74	1.00	78.43	49.51	34.68	259.30
20.	Sweet Potato	Kilogram	0.94	1.31	2.23	3.19	39.77	70.07	42.83	239.47
21.	Tomato	Kilogram	1.63	2.17	3.31	2.93	33.23	52.27	-11.37	79.79
22.	Vetch	Kilogram	2.04	3.96	5.40	6.83	93.81	36.30	26.50	234.17

Note:
(1) Period: I=1983-84 to 1987-88, II=1988-89 to 1992-93, III=1993-94 to 1997-98, IV=1998-99 to 2002-03
(2) Percentage Change: 1st={(II-I)/I}*100, 2nd={(III-II)/II}*100, 3rd={(IV-III)/III}*100, 4th={(IV-I)/I}*100.
Source: As per Table 1.

Rs. 112.53 per quintal was reflected during the first period, which has increased by Rs. 153.63 in the second period. The story is repeated in the third with Rs. 248.17. It has declined by Rs. 229.52 per quintal during the fourth period. The ups and down in the price were trends observed in Garlic and Onion during sub-periods.

The quantity of Cauliflower and Gourd is measured in term of number. The average price of Gourd has recorded at Rs. 0.71 for each number and Cauliflower has recorded a little as compared to Gourd with Rs. 0.35 per item. The story is again repeated in the second and third period, but in the fourth period, positional rank has changed and Cauliflower got higher price than Gourd.

The quantity of Chuka, Coriander Leaves, Fenugreek, Hemp, Shepu and Spinach is measured in term of bundles. The Coriander Leaves has recorded the first rank with a price of Rs. 0.57 per bundle in the market, followed by Fenugreek with Rs. 0.32 in the first period In the case of Coriander Leaves and Fenugreek have attained their rank repeatedly during the period second. But in the third period, picture has changed in the case of Fenugreek; Coriander Leaves has increased by Rs. 1.66 per bundle and Shepu with Rs. 0.87 attained second position. In the recent past Coriander Leaves has increased price with Rs. 1.89 per bundle and followed by Fenugreek with Rs.1.24 per bundle.

Most of the vegetables; Bitter gourd, Brinjal, Cabbage, Carrot, Cucumber, Dodaka, Green Chilies, Lady's finger, Potato, Sweet Potato, Tomato and Vetch quantity are measured in terms of kilogram. Lady's finger has recorded the prime position in the price with Rs. 2.33 per kilogram daring the first period. Green chili was next vegetable with Rs. 2.19 per kilogram. The Vetch with a price of Rs. 3.96 per kilogram has attaimed first position followed by Green chili with Rs. 3.76. Green chili has achieved first position in the prices with Rs. 5.99 per kilogram followed by Lady's finger with Rs. 5.88 per kilogram in the third period. In the recent past the prime position in prices has been achieved by Lady's finger with Rs. 7.09 per kilogram followed by Green chili with Rs. 6.37 per kilogram.

The overall change in price behaviour is seen with Cauliflower among the vegetables with 1288.51 per cent change. Shepu is the next vegetable by 350.88 per cent change during entire period. Remaining vegetables, except Gourd and Tomato, have reflected a change between 100 to 300 per cent.

COMPOUND GROWTH RATES IN THE PRICES OF VEGETABLES

The annual growth rate in the prices of Vegetables is exhibited in Table 6. The observations therein are explained as under:

Period-I

Except Bitter gourd and Shepu, almost all vegetables show a positive growth rate in the vegetable prices. Among the vegetables, Garlic has recorded a highest growth rate of 362.81 per cent. Nearly 40 per cent of vegetables have registered growth rates within the range of 10 to 20 per cent. Out of total number of vegetables, 40 per cent vegetables have recorded a single-digit growth rate within the range of 1 to 9 per cent.

Table 6
Compound Growth Rates in the Prices of Vegetables

Sl. No.	*Vegetables*	*CGR Period* I	II	III	IV	V
1.	Bitter gourd	-0.26	8.29	10.16	8.80	8.60
2.	Brinjal	7.80	-0.05	18.08	-5.00	7.11
3.	Cabbage	10.73	13.28	9.52	-1.83	5.24
4.	Carrot	11.11	11.97	15.95	-1.44	7.20
5.	Cauliflower	1.09	-0.70	23.51	70.80	13.59
6.	Chuka	17.38	22.90	-4.17	5.44	8.79
7.	Coriander Leaves	21.25	20.92	18.60	3.89	9.38
8.	Cucumber	10.05	12.19	7.14	1.72	6.50
9.	Dodaka	4.34	10.10	10.59	4.27	7.27
10.	Fenugreek	12.63	17.79	4.34	3.92	9.10
11.	Garlic	362.81	14.23	-9.72	14.68	18.29
12.	Gourd	1.00	1.16	-2.59	7.38	3.17
13.	Green Chilies	13.07	10.58	11.57	6.15	7.86
14.	Hemp	6.74	27.44	0.72	5.17	8.54
15.	Lady's finger	8.09	12.70	8.64	5.66	8.14
16.	Onion	10.79	7.64	3.84	-2.40	5.31
17.	Potato	7.08	11.25	9.95	-5.91	8.89
18.	Shepu	-5.50	20.34	13.45	2.51	11.79
19.	Spinach	10.14	18.19	13.22	0.86	8.96
20.	Sweet Potato	9.16	15.99	17.27	15.25	8.89
21.	Tomato	10.73	5.90	14.86	6.29	4.68
22.	Vetch	3.78	11.53	9.38	6.71	8.12

Note: (1) CGR calculated as Antilog (b-1)*100
(2) Period: I=1983-84 to 1987-88, II=1988-89 to 1992-93, III=1993-94 to 1997-98, IV=1998-99 to 2002-03, V=1983-84 to 2002-03.

Source: As per Table 1.

Period-II

The second period was little better than the first period. Good numbers of vegetables have a significant growth rate in the prices. Most of the vegetables show a positive trend, except two vegetables that have registered a marginal negative trend of less than 1 per cent. Hemp has recorded a highest growth rate among the vegetables with 27.44 per cent.

Period-III

Cauliflower stood first in the rank among all vegetables with 23.51 per cent per annum growth rate in the prices. Coriander Leaves was next to

Cauliflower with a share of 18.60 per cent. Some vegetables shows a negative trend namely; Chuka, Garlic and Gourd, which have registered a better performance during the first two periods.

Period-IV

Cauliflower again has attained the first rank among the vegetables with a share of 70.80 per cent per annum growth rate in the prices. Garlic and Sweet Potato shows a significant performacne. Some important vegetables like Brinjal, Cabbage, Carrot, Onion and Potato have performed a negative trend. Growth rates of remaining vegetables was registered a single-digit grow the rate confining within the range of 1-9 per cent.

Period-V

Diagram 3 has shows an annual compound growth rate in the prices of vegetables during the study period. A general feature of this period has been observed positive. Garlic has showed a highest growth rate of 18.29 per cent. Cauliflower was the next to Garlic with a share of 13.59 per cent. A growth rate in prices of Shepu is also significant.

Out of 22 vegetables, more than 85 per cent of vegetables have performed a single-digit growth rates within the range of 3-9 per cent.

Diagram 3
CGR in the Prices of Vegetables
(1983-84 to 2002-03)

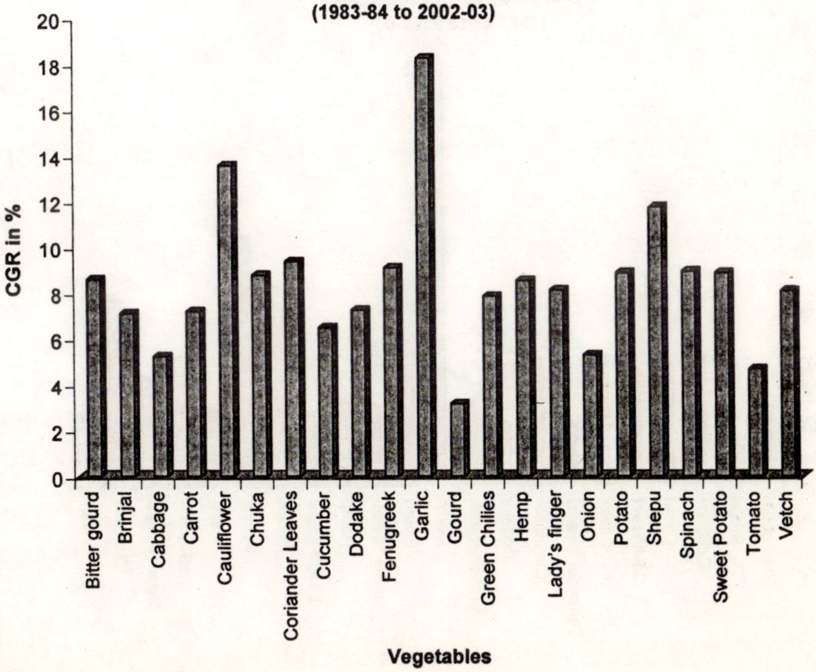

VARIATIONS IN ARRIVAL OF VEGETABLES

The quantitative techniques like, relative range, standard deviation, coefficient of variation and skewness were applied for analyzing the overall arrival of vegetables in the market yard.

The variation in arrival of vegetables has been analyzed in Table 7. Variations in arrival of major vegetables in their various quantities have created some interesting picture.

There is a difference of relative range among the Vegetables. The range coefficient of arrival of Fenugreek is higher than other Vegetables with 0.99. Garlic has next to Fenugreek with 0.96 relative range. Cauliflower, Chuka, Gourd, Onion, Potato, and Spinach have registered a higher variability. Brinjal has showed a lowest relative range of 0.25 among the vegetables. Remaining vegetables have showed moderate coefficient of range. Standard deviation for major vegetables is considered for the entire period.

Coefficient of variation in arrival of vegetables is shown in Diagram 4 for the 1983-84 to 2002-03. The coefficient of variations in arrival of major vegetables is calculated for the entire period of the study. Among the Vegetables, Brinjal has registered a lowest coefficient of variation by 13.53 per cent. Coriander Leaves is the next to Brinjal with 20.07 per cent.

Diagram 4
C.V. in Arrival of Vegetables
(1983-84 to 2002-03)

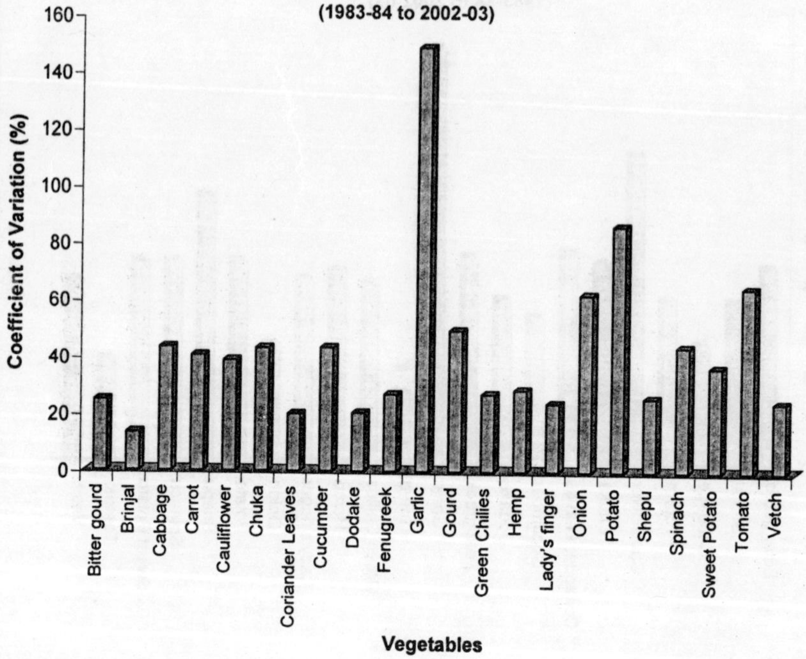

Table 7
Variations in Arrival of Vegetables

Sl. No.	Vegetables	Quantity	Range Min.	Range Max.	RR	Standard Deviation I	II	III	IV	V	Coefficient of Variation 1st	2nd	3rd	4th	5th	Skew
1.	Bitter gourd	Kilogram	96877	283676	0.49	41567	13103	11755	29071	46355	27.57	8.04	6.31	11.68	24.76	0.43
2.	Brinjal	Kilogram	1789408	2991379	0.25	113919	414301	108138	281426	321857	5.14	16.21	4.99	10.94	13.53	0.37
3.	Cabbage	Kilogram	436706	1787700	0.61	73546	82933	215224	320843	421852	13.51	11.48	19.43	21.28	43.47	0.79
4.	Carrot	Kilogram	344211	1592217	0.64	25726	262768	173039	281526	332826	5.08	37.42	19.96	23.32	40.55	0.70
5.	Cauliflower	Number	230139	1279000	0.70	267774	130576	163156	322984	288787	51.84	20.28	18.14	35.45	38.88	0.35
6.	Chuka	Bundle	314345	1488226	0.65	67668	392138	65489	65873	236202	11.79	53.83	15.54	14.18	43.17	3.32
7.	Coriander Leaves	Bundle	2565252	4870675	0.31	138589	271638	90454	695384	660675	5.07	8.96	2.80	16.66	20.07	1.49
8.	Cucumber	Kilogram	286483	1082769	0.58	42356	56700	57393	209059	238313	12.85	12.72	10.77	23.50	43.37	1.31
9.	Dodaka	Kilogram	265327	596100	0.38	40435	45804	32926	92320	79612	12.61	12.61	8.13	19.68	20.44	0.96
10.	Fenugreek	Bundle	23687	3687501	0.99	139150	290132	1094258	505811	733234	5.37	9.43	51.39	19.65	27.06	-2.38
11.	Garlic	Quintal	2102	113013	0.96	43240	805	5137	4267	24407	126.04	13.45	49.57	28.68	148.99	3.43
12.	Gourd	Number	68507	337300	0.66	13255	81252	61347	83181	90999	14.58	48.50	28.13	32.17	49.52	0.50
13.	Green Chilies	Kilogram	667030	2311645	0.55	215978	154585	237751	188587	421838	21.28	9.69	15.32	9.15	27.12	-0.21
14.	Hemp	Bundle	60586	235672	0.59	17523	5333	59674	15360	33394	13.63	5.11	49.36	13.64	28.64	2.23
15.	Lady's finger	Kilogram	313262	663459	0.36	102556	103989	31866	95509	117328	26.12	19.22	7.19	16.28	23.91	0.05
16.	Onion	Quintal	289647	2037936	0.75	20402	118752	156934	361371	525684	6.42	24.60	15.02	26.43	62.07	0.75
17.	Potato	Kilogram	2679620	26014496	0.81	432210	336095	1807742	6473058	7195845	13.98	9.61	22.92	34.34	86.38	1.43
18.	Shepu	Bundle	817674	2066973	0.43	167959	318810	178344	459239	351673	15.49	22.53	13.05	29.29	25.89	0.47
19.	Spinach	Bundle	223423	1568862	0.75	158045	94671	54159	343289	377928	45.78	10.27	5.82	27.73	44.01	-0.11
20.	Sweet Potato	Kilogram	118693	425518	0.56	57489	102462	43878	29897	89635	17.20	38.63	21.59	17.41	36.80	0.74
21.	Tomato	Kilogram	3319931	21096658	0.73	728686	496056	2487030	1924187	6033020	18.45	9.11	27.44	10.20	64.68	0.91
22.	Vetch	Kilogram	223691	583934	0.45	66537	49868	14800	100846	91708	21.08	15.93	9.78	22.73	24.46	0.31

Note:

(1) Standard Deviation: I=1983-84 to 1987-88, II=1988-89 to 1992-93, III=1993-94 to 1997-98, IV=1998-99 to 2002-03 V=1983-84 to 2002-03

(2) Coefficient of Variation: 1st=1983-84 to 1987-88, 2nd=1988-89 to 1992-93, 3rd=1993-94 to 1997-98, 4th=1998-99 to 2002-03 5th=1983-84 to 2002-03

Source: As per Table 1.

Coefficient of variation is slightly higher than the Dodaka and Coriander Leaves with 20.44 per cent. Bitter gourd, Fenugreek, Green Chilies, Hemp, Lady's finger, Shepu and Vetch has recorded a lower coefficient of variation between 23 and 29 per cent. Garlic has showed the highest coefficient of variation by 148.99 per cent among the vegetables, followed by Potato with 86.38 per cent. Tomato and Onion have also registered the highest coefficient of variation with 64.68 per cent and 62.07 per cent respectively.

Skewness of arrival of Vegetables is exhibited in Table 7. Most of the vegetables' arrivals show a positive skewness for the entire period except Fenugreek, Green Chilies and Spinach. Distribution in the arrival of Fenugreek shows a highly negative skewness with 2.38; it implies that the curve of distribution of arrival of Fenugreek has a very longer tail towards the left. Green Chilies and Spinach have showed slightly negative skewness; it implies that the curve of distribution have little longer tail towards the left. On the other hand, Garlic and Chuka have showed a very high skewness with 3.43 and 3.32 respectively; it implies that the curve of distribution of arrival of Garlic and Chuka have a very longer tail towards the right. Coriander Leaves, Cucumber, Hemp and Potato have also showed a positive skewness at the higher level between 1 and 2.3. Most of the vegetables like Cabbage, Carrot, Gourd, Onion and Sweet Potato reflects a moderately positive skewed. Meanwhile, distribution in the arrival of Lady's finger shows a slightly positive skewed with 0.05; it implies that the curve of distribution of arrival of Guava has little long tail towards the right. Thus the distribution of Lady's finger in the arrival is likely to symmetric during the study period.

VARIATIONS IN THE VALUE TRANSACTION OF VEGETABLES

The variation in the sale of vegetables is analyzed in Table 8. There is different relative range among the Vegetables. Sale of Cauliflower and Fenugreek have a highest range of coefficient among the Vegetables with 0.99. Garlic is next to Fenugreek with 0.97 relative ranges, followed by Shepu with 0.96. Bittergourd, Carrot, Coriander Leaves, Cucumber, Gourd, Green Chilies, Lady'sfinger, Onion, Potato,

Tomato and Spinach have registered higher variability between 0.80 and 0.94. Sweet Potato has showed a lowest relative range of 0.59 among the vegetables. Remaining other vegetables have a higher coefficient of rage. Standard deviation is also considered for the entire period for major vegetables.

Coefficient of variation in value transaction of vegetables is shown in the Diagram 5 for the period from 1983-84 to 2002-03. The coefficient of variations as calculated in respect of the value transaction of major vegetables shows that Vegetables, Sweet Potato have registered a lowest

Table 8

Variations in Value Transaction of Vegetables

Sl. No.	Vegetables	Quantity	Range			Standard Deviation					Coefficient of Variation					Skew
			Min.	Max.	RR	I	II	III	IV	V	1st	2nd	3rd	4th	5th	
1.	Bitter gourd	Kilogram	150973	1510311	0.82	19178	69565	148776	225114	428450	21.80	18.01	19.16	17.67	64.37	0.71
2.	Brinjal	Kilogram	2350384	10267360	0.63	488356	417656	1513421	379570	2599995	15.60	8.77	21.95	3.91	42.47	0.33
3.	Cabbage	Kilogram	542893	4501328	0.78	69422	154750	420070	660066	1171210	1153	14.65	19.71	19.09	64.64	0.78
4.	Carrot	Kilogram	278127	2949810	0.83	65135	383138	290609	398893	846380	17.47	37.48	19.09	15.80	62.22	0.45
5.	Cauliflower	Number	88378	23377720	0.99	45760	96388	124880	8861311	4975582	28.37	20.19	15.62	156.05	279.66	4.41
6.	Chuka	Bundle	117960	794068	0.74	21915	224329	34526	73998	155327	13.90	64.22	10.17	17.33	48.79	1.42
7.	Coriander Leaves	Bundle	890115	10177843	0.84	425334	575725	1362654	1608000	2699030	27.30	20.66	25.40	20.24	61.15	0.64
8.	Cucumber	Kilogram	370665	4301052	0.84	100975	143130	200087	828047	1169176	20.57	15.84	13.28	24.86	75.06	1.20
9.	Dodaka	Kilogram	477277	3303910	0.75	122108	298825	360591	471493	855561	17.95,	25.71	18.28	17.20	52.21	0.46
10.	Fenugreek	Bundle	11886	4590187	0.99	167920	419979	951769	694167	1227892	20.24	21.97	50.50	18.48	58.59	0.42
11.	Garlic	Quintal	342067	23164017	0.97	1203869	1339582	1937185	3192165	7159441	60.52	38.97	17.07	16.70	79.80	0.61
12.	Gourd	Number	46886	456400	0.81	10978	63447	50649	121543	117949	16.89	41.33	23.17	38.22	62.47	0.75
13.	Green Chilies	Kilogram	1159020	17891062	0.88	880086	1459924	2106572	2450435	4417085	38.38	24.66	22.66	18.63	57.62	0.38
14.	Hemp	Bundle	14220	102881	0.76	5930	12814	25401	14282	24980	23.30	36.02	44.17	19.21	51.81	0.74
15.	Lady's finger	Kilogram	560171	5100650	0.80	312308	137584	403635	804441	1285513	33.57	7.68	15.50	19.31	54.18	0.67
16.	Onion	Quintal	26311970	418381965	0.88	8368004	23723646	69967586	83860803	139913919	23.20	32.91	27.16	24.28	78.69	0.55
17.	Potato	Kilogram	4017795	102147576	0.92	1330358	1143485	10657343	18110380	30334413	21.590	13.91	34.43	23.58	99.42	1.12
18.	Shepu	Bundle	45823	2430600	0.96	171979	94699	89945	558396	656268	58.42	12.96	7.75	29.75	64.60	0.80
19.	Spinach	Bundle	48528	1700997	0.94	60376	112997	166361	334464	448777	59.87	24.74	23.98	27.64	72.93	0.77
20.	Sweet Potato	Kilogram	214323	828941	0.59	58106	76986	92016	162073	139992	18.64	23.62	21.00	30.00	34.65	1.37
21.	Tomato	Kilogram	4202064	64694278	0.88	1687029	1757973	11664882	9299320	20391060	26.15	14.84	38.96	16.93	79.06	0.76
22.	Vetch	Kilogram	415092	3603798	0.79	158086	369943	474352	658537	1014391	24.39	29.33	20.45	22.05	56.23	0.40

Note:

(1) Standard Deviation: I =1983-84 to 1987-88, II=1988-89 to 1992-93, III=1993-94 to 1997-98, IV=1998-99 to 2002-03 V=1983-84 to 2002-03

(2) Coefficient of Variation: 1st =1983-84 to 1987-88, 2nd=1988-89 to 1992-93, 3rd=1993-94 to 1997-98, 4th=1998-99 to 2002-03 5th=1983-84 to 2002-03

Source: As per Table 1.

Diagram 5
C.V. in Value Transaction of Vegetables
(1983-84 to 2002-03)

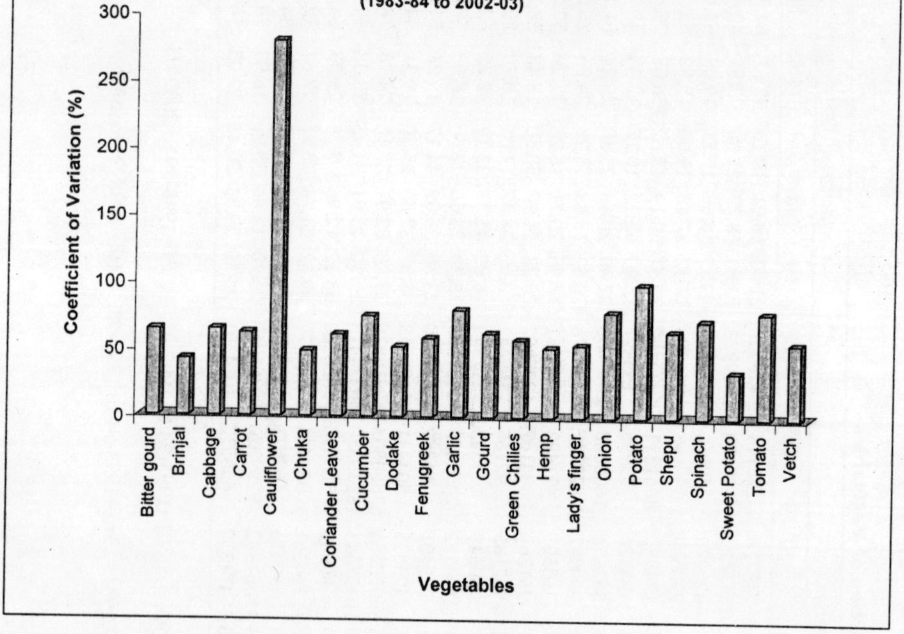

coefficient of variation by 34.65 per cent. Brinjal is next commodity with 42.47 per cent of variation. Bittergourd, Cabbage, Carrot, Coriander Leaves, Dodake, Fenugreek, Gourd, Green Chilies, Hemp, Lady's finger, Shepu and Vetch have recorded a moderate coefficient of variation between 51 and 65 per cent. Cauliflower showed a highest coefficient of variation by 279.66 per cent, followed by Potato with 99.42 per cent. Tomato and Onion have registered high coefficient of variation with 78.69 per cent and 79.06 per cent respectively.

Distribution of sale of Vegetables shows a positive skewed Distribution in the sale of Cauliflower has reflected a very high skewed with 4.41; which implies that the curve of distribution of sale has very longer tail towards the right. Chuka, Cucumber, Sweet Potato and Potato have also a positive skewed between 1 and 1.5. Most of the vegetables have moderately positive skewed. Meanwhile, distribution in sale of Brinjal shows a lowest positive skewed with 0.33, followed by Green Chilies with 0.38; indicating the fact that the curve of distribution of sales has little long tail towards the right.

REFERENCE

Agarwal D.R. (2003), "Quantitative Methods", Vrinda Publicatios Pvt. Ltd., 3rd Revised & Enlarged Edition, Delhi, pp. 744-745.

Bhatia D.K. & Gupta Vijay (1986), "Business Statistics", Vani Educational Books, New Delhi, pp. 141-143.

Gupta S.C. (1996), "Fundamentals of Statistics", Himalaya Publishing House, New Delhi.

Monga G.S. (2000), "Mathematics and Statistics for Economics", Vikas Pub. House Pvt. Ltd., Second Revised Edition, New Delhi, p. 648.

Prasad A.S. (1985), "Agricultural Marketing in India", Mittal Publications, Delhi, pp. 38-46.

Reddy A.V. (1991), "Agricultural Marketing, Printwell", Jaipur, pp. 158-159.

Reddy P.I. (1995), "Marketing of Vegetables", Printwell, Jaipur, pp. 206-209.

Indian Journal of Agricultural Marketing (2002), Vol. 16, No. 2, Nagpur.

Indian Journal of Agricultural Marketing (2000), (Conference Special), Vol. 14, No. 3, Nagpur.

The Bihar Journal of Agricultural Marketing (2000), Vol. VIII, No. 1, Patna.

The Bihar Journal of Agricultural Marketing (1997), (Silver Jubilee Special Number), Vol. V, No. 3, Patna.

7

INTERPRETATION OF MARKETING ACTIVITIES OF A.P.M.C. SOLAPUR: CORRELATION BETWEEN ARRIVALS AND PRICES

This chapter explains an interpretation of marketing activities of Agricultural Produce Market Committee, Solapur in terms association with arrivals and prices in respect of agricultural commodities namely, food grains, fruits and vegetables during 1983-84 to 2002-03.

ASSOCIATION WITH ARRIVALS AND PRICES

'Correlation analysis deals with the association with two or more variables'. In the present study, an association is calculated between arrival of agricultural commodities and their prices in the market yard, especially for food grains, fruits and vegetables, which is also known as supply responses to the prices. Generally we have seen a negative relationship between arrival (Supply) and their price. When arrival of a particular commodity increases the prices tends to fall down. Relationship (r) between arrival and prices of Food grains, Fruits and Vegetables is measured; moreover, coefficient of determination (r square), t-statistic and F significance are also measured. Some of these tools are discussed below.

Coefficient of Determination: For the proper interpretation of correlation coefficient, coefficient of determination is calculated. Coefficient of determination is the square of correlation coefficient.

Coefficient of correlation = r

Coefficient of determination = r^2

Coefficient of non-determination = $1- r^2$

We have taken as trend free component of arrival and their prices for analysis of relationship between these two variables. Therefore, error term (e) is computed for each variable. Error in the arrival of agricultural commodity has been calculated in the following way.

$$Y = a + bt + e$$

Where,

Y = arrival (food grains, fruits and vegetables)
t = period
a = constant value
b = regression coefficient
e = error in arrival

Where a and b are the estimators of parameter a and b and calculated as

$$a = \frac{\Sigma Y}{N} - b\frac{\Sigma X}{N}$$

$$b = \frac{N^*\Sigma XY - (\Sigma X^*\Sigma Y)}{N^*\Sigma X^2 - (\Sigma X)^2}$$

For free trend component in the case of arrival of agricultural commodities, error is calculated in the term (e) as:

$$e_y = Y - \hat{Y}$$

Where,

$\hat{Y}$ = Predicted Value of arrival

Error in the prices in the food grains, fruits and vegetables has been calculated in the following way.

$$X = a' + b't + e$$

Where,

X = prices (food grains, fruits and vegetables)
t = period
a′ = constant value
b′ = regression coefficient
e = error in prices

Where a and b are the estimators of parameter a and b and calculated as

$$a' = \frac{\Sigma X}{N} - b\frac{\Sigma Y}{N}$$

$$b' = \frac{N^*\Sigma XY - (\Sigma X^*\Sigma Y)}{N^*\Sigma Y^2 - (\Sigma Y)^2}$$

For free trend component in case of price for agricultural commodities in the market yard, error is calculated in the term (e) as:

$$e_x = X - \hat{X}$$

Where,

$\hat{X}$ = Predicted Value of prices

Then the calculated Correlation coefficient between e_y and e_x as:

$$\hat{X}r = \frac{N^*\sum e_x e_y - (\sum e_x {}^* \sum e_y)}{\sqrt{N^*\sum e_{x^2} - (\sum e_x)^2} * \sqrt{N^*\sum e_{y^2} - (\sum e_y)^2}}$$

The test of significance of Correlation Coefficient: Once the correlation coefficient has been calculated from sample data, one is normally interested in asking the question; is there an association between the variables? Or with the confidence can we make a statement about the association between the variables? Providing the confidence limits for the population correlation coefficient form the sample size n, and the sample correlation coefficient r. If this confidence interval includes the value zero, then we say that r is not significant; implying thereby that the population correlation coefficient may be zero and the value of r may be due to sampling variability. The test of significance of correlation coefficient means to test the hypothesis, whether or not the correlation coefficient (population b) is zero. We test:

$$H_0 : b = 0 \text{ vs } H_1 : b < 0$$

The test statistic

$$t = \frac{r}{\sqrt{(1 - r^2)/N - 2}}$$

Degrees of Freedom: Number associated with a test statistic is used in determining the observed significance level.

$$df = N-2$$

Number of observations taken as 20 years (study period), minus 2 taken for calculating degree of freedom because we lose two value of parameters i.e. a and b.

Significance of F: If observed significance level of F, probability is small enough, usually less than 0.05 or 0.01, then the null hypothesis is the outcome indicating the fact that there is no linear relationship between the dependent and independent variables, hence it is rejected. F is the ratio of two mean squares. The larger mean square is conventionally placed in the numerator and the smaller in the denominator. The degrees of freedom associated with the numerator and denominator is used in the evaluation of F statistics.

RELATIONSHIP BETWEEN ARRIVAL OF FOOD GRAINS AND THEIR PRICES

First hypothesis taken as, "An arrival of the food grains and their prices are negatively associated during the study period." For testing the hypothesis, null hypothesis (H_0) and alternative hypothesis (H_1) are represented by:

$H_{0:}$ r = 0

H_1: r < 0 (one way)

Where,

r = correlation coefficient

Null hypothesis represent no association between the arrival and prices of food grains. In the other word, correlation coefficient is equal to zero. A null hypothesis H_0 is assumed to be true unless the sample evidence points against it. If null hypothesis is not true, then some alternate must be true and in carrying out a hypothesis test, the researcher formulates an alternative hypothesis against which the null hypothesis is tested. The alternative hypothesis is correlation coefficient is less than zero (one way hypothesis). It means that when arrival is increased their adverse effect is seen in the price level of food grains in the market yard.

Relationship between arrival and prices of food grains and other commodity is revealed in Table 1. It is observed that the coefficient of correlations (r) of food grains and other commodity has not equated to zero. Some of the commodities like Bajra, Blackgram, Capsicum, Groundnut, Jowar, Pigeon pea, Sunflower and Jaggery have noticed less than zero coefficient of correlation. In other words a negative relationships has been noticed between arrival and price among the commodities during the study period. On the other hand Gram, Green gram, Maize, Rice and Wheat have noticed more than zero coefficient of correlation. It means that among these commodities positive relationships has been noticed between their arrival and price.

Table 1

Correlation with Arrivals of Food Grains and their Prices

Sl. No.	*Food grains*	*r*	*r square*	*t statistic*	*df(N-2)*	*F sig*
1.	Bajra	-0.045	0.002	-0.191	18	0.851
2.	Black gram	-0.118	0.014	-0.506	18	0.619
3.	Capsicum	-0.553	0.306	-2.815	18	0.011
4.	Gram	0.035	0.001	0.147	18	0.885
5.	Green gram	0.246	0.061	1.078	18	0.295
6.	Groundnut	-0.228	0.052	-0.996	18	0.333
7.	Jowar	-0.014	0.000	-0.061	18	0.952
8.	Maize	0.120	0.014	0.511	18	0.616
9.	Pigeon pea	-0.391	0.153	-1.804	18	0.088
10.	Rice	0.007	0.000	0.030	18	0.976
11.	Sunflower	-0.084	0.007	-0.358	18	0.725
12.	Wheat	0.179	0.032	0.773	18	0.449
13.	Jaggery	-0.416	0.173	-1.940	18	0.068

Source: Processed data on the basis of Annual Report of APMC, Solapur, period from 1983-84 to 2002-03.

Coefficient of determination (r square) of all commodities is also revealed in the same table. Almost all commodities have a very less coefficient of determination. Some of them namely, Rice and Jowar have showed a zero percent coefficient of determination.

Test statistic (t ratio) is computed with the help of sample data. Table value is 1.33 at 1% level of significance with 18 degree of freedom. Values of 't' in the case of Capsicum, Pigeon pea and Jaggery have a greater value than table value by -2.815, -1.804 and -1.94 respectively. Therefore, we can say that they are significant and the null hypothesis is rejected at level of significance of 1% per cent.

In the case of cereals, the computed value of 't' of Rice, Wheat, Jowar, Bajra and Maize are less than table value, moreover these cereals have a very insignificant and positive relationship noticed between arrival and price. Therefore, we can say that, the arrival is not price sensitive. It means that the difference is just due to fluctuations of sampling and the sample data do not provide us sufficient evidence against the null hypothesis, which may, therefore, be accepted.

Among the pulses, except Pigeon pea, table value is greater than computed value of 't' in the case of Black gram, Gram and Green gram and the value of difference is not significant. The story of cereals apply to pulses, the sample data of above pulses do not provide us sufficient evidence against the null hypothesis.

On the whole, the analyses indicate that there are no significant relationships between prices and arrival of all commodities in the market yard. The analysis, on the whole, for the food grains, both cereals and pulses, reveals that the price changes do not influence the marketing decisions of the farmers regarding the disposal of the food grains' surplus. Although in most of the cases (r) values are positive; they are not significant.

RELATIONSHIP BETWEEN ARRIVAL OF FRUITS AND THEIR PRICES

Second hypothesis is taken as, "An arrival of Fruits and their prices are negatively associated during the study period." For this purpose, simple and composite hypotheses were constructed. In this order null hypothesis (H_0) and alternative hypothesis (H_1) are represented by:

$$H_{0:}\ r = 0$$

$$H_1\!:\ r < 0 \text{ (one way)}$$

Where,

r = correlation coefficient

Null hypothesis represent no association between the arrival and prices of Fruits. It is nothing but correlation coefficient is equal to zero. A null hypothesis H_0 is assumed to be true unless the sample evidence points against it. If null hypothesis is not true, then some alternate must be true and in carrying out a hypothesis test, the researcher formulates an alternative hypothesis against which the null hypothesis is tested. The alternative hypothesis is correlation coefficient is less than zero (one way hypothesis). It means that when arrival is increased their adverse effect is seen in the price level of Fruits in the market yard.

Relationship between arrival and prices of Fruits is revealed in Table 2. Moreover, r square, t-statistic, degree of freedom and F significance are calculated in the same table by co-relating the arrival and prices of Fruits. It is observed that coefficient of correlations (r) of almost all Fruits has no results equal to zero. Most of the Fruits have noticed less than zero coefficient of correlation between prices and arrival. In other words negative relationships has been noticed between arrival and price among many Fruits during the study period. Only Apple and Custard apple have noticed more than zero coefficient of correlation between the prices and arrivals. It means that these Fruits have noticed positive relationships between their arrival and price.

The square of the correlation coefficient is called the coefficient of determination. The coefficient of determination = r^2 is the proportion of total variation in arrival that is explained by the linear relation between price and arrival. Coefficient of determination (r square) of major Fruits is revealed in the same table. Most of the Fruits have observed less coefficient of determination. Some of them have noticed a very less coefficient of determination namely, Orange and Custard apple with .011 and .024 respectively.

Table 2

Correlation with Arrivals of Fruits and their Prices

Sl. No.	*Fruits*	*r*	*r square*	*t statistic*	*df(N-2)*	*F sig*
1.	Apple	0.652	0.426	3.444	18	0.003
2.	Banana	-0.558	0.311	-2.851	18	0.011
3.	Ber	-0.617	0.380	-3.033	18	0.008
4.	Custard apple	0.156	0.024	0.670	18	0.511
5.	Grapes	-0.242	0.058	-1.057	18	0.305
6.	Guava	-0.606	0.367	-3.230	18	0.005
7.	Lemon	-0.722	0.521	-4.422	18	0.000
8.	Mango	-0.361	0.131	-1.644	18	0.118
9.	Orange	-0.103	0.011	-0.413	18	0.685
10.	Papaya	-0.375	0.141	-1.618	18	0.125
11.	Pomegranate	-0.797	0.635	-5.281	18	0.000
12.	Sapota	-0.752	0.566	-4.847	18	0.000
13.	Watermelon	-0.510	0.260	-2.516	18	0.022

Source: As per Table 1.

For testing purpose, test statistic (t ratio) is computed with the help of sample data. Table value is 1.33 at 1% level of significance with 18 degree of freedom. Computed 't' values of most of the Fruits have noticed greater than table value. In the case of Orange, Custard apple and Grapes have observed the computed value of 't' is less than table value, moreover Orange and Custard apple have noticed a very insignificant relationship with arrival and price, therefore, we can say that, the arrivals of the fruits are not price sensitive. By this, we mean that the difference is just due to fluctuations of sampling and the sample data do not provide us sufficient evidence against the null hypothesis, which may, therefore, in above case, be accepted.

But on the other hand most of the Fruits have noticed the picture against the null hypothesis. Banana, Ber, Guava, Lemon, Mango, Papaya, Pomegranate, Sapota and Watermelon have noticed the greater value of computed t-statistic than table value and these value has registered between -1.618 to -5.281 (t-ratio). Moreover, the differences between prices and arrival of these fruits have noticed a highly significant. In the case of Lemon, Pomegranate and Sapota have observed a very high significant with 0.000, therefore, we can say that, the sample data do provide us sufficient evidence against the null hypothesis, which may, therefore, in above case, the null hypothesis is rejected at 1% per cent level of significance.

On the whole, the analysis indicates that there are highly significant relationships between prices and arrival of most of the fruits except Orange, Custard apple and Grapes in the market yard. The analysis, on the whole, for the Fruits, reveals that the price changes much be more influencing the marketing decisions of farmers regarding the disposal of Fruits. Although in some of the cases (r) values are positive, which they are insignificant.

RELATIONSHIP BETWEEN ARRIVAL OF VEGETABLES AND THEIR PRICES

Third hypothesis is taken as, "An arrival of Vegetables and their prices are negatively associated during the study period." For this the simple and composite hypotheses constructed. In this order, null hypothesis (H_0) and alternative hypothesis (H_1) are represented by:

$H_{0:}$ r = 0

H_1: r < 0 (one way)

Where,

r = correlation coefficient

Null hypothesis represents no association between the arrival and prices of Vegetables. It means that correlation coefficient is equal to zero. A null hypothesis H_0 is assumed to be true unless the sample evidence points against it. If null hypothesis is not true, then some alternate must be true and in carrying out a hypothesis test, the researcher formulates an alternative hypothesis against which the null hypothesis is tested. The alternative hypothesis is correlation coefficient is less than zero (one way hypothesis). It means that when arrival is increased the adverse effect is seen in the price level of Vegetables in the market yard and vice versa.

Correlation coefficient, r square, t-statistic, degree of freedom and F significance between arrival and prices of Vegetables are revealed in Table 3. It is observed from the table, that coefficient of correlations (r) of almost all Vegetables are not equal to zero.

Table 3

Correlation between Arrivals of Vegetables and their Prices

Sl. No.	*Vegetables*	*r*	*r square*	*t statistic*	*df(N-2)*	*F sig*
1.	Bitter gourd	-0.460	0.212	-2.198	18	0.041
2.	Brinjal	-0.806	0.649	-5.775	18	0.000
3.	Cabbage	-0.721	0.519	-4.408	18	0.000
4.	Carrot	-0.752	0.566	-4.843	18	0.000
5.	Cauliflower	0.244	0.060	1.068	18	0.300
6.	Chuka	-0.238	0.056	-1.038	18	0.313
7.	Coriander Leaves	-0.576	0.332	-2.989	18	0.008
8.	Cucumber	-0.317	0.100	-1.417	18	0.173
9.	Dodake	-0.630	0.397	-3.444	18	0.003
10.	Fenugreek	0.523	0.273	2.603	18	0.018
11.	Garlic	-0.349	0.122	-1.580	18	0.131
12.	Gourd	-0.183	0.033	-.789	18	0.441
13.	Green Chilies	-0.404	0.163	-1.875	18	0.077
14.	Hemp	-0.349	0.122	-1.582	18	0.131
15.	Lady's finger	-0.744	0.554	-4.729	18	0.000
16.	Onion	-0.453	0.205	-2.157	18	0.045
17.	Potato	-0.536	0.287	-2.693	18	0.015
18.	Shepu	-0.508	0.258	-2.503	18	0.022
19.	Spinach	-0.597	0.356	-3.157	18	0.005
20.	Sweet Potato	-0.056	0.003	-.238	18	0.815
21.	Tomato	-0.643	0.414	-3.563	18	0.002
22.	Vetch	-0.503	0.253	-2.470	18	0.024

Source: As per Table 1.

Most of the Vegetables have noticed less than zero coefficient of correlation between prices and arrival. It means that a negative relationship has noticed between arrival and price of Vegetables except Cauliflower and Fenugreek during the study period. Cauliflower and Fenugreek have noticed more than zero coefficient of correlation between the prices and arrivals. It means that these Vegetables have noticed a positive relationship between arrival and price.

The coefficient of determination = r^2 is the proportion of total variation in arrival that is explained by the linear relation between price and arrival. Coefficient of determination (r square) of major Vegetables is revealed in the same table. Many Vegetables such as; Brinjal, Cabbage Carrot and Lady's finger has reflected a high coefficient of determination between 0.519 and 0.649. Some of Vegetables such as Potato, Shepu, Spinach, Tomato and Vetch have experienced less coefficient of determination between the arrivals and prices. Sweet Potato, Gourd, Cucumber and Chuka have noticed very less coefficient of determination.

For testing, test statistic (t ratio) is computed with the help of sample data. Table value is 1.33 at 1% level of significance with 18 degree of freedom. Most of the Vegetable's Computed 't' values have noticed a greater than table value except Cauliflower, Chuka, Gourd and Sweet Potato. In the case of Cauliflower, Chuka, Gourd and Sweet Potato have computed value of 't' less than table value, moreover Sweet Potato has noticed a very insignificant between arrival and price, therefore, we can say that, the arrival of these Vegetables are not price sensitive. By this we mean that the difference is just due to fluctuations of sampling and the sample data, which do not provide us sufficient evidence against the null hypothesis, which may, therefore, in above case, be accepted.

But on the other hand, 18 out of 22 Vegetables have showed the situation against the null hypothesis. Bitter gourd, Brinjal, Cabbage, Carrot, Coriander Leaves, Cucumber, Dodake, Fenugreek, Garlic, Green chilies, Hemp, Lady's finger, Onion, Potato, Shepu, Spinach, Tomato and Vetch have noticed a greater value of computed t-statistic than the table value and these values are seen between –1.417 to –5.775 (t-ratio). Moreover, the differences between prices and arrival of these Vegetables have noticed highly significant. Some of them namely; Brinjal, Cabbage, Carrot and Lady's finger have observed a very high significant with 0.000, therefore, we can say that, the sample data do provide us sufficient evidence against the null hypothesis. Therefore, the null hypothesis is rejected at 1% percent level of significance with 18 degree of freedom.

On the whole, the analyses indicate that there are highly significant relationships between prices and arrival of most of the Vegetables except Cauliflower, Chuka, Gourd and Sweet Potato in the market yard. The analysis, on the whole, reveals that the price change has much more influence on the marketing decisions of farmers regarding the disposal of Vegetables.

REFERENCE

Bhatia D.K. and Gupta Vijay (1986), "Business Statistics", Vani Educational Books, New Delhi.

Gupta S.C. (1996), "Fundamentals of Statistics", Himalaya Publishing House, New Delhi.

Monga G.S. (2000), "Mathematics and Statistics for Economics", Vikas Pub. House Pvt. Ltd., Second Revised Edition, New Delhi.

Prasad A.S. (1985), "Agricultural Marketing in India", Mittal Publications, Delhi.

Reddy P.I. (1995), "Marketing of Vegetables", Printwell, Jaipur.

Indian Journal of Agricultural Marketing (2002), Vol. 16, No. 2, Nagpur.

Indian Journal of Agricultural Marketing (2000), (Conference Special), Vol. 14, No. 3, Nagpur.

The Bihar Journal of Agricultural Marketing (2000), Vol. VIII, No. 1, Patna.

The Bihar Journal of Agricultural Marketing (1997), (Silver Jubilee Special Number), Vol. V, No. 3, Patna.

8

INTERPRETATION OF MARKETING ACTIVITIES OF A.P.M.C. SOLAPUR: REGRESSION ANALYSIS OF REGULATED COMMODITIES

In this chapter regression model is applied for the analysis of arrival of food grains, fruits and vegetables. Economic Theory is mainly concerned with relations with economic variables. In economics, we deal exclusively with these stochastic relations. The simplest type of stochastic relation between two variables X and Y is a linear one. This model is called a simple linear regression model and is described as:

$$Y = a + bt + e$$

Here Y is known as dependent variable; *t* the independent or explanatory variable indicating movement in Y is being explained with the help of changes in *t*; and *e* the stochastic disturbance (error), *a* and *b* are the parameters of the model.

Fitting the Line of Best fit

$$Y = a + bt$$

Where *a* and *b* are the estimators of parameter a and b. The value of 'a' and 'b' is found by the following equations:

$$b = \frac{N^{*}\Sigma XY - (\Sigma X^{*}\Sigma Y)}{N^{*}\Sigma X^{2} - (\Sigma X)^{2}}$$

$$a = \frac{\Sigma Y}{N} - b\frac{\Sigma X}{N}$$

Standard Error (b): The slope is a measure of the amount of change in the dependent variable associated with each unit of change in the independent variable. If the slope is 0, there is no linear relationship between the dependent variable and the independent variable. The number in parentheses is the standard error of the slope.

$$SE(b) = \sqrt{\frac{\sum e^2/N-2}{\sum x^2}}$$

Where,

$$e^2 = (Y\text{-}Ycap)^2$$
$$x^2 = X\text{-}Xbar$$

t-statistic calculated as:

$$t = \frac{b}{SE(b)}$$

Correlation coefficient calculated as:

$$r = \frac{N^*\sum XY-(\sum X^*\sum Y)}{\sqrt{N^*\sum X^2-(\sum X)^2} * \sqrt{N^*\sum Y^2-(\sum Y)^2}}$$

Explanatory Power of Regression Equations calculated as:

$$r^2 = 1-\frac{\sum e^2}{\sum y^2}$$

Where,

$$y^2 = (Y\text{-}Ybar)^2$$

TRENDS IN ARRIVAL OF FOOD GRAINS

Fourth hypothesis is taken as, "Arrivals of the major food grains in the regulated market have shown a positive trend (performance) during the study period." In regression equation we encounter the issue one or two-sided test. In the present study we considered two-side test. The null hypothesis is that arrival of major food grains does not increase during the study period. The alternative hypothesis is that arrival of major food grains does increase or have a positive trend during the study period.

$H_{0:}$ b = 0

Where b is the population parameter (slope) (Null hypothesis is taken as performance of arrival as unrelated to the study period). This implies that alternative hypothesis is that performance of arrival of food grains is related to the study period.

H_1: b > 0 (positive way)

H_1: b < 0 (negative way)

H_1: b ≠ 0 (Two sided hypothesis)

We used the test statistic t on the data collected for our study period. In order to examine the trend of the arrival of the selected food grains, the annual arrival is taken for twenty years (1983-84 to 2002-03). The trend values have been computed with least square method. The trend values (line of best fit) are computed by the equation:

$$Y = a + bX$$

Where,

Y = arrival of food grains

a = constant value (intercept)

b = regression coefficient (slope)

X = time

The trend values are computed for the arrival of selected food grains in the regulated markets in Table 1. The performance of arrival of foodgrains as revealed in the table is discussed below.

Table 1
Regression Analysis of Arrival of Foodgrains

Sl. No.	*Foodgrains*	*a*	*b*	*SE (b)*	*t statistic*	*r*	*r square*	*F. sig.*
1.	Bajra	7880	-101	171	-0.593	-0.139	0.019	0.560
2.	Black gram	9211	195	227	0.857	0.198	0.039	0.403
3.	Capsicum	17803	-486	120	-4.053	0.691	0.477	0.001
4.	Gram	7842	101	127	0.796	0.184	0.034	0.436
5.	Green gram	4649	-183	70	-2.601	-0.523	0.273	0.018
6.	Groundnut	22749	-978	258	-2.732	-0.541	0.193	0.014
7.	Jowar	162431	546	2041	0.268	0.063	0.004	0.792
8.	Maize	4755	120	89	1.348	0.303	0.092	0.194
9.	Pigeon pea	49151	-1943	573	-3.389	-0.624	0.390	0.003
10.	Rice	105690	19597	3276	5.981	0.816	0.665	0.000
11.	Sunflower	19257	-437	564	-0.775	-0.180	0.032	0.448
12.	Wheat	74624	9858	1633	6.038	0.818	0.669	0.000
13.	Jaggery	88182	9953	3394	2.933	0.569	0.323	0.009

Source: Processed data on the basis of Annual Report of APMC, Solapur period from 1983-84 to 2002-03.

The arrival of food grains, among the cereals, showed an increasing tendency except Bajra during the period under study. The trend equations for the arrival of cereals are given below:

Rice Y = 105690 + 19597x

Wheat Y = 74624 + 9858x

Jowar Y = 162431 + 546x

Maize Y = 4755 + 120x

Bajra Y = 7880 - 101x

From these linear equations it can be said that, the arrival of Rice has increased by 19597 quintals every year in the market yard, which is higher than other cereals, followed by Wheat with 9858 quintals every year. While

Bajra showed a decreasing trend by 101 quintals every year, which is mainly due to the preference of the farmers to other cereals crops, which gives high remunerations.

Among the pulses, annual increasing trend is observed particularly, in the case of Black gram and Gram by 195 and 101 quintals respectively. On the other hand, arrival of Pigeon pea and Green gram is seen decreasing during the study period. The rate of decrease in arrival of Pigeon pea is relatively high when compared to the annual decrease in arrival of Green gram. The linear equations for the arrival of pulses are given below:

Black gram	Y	= 9211 + 195x
Gram	Y	= 7842 + 101x
Pigeon pea	Y	= 49151 - 1943x
Green gram	Y	= 4649 - 183x

In the case of processed product, Jaggery showed a positive and relatively higher regression coefficient than some other commodities in arrival. The linear equation of Jaggery in arrival is given below:

Jaggery	Y	= 88182 + 9953x

But negative performance is seen in the arrival of Capsicum, Groundnut and Sunflower. The negative trend of these items is given in following equations:

Groundnut	Y	= 22749 – 978x
Capsicum	Y	= 17803 – 486x
Sunflower	Y	= 19257 – 437x

Values of 'a' and 'b' are taken, as reliable or not, therefore, we prefer to test 'b', which is called as standard error of estimate 'b' {SE (b)}. Table 1 gives the SE (b) of food grains and other commodities during the study period.

The tabular value of 't' at 1% level of significance for 18 degree of freedom is estimated at (*df*) = 1.73. For testing the test statistic (t ratio) the computed 't' values of Wheat and Rice have noticed at the greater side than the table value among the cereals with a (t-statistic) registered value of 6.038 and 5.981 respectively. Moreover, the F significance of these cereals is also notice a highly significant level with 0.000. In the case of Jaggery, also the computed t-statistic is greater with positive value than table value with 2.933. Moreover, F sig. of arrival of Jaggery is also noticed a high significant level with 0.008. Therefore, we can say that, the data provides sufficient evidence against the null hypothesis, which means the null hypothesis, is rejected at 1% per cent level of significance and accept alternative hypothesis for arrival of Wheat, Rice and Jaggery.

But on the other hand most of the food grains and other commodities have noticed the situation against the null hypothesis. Capsicum, Groundnut, Green gram and Pigeon pea have noticed the greater but negative value of computed t-statistic than the table value and these values have been registered between -2.601 and -4.053. Moreover, the differences between years and arrival of these commodities have noticed highly significant. In the case of Capsicum and Pigeon pea have observed a very high significant with 0.001 and 0.003 respectively, therefore, we can say that, the sample data do provide an evidence against the null hypothesis, which may, therefore, be said as null hypothesis is rejected at 1% percent level of significance. It means that the performance arrival of food grains is related to the study period but in a negative way.

But, in case of Bajra, Jowar, Black gram, Gram, Maize and Sunflower have observed the computed value of 't' is less than table value (some are positive and some are negative). Moreover the arrival of Bajra and Jowar have noticed a very insignificant among the cereals, therefore, we can say that, the data do not provide us sufficient evidence against the null hypothesis, which may, be accepted.

Same table gives the information about coefficient of determination (r square) of food grains and other commodities. Concept of coefficient of determination (r^2 notation) is applied to test the explanatory power of regression equations. It is observed that, Wheat has high explanatory power with 0.669 during the study period, followed by Rice with 0.665 (r^2). It means that explanatory power of regression equation of Wheat is 0.67 or 67% that is 67% variation in arrival (Y) is because of variation in period (X). While explanatory power of Jowar is very less with 0.004 or 0.4%.

On the whole, the analyses indicate that there are highly significant relationships between arrival of most of the food grains and other commodity except Bajra and Jowar. The analysis, on the whole, for the food grains and other commodity, reveals that some positive and some negative trends exist in the market yard.

TRENDS IN ARRIVAL OF FRUITS

The fifth hypothesis is taken as, "Arrivals of the major Fruits in the regulated market have shown a positive trend (performance) during the study period." For this purpose, we considered two-sided test. The Null hypothesis is that arrival of major Fruits does not relate to the study period.

$$H_{0:}\ b = 0$$

Where b is population parameter (slope). This implies the alternative hypothesis is related to the study period (it may be positive or negative). Explanation of alternative hypothesis is given as:

$$H_1\text{: } b > 0 \text{ (positive way)}$$
$$H_1\text{: } b < 0 \text{ (negative way)}$$
$$H_1\text{: } b \neq 0 \text{ (Two sided hypothesis)}$$

We used test statistic t on the data computed so far. In order to examine the trend of the arrival of selected Fruits, the annual arrival is taken for twenty years period (1983-84 to 2002-03). The trend values have been computed by least square method. The trend values (the Line of Best Fit) are computed by the equations:

$$Y = a + bX$$

Where,

Y = arrival of fruits

a = constant value (intercept)

b = regression coefficient (slope)

X = time

The value of 'a' and 'b' are found as explained (equations) in Table 2. The trend values computed for the arrival of selected Fruits in the regulated markets is presented in Table 2. The performance of arrival of Fruits as revealed in the table is discussed below.

Table 2
Regression Analysis of Arrival of Fruits

Sl. No.	*Fruits*	*Quantity*	*a*	*b*	*SE (b)*	*t statistic*	*r*	*r square*	*F. sig.*
1.	Apple	Dozen	163082	20880	6195	3.371	0.644	0.415	0.004
2.	Banana	Quintal	685123	-41835	14486	-2.888	-0.563	0.317	0.010
3.	Ber	Kilogram	-1663232	329221	35733	9.213	0.922	0.850	0.000
4.	Custard apple	Quintal	57454	-3801	1060	-3.586	-0.646	0.417	0.002
5.	Grapes	Boxes	28743	5638	1295	4.356	0.716	0.513	0.000
6.	Guava	Kilogram	458444	-479	6411	-0.075	-0.018	0.000	0.941
7.	Lemon	Kilogram	831090	95132	33535	2.837	0.556	0.390	0.011
8.	Mango	Dozen	369257	-12805	5337	-2.399	-0.492	0.242	0.027
9.	Orange	Dozen	-7045	3917	1296	3.023	0.603	0.364	0.008
10.	Papaya	Dozen	-4856	1020	440	2.319	0.501	0.251	0.034
11.	Pomegranate	Dozen	-322129	63719	12916	4.934	0.777	0.603	0.000
12.	Sapota	Dozen	-59837	12955	9926	1.305	0.294	0.086	0.208
13.	Watermelon	Number	707705	-6538	6870	-0.952	-0.219	0.048	0.354

Source: As per Table 1.

The arrival of major Fruits, (most of the fruits) showed an increasing tendency during the period under study. The trend equations for arrival of some fruits are given below, which shows a positive regression coefficient.

Apple $Y = 163082 + 20880x$

Grapes $Y = 28743 + 5638x$

Lemon $Y = 831090 + 95132x$

The annual arrival of Apple has increased by 20880 dozen during the twenty years. The arrival of Grapes has also increased by 5638 boxes and that of Lemon has increased by 95132 kilogram. On the contrary some fruits however experienced a negative regression coefficient. The trend equations are given below:

Banana	Y	= 685123 - 41835x
Mango	Y	= 369257 - 12805x
Watermelon	Y	= 707705 - 6538x

Annual arrival of Banana has decreased by 41835 quintal and that of Mango by 12805 dozen. Some fruits, however experience a positive regression coefficient but noticed a negative intercept value, some of these trend equations are given as:

Ber	Y	= 329221x –1663232
Pomegranate	Y	= 63719x - 322129
Sapota	Y	= 12955x - 59837

From these linear equations it can be observed that, the annual arrival of Ber has increased by 329221 kilogram. The annual rate of increase in arrival of Pomegranate is 63719 dozen. But, a fruits experience a negative intercept value during the study period.

Value of 'a' and 'b' is taken, as reliable or not, therefore, we have tested 'b'. Testing of 'b', is called as standard error of estimate 'b' {SE (b)}. Table 2 gives the SE (b) of fruits during the study period.

The tabular value of 't' at 1% level of significance for 18 degree of freedom is (*df*) = 1.73. For the testing the computed test statistic (t ratio) of Apple, Ber, Grapes, Lemon, Orange, Papaya and Pomegranate have noticed a greater than table value among the Fruits with values registered (t-statistic) between 2.319 and 8.213. Moreover, the F sig. of these fruits has noticed highly significant. The Ber, Grapes and Pomegranate have registered a very high significant with 0.000. Therefore, we can say that, the data provides us sufficient evidence against the null hypothesis, which means the null hypothesis is rejected at 1% percent level of significance and accepted the alternative hypothesis for these fruits. It means that a very positive performance has been seen during the study period.

On the other hand most of the fruits have observed a negative trend. Custard apple, Banana and Mango have noticed the situation against the null hypothesis. Custard apple, Banana and Mango have noticed a greater but negative value of computed t-statistic than table value with registered values of –3.586, -2.888 and –2.399 respectively. Moreover, the differences between the years and arrival of these fruits have noticed a high significance. In the case of Custard apple, Banana and Mango are experience a very high significant with 0.002, 0.010 and 0.027 respectively. Therefore, we can say that, the data provides sufficient evidence against the null hypothesis, which may, therefore, in above case; the null hypothesis is rejected at 1% percent level of significance. It means that a negative performance in arrival of these fruits is experienced during the study period.

But, in the case of Guava, Sapota and Watermelon computed value of 't' is less than table value (Sapota is positive and other are negative). Moreover arrival of Guava has noticed a very insignificant among the fruits with 0.941. So, the data not provides sufficient evidence against the null hypothesis, which may, be accepted.

The information about coefficient of determination (r square) of Fruits is exhibited in the same Table. Concept of coefficient of determination (r^2 notation) is applied for testing the explanatory power of regression equations. Ber has showed a high explanatory power with 0.85 during the study period, followed by Pomegranate with 0.603 (r^2). It means that explanatory power of regression equation of Ber is 0.85 or 85%; i.e. 85% variation in arrival (Y) of Ber is because of variation in period (X). While explanatory power of Guava is very less with 0.000 or 0 %.

In brief, the analyses indicate that there are highly significant relationships between arrivals of most of the fruits during the study period. The analysis, on the whole, reveals that many fruits have noticed positive performance in the market yard during the study period.

TRENDS IN ARRIVAL OF VEGETABLES

The sixth hypothesis is taken as, "Arrivals of the Vegetables in the regulated market have shown positive trend (performance) during study period." For this purpose, we have considered two-sided tests. The Null hypothesis is that arrival of major Fruits does not relate to the study period.

$$H_0: b = 0$$

Where b is in above notation indicate the population parameter (slope). This implies the alternative hypothesis is that arrival of Vegetables does related to study period (it may be positive or negative). Explanation of alternative hypothesis is given as:

$H_1: b > 0$ (positive way)

$H_1: b < 0$ (negative way)

$H_1: b \neq 0$ (Two sided hypothesis)

In order to examine the trend of the arrival of selected Vegetables, the annual arrivals are taken for twenty years data (1983-84 to 2002-03). The trend values have been computed for them by the method of least square. The trend values (the Line of Best Fit) are computed by the equations:

$$Y = a + bX$$

Where,

Y = arrival of Vegetables

a = constant value (intercept)

b = regression coefficient (slope)

X = time

The trend values are computed for the arrival of selected Vegetables in the regulated markets, which are presented in Table 3. The performances of arrival of Vegetables as revealed in the table are discussed below.

Table 3
Regression Analysis of Arrival of Vegetables

Sl. No.	*Vegetables*	*Quantity*	*a*	*b*	*SE (b)*	*t statistic*	*r*	*r square*	*F. sig.*
1.	Bittergourd	Kilogram	119831	6420	1140	5.631	0.799	0.638	0.000
2.	Brinjal	Kilogram	2202303	16767	12549	1.336	0.300	0.090	0.198
3.	Cabbage	Kilogram	299722	63888	8401	7.605	0.873	0.763	0.000
4.	Carrot	Kilogram	338796	45901	8248	5.565	0.795	0.632	0.000
5.	Cauliflower	Number	430188	29773	9492	3.137	0.594	0.353	0.006
6.	Chuka	Bundle	681044	-12760	9175	-1.391	-0.312	0.097	0.181
7.	Coriander Leaves	Bundle	2342424	90455	16575	5.457	0.789	0.623	0.000
8.	Cucumber	Kilogram	178868	35293	5069	6.963	0.854	0.729	0.000
9.	Dodaka	Kilogram	279660	10458	2124	4.923	0.757	0.574	0.000
10.	Fenugreek	Bundle	2648204	5830	29940	0.195	0.046	0.002	0.848
11.	Garlic	Quintal	31283	-1419	940	-1.510	-0.335	0.112	0.148
12.	Gourd	Number	54406	12321	2324	5.301	0.781	0.610	0.000
13.	Green Chilies	Kilogram	909418	61542	9323	6.601	0.841	0.708	0.000
14.	Hemp	Bundle	116350	21	1365	0.015	0.004	0.000	0.988
15.	Lady's finger	Kilogram	385912	9980	4179	2.388	0.490	0.241	0.028
16.	Onion	Quintal	-50219	85438	7496	11.397	0.937	0.878	0.000
17.	Potato	Kilogram	-2438497	1025659	167551	6.121	0.822	0.676	0.000
18.	Shepu	Bundle	1072428	27239	12862	2.118	0.447	0.199	0.048
19.	Spinach	Bundle	281226	55005	8400	6.548	0.839	0.704	0.000
20.	Sweet Potato	Kilogram	365427	-11607	2437	-4.762	-0.747	0.558	0.000
21.	Tomato	Kilogram	-635755	948927	103868	9.136	0.907	0.823	0.000
22.	Vetch	Kilogram	259745	10967	2715	4.040	0.690	0.476	0.001

Source: As per Table 1.

The arrivals of Vegetables have an (19 out of 22) increasing tendency during under the study. The trend equations for some vegetables are given below, which also showed a positive regression coefficient.

Cabbage $Y = 299722 + 63888x$

Cauliflowe: $Y = 430188 + 29773x$

Coriander Leaves $Y = 2342424 + 90455x$

The annual arrivals of Apple has increased by 20880 dozen. The arrival of Grapes has also increased by 5638 boxes and that of Lemon has increased by 95132 kilogram. On the other hand, some fruits have observed a negative regression coefficient. Their trend equations are given below:

Banana $Y = 685123 - 41835x$

Mango $Y = 369257 - 12805x$

Watermelon $Y = 707705 - 6538x$

The annual arrivals of Banana has decreased by 41835 quintals and the Mango has decreased by 12805 dozen. Some of the fruits have showed a positive regression coefficient but noticed a negative intercept value; some of these trend equations are given below:

Ber	Y = 329221x -1663232
Pomegranate	Y = 63719x - 322129
Sapota	Y = 12955x - 59837

From these linear equations it is seen that, the annual arrivals of the Ber has increased by 329221 kilogram. The rate of increase in arrivals of Pomegranate was 63719 dozens. All these fruits have observed a negative intercept value during the study period.

We used the test statistic t on the basis of the data. Value of 'a' and 'b' is taken, as standard error of estimate 'b' {SE (b)}. Table 3 gives the SE (b) of vegetables during the study period. The tabular value of 't' at 1% level of significance for 18 degree of freedom is (*df*) = 1.73. For the testing purpose, test statistic (t ratio) is computed with the help of twenty years annual data.

Computed 't' values of Bitter gourd, Cabbage, Carrot, Cauliflower, Coriander Leaves, Cucumber, Dodaka, Gourd, Green Chilies, Lady's finger, Onion, Potato, Shepu, Spinach, Tomato and Vetch have (16 vegetables out of 22) noticed a greater values than the table value among the Vegetables and these value have (t-statistic) registered between 2.118 and 11.397. Moreover, the F significance of these fruits has noticed highly significant. In the case of Bitter gourd, Cabbage, Carrot, Coriander Leaves, Cucumber, Dodaka, Gourd, Green Chilies, Onion, Potato, Spinach and Tomato registered a very high significance with 0.000 values. Therefore, we can say that, the twenty years data of arrival of Vegetables provide sufficient evidence against the null hypothesis. Therefore, in above case, the null hypothesis is rejected at 1% percent level of significance and accept alternative hypothesis for these Vegetables, it means that a very good positive performance has been observed during the study period. But on the other hand, Sweet Potato has observed a negative trend. It has noticed the greater but negative value of computed t-statistic than table value by –4.762. Moreover, the differences between the years and the arrivals of Sweet Potato noticed a very high significance with 0.000 values. Therefore, we can say that, the data do not provide sufficient evidence against the null hypothesis, which may, therefore, in case of Sweet Potato; the null hypothesis is rejected at 1% percent level of significance. It means that a negative performance in arrivala of Sweet Potato is observed during the study period.

However, in the case of Brinjal, Chuka, Fenugreek, Garlic and Hemp have observed the computed value of 't' as less than table value (Chuka and Garlic are negative). Moreover the arrivals of Hemp and Fenugreek have noticed a very insignificant among the Vegetables by 0.99 and 0.85 respectively. Therefore, the data of arrivals do not provide sufficient evidence against the null hypothesis, which may, therefore, in above case, be accepted.

The same table gives the information about the coefficient of determination (r square) of Vegetables. Coefficient of determination (r^2 notation) is used to test the explanatory power of regression equations. It is observed that, Onion has showed a highest explanatory power with 0.88 during the study period among the vegetables, followed by Tomato with 0.82 (r^2). It means that explanatory power of regression equation of Onion is 0.88 or 88% that is 88% variation in arrival (Y) of Onion is because of variation in period (X). Some other vegetables also have a high explanatory power e.g. Bitter gourd, Cabbage, Carrot, Coriander Leaves, Cucumber, Dodaka, Gourd, Green Chilies, Potato and Sweet Potato was between the range of 55% and 77% (r^2). While explanatory power of Hemp is very less with 0.000 or 0 %.

In brief, this analysis indicates that there is a highly significant relationship between time and arrival of most of the Vegetables (20 Vegetables out of 22). The analysis, on the whole, for the Vegetables, reveals that the maximum vegetables have noticed a positive performance in the market yard for their arrival during under study period.

TRENDS IN THE VALUE TRANSACTION OF FOOD GRAINS

The Seventh hypothesis is taken as, "Value transaction of the major food grains and other agricultural commodities in the regulated market shows a positive trend during study period." For testing this hypothesis we have considered one-sided test. The Null hypothesis is that the performance of value transaction of major food grains and other commodities does not relate to the study period.

$$H_0: b = 0$$

Where b is in above notation indicate the population parameter (slope). This implies the alternative hypothesis as the performance of value transaction of major Food grains and other commodities, which does relate to the study period. Explanation of alternative hypothesis is given as under:

$$H_1: b > 0 \text{ (one way)}$$

We used the test statistic t for the data collected period. In order to examine the trend of the value transaction of selected food grains, the annual value transactions is taken into account for twenty years (1983-84 to 2002-03). The trend values have been computed by least square method. The trend values (the Line of Best Fit) are computed by the equations:

Y = a + bX

Where,

Y = value transaction of foodgrains

a = constant value (intercept)

b = regression coefficient (slope)

X = time

The value of 'a' and 'b' are taken as explained (equations) in Table 4. The trend values computed for the value transaction of food grains and other commodities in the regulated markets, which are also presented in Table 4.

The performance of value transaction of these commodities as revealed in the table is discussed below.

Table 4
Regression Analysis of Value Transaction of Foodgrains

Sl. No.	*Foodgrains*	*a*	*b*	*SE (b)*	*t statistic*	*r*	*r square*	*F. sig.*
1.	Bajra	2810522	7317	138612	0.053	0.012	0.000	0.958
2.	Black gram	832730	963068	269809	3.569	0.644	0.414	0.002
3.	Capsicum	16120697	472998	272998	1.733	0.378	0.143	0.100
4.	Gram	1112386	677802	144022	4.706	0.743	0.552	0.000
5.	Green gram	1555153	78331	43756	1.790	0.389	0.151	0.090
6.	Groundnut	12230288	-221075	318817	-0.693	-0.161	0.026	0.497
7.	Jowar	10584785	7047735	1428039	4.935	0.758	0.575	0.000
8.	Maize	503276	147698	36352	4.063	0.692	0.478	0.001
9.	Pigeon pea	13936326	1784402	596393	0.346	0.081	0.007	0.733
10.	Rice	-105163074	39615210	5299288	7.476	0.870	0.756	0.000
11.	Sunflower	13191181	12621	589115	0.021	0.005	0.000	0.983
12.	Wheat	-18844429	12835395	1072423	11.969	0.943	0.888	0.000
13.	Jaggery	-14055351	13509764	1967492	6.407	0.834	0.695	0.000

Note: Figures of a & b is in rupees.
Source: As per Table 1.

The value transaction of food grains, among the cereals, shows an increasing tendency during under the study. The trend equations for the value transaction of cereals are given below:

Rice	Y	=	39615210x – 105163074
Wheat	Y	=	12835395x –18844429
Jowar	Y	=	7047735x + 10584785
Maize	Y	=	147698x + 503276
Bajra	Y	=	7317x + 2810522

For these linear equations it is seen that, the annual value transaction of the Rice crop has increased by Rs. 396 lakhs, which is higher than other cereals, followed by Wheat with Rs. 128 lakhs. Jowar showed a higher regression coefficient by Rs. 70 lakhs. While Bajra showed a lower positive slope by Rs. 0.07 lakhs which is mainly due to the preference of farmers to Rice, Wheat and Jowar, which accounts a high remunerations. Among the pulses, almost all pulses were having an increasing trend during the study period. Pigeon pea has increased by Rs. 17.84 lakh every year. It is higher in the pulses, followed by Black gram, which has increased by Rs. 8.63 lakh. The linear equations for the value transaction of pulses are given below:

Pigeon pea	Y = 13936326 + 1784402x
Black gram	Y = 832730 + 963068x
Gram	Y = 1112386 + 677802x
Green gram	Y = 1555153 + 78331x

In the case of processed products, Jaggery shows a positive and relatively higher regression coefficient than other commodities in the value transaction. The linear equation of Jaggery in value transaction is given below:

Jaggery	Y = - 14055351 + 13509764x

But a negative performance is seen in the case of value transaction of Groundnut. The negative trend of Groundnut is given in following equations:

Groundnut	Y = 12230288 – 221075x

Value of 'a' and 'b' taken, as reliable or not, is therefore, called as standard error of estimate 'b' {SE (b)}. Table 4 gives the SE (b) of food grains and other commodities during the study period.

The tabular value of 't' at 1% level of significance for 18 degree of freedom is (*df*) = 1.33 (one way). For the testing the test statistic of annual data for value transaction of food grains and other commodities is computed for 't' values of Wheat, Rice, Jowar, Maize, Black gram, Gram, Green gram, Capsicum and Jaggery (9 out of 13 commodity) which are noticed a greater value than table value among all commodities and these value (t-statistic) have registered between 1.733 and 11.968. Moreover, the F significance of some commodities namely, Wheat, Rice, Jowar, Gram and Jaggery have noticed very high significance with 0.000 values. Maize, Black gram, Green gram and Capsicum have also noticed a higher significance. Therefore, we can say that, the data of value transaction of food grains and other commodities provide sufficient evidence against the null hypothesis, which may, therefore, is rejected at 1% percent level of significance and accept the alternative hypothesis.

In the case of Bajra, Pigeon pea, Sunflower and Groundnut, we observed the computed value of 't' is less than table value, moreover F significance of Sunflower, Bajra and Pigeon pea have noticed a very insignificant trend among all commodities by 0.983, 0.958 and 0.733 respectively. Therefore, we can say that, the twenty years data do not provide sufficient evidence against the null hypothesis, which may, therefore, be accepted.

Same table gives the information about coefficient of determination (r^2) of food grains and other commodity. This r^2 notation is used to test the explanatory power of regression equation. It is observed that, Wheat has showed a highest explanatory power with 0.888 during the study period, followed by Rice with 0.756 (r^2). Gram, Jowar, Maize and Jaggery has also noticed a higher explanatory power. It means that explanatory power of regression equation of Wheat is .89 or 89% that is 89% variation in value transaction (Y) is because of variation in period (X). While explanatory power of Sunflower and Bajra are a very less variation with 0.000.

On the whole, the analysis indicates that there are highly significant relationships between time and value transaction of most of the food grains and other commodity except Bajra and Sunflower. The analysis, on the whole, for many food grains and other commodities, revealed that the positive trends in the market yard for their value transaction.

TRENDS IN THE VALUE TRANSACTION OF FRUITS

The eighth hypothesis is taken as, "Value transaction of the major Fruits in the regulated market have shown a positive trend during study period." For that purpose we have considered one-sided test. The Null hypothesis is that performance of value transaction of major Fruits does not relate to the study period.

$$H_0: b = 0$$

Where b is in the above notation indicate the population parameter (slope). This implies the alternative hypothesis that, the performance of value transaction of major Fruits is related to the study period. Explanation of alternative hypothesis given as:

$$H_1: b > 0 \text{ (one way)}$$

We used test statistic t on the basis of our study period. In order to examine the trend of the value transaction of selected Fruits, the annual value transactions are taken for twenty-year period (1983-84 to 2002-03). The trend values have been computed by the method of least squares. The trend values (the Line of Best Fit) are computed by the equations:

$$Y = a + bX$$

Where,

Y = value transaction of fruits

a = constant value (intercept)

b = regression coefficient (slope)

X = time

The trend values computed for the Value transaction of selected Fruits in the regulated markets is presented in Table 5. The performance of value transaction of Fruits as revealed in the table is discussed below.

Table 5
Regression Analysis of Value Transaction of Fruits

Sl. No.	*Fruits*	*Quantity*	*a*	*b*	*SE (b)*	*t statistic*	*r*	*r square*	*F. sig.*
1.	Apple	Dozen	-4127066	1072994	183502	5.847	0.817	0.668	0.000
2.	Banana	Quintal	2069984	500739	99809	5.017	0.764	0.583	0.000
3.	Ber	Kilogram	-3654211	933291	100717	9.267	0.918	0.843	0.000
4.	Custard apple	Quintal	95874	14131	4063	3.478	0.634	0.402	0.003
5.	Grapes	Boxes	-850821	403794	62623	6.448	0.835	0.698	0.000
6.	Guava	Kilogram	376947	37197	11871	3.133	0.594	0.353	0.006
7.	Lemon	Kilogram	-590605	749302	112455	6.666	0.844	0.712	0.000
8.	Mango	Dozen	1692212	-4030	45054	-0.089	-0.021	0.000	0.930
9.	Orange	Dozen	-204961	48447	11746	4.125	0.707	0.500	0.001
10.	Papaya	Dozen	-56509	9858	1541	6.396	0.841	0.706	0.000
11.	Pomegranate	Dozen	-8327437	1639591	237176	6.913	0.859	0.738	0.000
12.	Sapota	Dozen	-404745	83361	37741	2.209	0.462	0.213	0.040
13.	Watermelon	Number	1080275	173819	29293	5.934	0.813	0.662	0.000

Note: Figures of a & b in rupees.
Source: As per Table 1.

The value transaction of major Fruits shows an increasing tendency except Mango during the period under study. The trend equations for value transaction of some major fruits, which noticed a higher positive regression coefficient, are given below:

Pomegranate $Y = 1639591x - 8327437$

Apple $Y = 1072994x - 4127066$

Ber $Y = 933291x - 3654211$

The annual value transaction of Pomegranate has increased by Rs. 16.39 lakhs during the period under study, followed by Apple by Rs. 10.72 lakhs. Ber has also noticed a higher positive change with Rs. 8.33 lakh, but the intercept of each fruit has been observed a negative value. In the case of Banana, Watermelon and Custard apple we observed both intercept and regression coefficient values are positive.

Banana $Y = 2069984 + 500739x$

Watermelon $Y = 1080275 + 173819x$

Custard apple $Y = 95874 + 14131x$

The annual value transaction of Banana has increased by Rs. 5 lakh. Papaya has noticed a lowest regression coefficient by Rs. 0.09 lakh. The judge the values of 'a' and 'b' as taken, are reliable or not, we test 'b', which is called as standard error of the estimate 'b' {SE (b)}. Table 5 gives the SE (b) of fruits during the study period.

The tabular value of 't' at 1% level of significance for 18 degree of freedom is (*df*) = 1.33. For the testing the test statistic computed with the help of (twenty years annual) data of value transaction of fruits, we computed 't' values of Apple, Banana, Ber, Custard apple, Grapes, Guava, Lemon, Orange, Papaya, Pomegranate, Sapota and Watermelon (12 fruits out of 13) which have noticed a greater values than the table values and these values have (t-statistic) registered a range of 2.209 and 8.267. Moreover, the F significance of these fruits in the value transaction has noticed a highly significant. In the case of Apple, Banana, Ber, Grapes, Lemon, Papaya, Pomegranate and Watermelon a high significant with 0.000 is registered and remaining fruits namely, Orange, Custard apple, Guava and Sapota have noticed highly significant values at 0.001, 0.003, 0.006 and 0.040 respectively. Therefore, we can say that, the data of value transaction of above fruits provides sufficient evidence against the null hypothesis, which may, therefore, is the null hypothesis and rejected at 1% percent level of significance and accept an alternative hypothesis for these fruits. It means that a very good positive performance in value transaction of fruits is seen during the study period.

Coefficient of determination (r^2 notation) is used to test the explanatory power of regression equations. It is observed that, Ber has a highest explanatory power with 0.84 during the study period, followed by Pomegranate with 0.74 (r^2). Apple, Banana, Grapes, Lemon, Orange and Watermelon have observed a higher explanatory power between 50% and 72%. While explanatory power of Mango is very less with 0.000 or 0 %.

In brief, the whole analysis indicates that there are highly significant relationships between time and value transaction of almost all fruits except Mango. The analysis, on the whole, reveals that the maximum fruits have noticed a positive and significant performance in the market yard for their value transaction during under study period.

TRENDS IN THE VALUE TRANSACTION OF VEGETABLES

The ninth hypothesis is taken as, "Value transaction of the major Vegetables in the regulated market have shown a positive trend during the study period." For this purpose, we considered one-sided test. The Null hypothesis is that performance of value transaction of Vegetables is not related to the study period.

$$H_0: b = 0$$

Where b is the population parameter (slope). This implies the alternative hypothesis as the performance of value transaction of Vegetables is related to study period. Explanation of alternative hypothesis is given as:

$$H_1: b > 0 \text{ (one way)}$$

We used test statistic t on the basis of our study period. In order to examine the trend of the value transaction of selected Vegetables, the annual value transactions is taken for twenty years period (1983-84 to 2002-03). The trend values have been computed by the method of least squares. The trend values (the Line of Best Fit) are computed by the equations:

$$Y = a + bX$$

Where,

Y = value transaction of vegetables

a = constant value (intercept)

b = regression coefficient (slope)

X = time

The trend values computed for the Value transaction of selected Vegetables in the regulated markets is presented in Table 6. The performance of value transaction of Vegetables as revealed in the table is discussed below.

Table 6
Regression Analysis of Value Transaction of Vegetables

Sl. No.	*Vegetables*	*Quantity*	*a*	*b*	*SE (b)*	*t statistic*	*r*	*r square*	*F. sig.*
1.	Bittergourd	Kilogram	-76993	70724	5370	13.170	0.952	0.906	0.000
2.	Brinjal	Kilogram	1569346	433584	29166	14.866	0.962	0.925	0.000
3.	Cabbage	Kilogram	-214558	193000	14918	12.937	0.950	0.903	0.000
4.	Carrot	Kilogram	-122448	142551	9432	14.973	0.962	0.926	0.000
5.	Cauliflower	Number	-2292718	387796	181685	2.134	0.449	0.202	0.047
6.	Chuka	Bundle	147399	16284	5058	3.220	0.605	0.365	0.005
7.	Coriander Leaves	Bundle	-312485	450131	30251	14.880	0.962	0.925	0.000
8.	Cucumber	Kilogram	-381313	203381	20797	9.779	0.917	0.842	0.000
9.	Dodaka	Kilogram	1322716	143483	8904	16.114	0.967	0.935	0.000
10.	Fenugreek	Bundle	258475	174961	28611	6.115	0.822	0.675	0.000
11.	Garlic	Quintal	-2959532	1136257	117969	9.632	0.915	0.838	0.000
12.	Gourd	Number	8021	19167	2537	7.557	0.872	0.760	0.000
13.	Green Chilies	Kilogram	-21706	732168	53081	13.794	0.956	0.914	0.000
14.	Hemp	Bundle	14693	3507	574	6.107	0.821	0.674	0.000
15.	Lady's finger	Kilogram	135522	213077	15454	13.787	0.956	0.913	0.000
16.	Onion	Quintal	-57401128	22400832	2204594	10.136	0.922	0.851	0.000
17.	Potato	Kilogram	-18553260	4672817	569564	8.204	0.888	0.789	0.000
18.	Shepu	Bundle	-81606	104521	10615	9.846	0.918	0.843	0.000
19.	Spinach	Bundle	-155209	73385	6109	12.012	0.943	0.889	0.000
20.	Sweet Potato	Kilogram	227856	19774	4137	4.055	0.691	0.477	0.001
21.	Tomato	Kilogram	-8963344	3309874	293434	11.280	0.936	0.876	0.000
22.	Vetch	Kilogram	53843	166677	13262	12.568	0.947	0.898	0.000

Note: Figures of a & b in rupees.
Source: As per Table 1.

The value transaction of Vegetables of almost all vegetables showed an increasing tendency. The trend equations for the value transaction of some vegetables is noticed as higher positive regression coefficient as given below:

Onion	Y = 22400832x - 57401128
Potato	Y = 4672817x - 18553260
Tomato	Y = 3309874x - 8963344

The annual value transaction of Onion has increased by Rs. 224 lakh, followed by Potato by Rs. 46.72 lakh. Tomato has also noticed a higher positive trend with Rs. 33.09 lakh. Cabbage, Cauliflower, Coriander Leaves, Garlic, Green Chilies and Cucumber have showed a higher regression coefficient, but the intercept of each vegetables has a negative value. However, for some vegetables both intercept and regression coefficient values are positive. The trend equations of some vegetables are given as:

Brinjal	Y = 1569346 + 433584x
Dodaka	Y = 1322716 + 143483x
Fenugreek	Y = 258475 + 174961x

Value transaction of Brinjal has increased by Rs. 4.33 lakh every year, value turnover of Dodaka and Fenugreek have increased by Rs. 1.43 lakh and Rs. 1.74 lakh along with a positive intercept value.

We have used the test statistic t on the basis of our study period. Value of 'a' and 'b' is taken, as reliable or not, is acknowledged by testing of 'b', which is called as standard error of estimate 'b' {SE (b)}. Table 6 gives the SE (b) of vegetables during the study period. The tabular value of 't' at 1% level of significance for 18 degree of freedom is (*df*) = 1.33 (one way).

It is remarkable to say, the computed 't' values of almost all Vegetables (22 vegetables out of 22) have noticed a greater values than table values. Among the Vegetables; Bitter gourd, Brinjal, Cabbage, Carrot, Coriander Leaves, Dodaka, Green Chilies, Lady's finger, Onion, Spinach, Tomato and Vetch have noticed a very high computed 't' value ranging between 10.136 and 16.114 and Potato, Shepu, Cucumber, Chuka, Cauliflower, Fenugreek, Garlic, Gourd, Hemp and Sweet Potato have a 't' value ranging between 2.134 and 8.846. Moreover, the F significance of all vegetables has noticed highly significant values. In the case of Bitter gourd, Brinjal, Cabbage, Carrot, Coriander Leaves, Cucumber, Dodaka, Fenugreek, Garlic, Gourd, Green Chilies, Onion, Potato, Shepu, Spinach, Vetch and Tomato a high significant with 0.000 values is noticed. The Sweet Potato and Chuka also observed a very high significant by 0.001 and 0.005 respectively. Therefore, we can say that, the data of value transaction of all Vegetables does provide sufficient evidence against the null hypothesis, which is therefore, a null hypothesis, is rejected at 1% percent level of significance and accept alternative hypothesis for all Vegetables. It means that a very good positive performance has been observed during the study period.

Coefficient of correlation and coefficient of determination (r^2) of vegetables are calculated in the same table. A very strong relationship between value transaction of vegetables and time is observed. Coefficient of determination (r^2 notation) is used to test the explanatory power of regression equations.

It is observed that, Dodaka has showed a highest explanatory power with 0.94 for the vegetables, followed by Carrot with 0.93 (r^2). It means that explanatory power of regression equation of Dodaka is 0.94 or 94% that is 94% variation in value transaction (Y) of Dodaka is because of variation in period (X). Remaining vegetables, except Cauliflower, Chuka and Sweet Potato have experienced a high explanatory power between 68% and 93% (r^2).

In brief, the analysis indicates that there is highly significant relationship between time and value transaction of all Vegetables (22 of out 22). The analysis, on the whole, for the Vegetables, revealed that all vegetables have noticed a positive and significant performance in the market yard for their value transaction during under study period.

PERFORMANCE OF SUB-MARKETS IN THE TOTAL TURNOVER

The tenth hypothesis is taken as, "The total turnover of Sub-markets have shown a positive trend during the study period." For this purpose, we considered one-sided test. The Null hypothesis is that performance of total turnover of sub-markets does not relate to the study period.

$$H_0: b = 0$$

Where b in above notation indicate the population parameter (slope). This implies the alternative hypothesis as positive performance of total turnover of sub-markets is seen in the market yard during study period. Explanation of alternative hypothesis is given as:

$$H_1: b > 0 \text{ (one way)}$$

We used the test statistic t in order to examine the trend of the total turnover of sub-markets. The annual turnover of sub-market is taken for twenty years period (1983-84 to 2002-03). The trend values have been computed by the method of least squares. The trend values (the Line of Best Fit) are computed by the equations as:

$$Y = a + bX$$

Where,

Y = total turnover of sub-markets

a = constant value (intercept)

b = regression coefficient (slope)

X = time

The trend values computed for the turnover of sub-markets in the regulated markets is presented in Table 7. The performance of total turnover of sub-markets as revealed in the table is discussed below.

Table 7

Regression Analysis of Total Turnover in Sub-markets

Sl. No.	*Sub-Markets*	*a*	*b*	*SE (b)*	*t statistic*	*r*	*r square*	*F. sig.*
1.	Food grains	-20010487	76594542	7282266	10.518	0.927	0.860	0.000
2.	Fruits & Vegetable	-106282153	44412611	3031334	14.651	0.961	0.923	0.000
3.	Straw Market	8900963	331749	96837	3.426	0.628	0.395	0.003
4.	Cattle Market	2001203	681971	95992	7.104	0.859	0.737	0.000
5.	Total Turnover	-115390475	122020874	9527379	12.807	0.949	0.901	0.000

Note: Figures of a & b in rupees.
Source: As per Table 1.

The total turnovers of all sub-markets have experienced an increasing tendency during the entire period. The trend equations for turnover of all sub-markets noticed a higher positive regression coefficient as given below:

Foodgrains & other	Y	= -20010487 + 76594542x
Fruits & Vegetable	Y	= -106282153 + 44412611x
Straw Market	Y	= 8900963 + 331749x
Cattle Market	Y	= 2001203 + 681971x

The annual turnover of Foodgrains and other commodities has increased by Rs. 765.94 lakh, followed by Fruits and Vegetable with an increase of Rs. 444.12 lakh every year. Cattle market and Straw market also noticed a lower but better regression coefficient with Rs. 6.81 lakhs and Rs. 3.31 lakhs. But, the intercept of food grains market and fruits and vegetable market has a negative value. However, Cattle market and Straw market have showed the intercept and regression coefficient values as positive. The total turnover of market yard has increased by Rs. 12.20 crores. The trend equations of total turnover (including all sub-market) is given as:

Total Turnover Y = -115390475 + 122020874x

We used the test statistic t on the basis of our study period. Value of 'a' and 'b' are taken as called standard error of estimate 'b' {SE (b)}. Table 7 gives the SE (b) of total turnover of various sub-markets during the study period. The tabular value of 't' at 1% level of significance for 18 degree of freedom is (*df*) = 1.33 (one way).

The computed 't' values of almost all sub-markets in the total turnover have noticed a greater than table values. Among the sub-markets, Food grains market and Fruits & Vegetable market have noticed a very high computed 't' value of 10.518 and 14.651 respectively. In the case of Straw market and Cattle market, we see the computed 't' value greater than table value with 3.426 and 7.104 respective. Moreover, the F significance of all sub-market has noticed a highly significant value. Food grains market, Fruits & Vegetable market and Cattle market also registered a very high significant with 0.000. The total turnover of market yard also observed a greater computed 't' value than table value and noticed a very high significant level. Therefore, we can say that, the total turnover of sub markets as well as total turnover of market yard provides a sufficient evidence against the null hypothesis, which may, therefore, the null hypothesis is rejected at 1% percent level of significance and accept alternative hypothesis. It means that a very good positive performance is observed during the study period for the total turnover of various sub-markets.

Coefficient of correlation and coefficient of determination (r^2) of sub-markets are calculated in the same table. A very strong relationship between total turnover of sub-markets and time has been seen. Fruits and Vegetable market has observed a very strong relationship with study period by 0.96 during the study period. Coefficient of determination (r^2 notation) is used to test the explanatory power of regression equation. Fruits and Vegetables market shows a highest explanatory power with 0.92 among the sub-markets, followed by Food grains and other commodity market with 0.86 (r^2).

In brief, the analysis indicates that there is highly significant relationship between time and total turnover of sub-markets. The analysis, on the whole, for the sub-markets, revealed that all sub-markets have noticed a positive and significant performance in the market yard during the study period.

REFERENCE

Agrawal A.N. and Kundan Lal (1996), "Agricultural Problems of India", Vikas Publishing House, New Delhi.

Bhatia D.K. & Gupta Vijay (1986), "Business Statistics", Vani Educational Books, New Delhi.

Desai R.G. (1998), "Agricultural Economics", Himalaya Publishing House, Bombay.

Gupta S.C. (1996), "Fundamentals of Statistics", Himalaya Publishing House, New Delhi.

Monga G.S. (2000), "Mathematics and Statistics for Economics", Vikas Pub. House Pvt. Ltd., Second Revised Edition, New Delhi.

Prasad A.S. (1985), "Agricultural Marketing in India", Mittal Publications, Delhi.

Reddy A.V. (1991), "Agricultural Marketing", Printwell, Jaipur.

Reddy P.I. (1995), "Marketing of Vegetables", Printwell, Jaipur.

Indian Journal of Agricultural Marketing (2002), Vol. 16, No. 2, Nagpur.

Indian Journal of Agricultural Marketing (2000), (Conference Special), Vol. 14, No. 3, Nagpur.

The Bihar Journal of Agricultural Marketing (2000), Vol. VIII, No. 1, Patna.

9

FINANCIAL TURNOVER OF A.P.M.C. SOLAPUR

This chapter explains the analysis and interpretation of financial turnover of Agricultural Produce Market Committee, Solapur in terms of performance and variation and other economic variables performed during 1983-84 to 2002-03.

PROGRESS IN FINANCIAL TURNOVER OF THE SUB-MARKET

Table 1 shows the progress of the Sub-markets in respect of financial turnover from 1983-84 to 2002-03. It is observed from the Table 1 that Siddheshwar Market Yard has been making progress in the financial turnover of sub-markets over a period of time.

The total turnover has increased continuously during the study period. During first period it has recorded Rs. 38.63 crores as its annual turnover, it has increased by Rs. 68.63 crores in the second period, Rs. 133.06 crores in the third period. It has also a record of Rs. 226 crores turnover in the recent period. The total turnover has increased by 485.09 per cent during the period from 1983-84 to 1987-88 and 1998-99 to 2002-03.

The Foodgrains market among the sub-markets has ranked the first position in the total turnover with Rs. 28.42 crores in the first period. Fruits and Vegetable market has attained the second position with Rs. 8.86 crores and third position has been attained by Straw market with Rs. 0.92 crores turnover. The Cattle market has record of least position with Rs. 0.43 crores during the same period. The story of first period is repeated in the second period, Food grains market stood first position in the total turnover with Rs. 50.21 crores and Cattle market has recorded a least position with Rs. 0.58 crores. But the rate of change in Fruits and Vegetable market was higher than Food grains market. In the case of Cattle market it is observed a higher rate of change in percentage than in Straw market.

Table 1
Progress of Financial Turnover of Sub-Markets

(Figures in Rs.)

Sl.		*Period*				*Percentage Change*			
No.	*Items*	*I*	*II*	*III*	*IV*	*1st*	*2nd*	*3rd*	*4th*
1.	Food grains & Others commodity	284159864	502141877	854361540	1496265551	76.71	70.14	75.13	426.56
2.	Fruits & Vegetable Market	88600697	166574110	448479223	736547038	88.00	169.24	64.23	731.31
3.	Straw Market	9215441	11762517	15236477	13322859	27.64	29.53	-12.56	44.57
4.	Cattle Market	4308910	5832726	12541425	13964551	35.36	115.02	11.35	224.08
5.	Total Turnover	386284912	686311229	1330618664	2260099999	77.67	93.88	69.85	485.09

Note:
(1) Period: I = 1983-84 to 1987-88, II = 1988-89 to 1992-93, III = 1993-94 to 1997-98, IV = 1998-99 to 2002-03
(2) Percentage Change: 1st = {(II-I)/I}*100, 2nd = {(III-II)/II}*100, 3rd = {(IV-III)/III}*100, 4th = {(IV-I)/I}*100
Source: Processed data on the basis of Annual Report of APMC, Solapur, period from 1983-84 to 2002-03.

No change in the positional ranks is observed in the turnover of sub-markets during the third period. However a relative change at the higher level was seen in the case of Fruits and Vegetable market compared to other sub-markets with a share of 169.24 per cent. Another important change, which has been observed in the third period, was that Cattle market performed better than the Food grains market.

In the fourth period positional rank was not the same as was in the three periods. Among the sub-markets, Foodgrains market has increased with Rs. 149.63 crores in the total turnover, followed by Fruits and Vegetable market with Rs. 73.65 crores and Cattle market achieved the third position with Rs. 1.40 crores turnover. Straw market has experienced a declining trend compared to earlier period.

Over a period of time the most prominent change has been observed in the total turnover of the sub-markets. Fruits and Vegetable market has a higher rate of change with 731.31 per cent, followed by Food grains market with 426.56 per cent change during 1983-84 to 1987-88 and 1998-99 to 2002-03.

COMPOUND GROWTH RATES OF THE TURNOVER IN SUB-MARKETS

Annual compound growth rates of turnover in sub-market of APMC, Solapur has give estimated in Table 2 for period from 1983-84 to 2002-03. Foodgains and other commodity market stood first in the turnover followed by Fruits and Vegetables Market. Straw Market stood the next and the Cattle Market recorded least.

Period-I

During the first period, Fruits and Vegetables Market has a positive trend with a record highest growth rate in turnover among the various sub-market with 20.82 per cent per annum. Cattle Market stood next with 14.50 per cent. Remaining two markets have registered a negative growth rates. However, total turnover shows a positive but lower growth rate with 2.15 per cent during the period.

Table 2
Compound Growth Rates in the Turnover of Sub-Markets

Sl.		*CGR Period*				
No.	*Item*	*I*	*II*	*III*	*IV*	*V*
1.	Food grains & other	-2.89	12.90	11.02	-2.45	11.20
2.	Fruits & Vegetables	20.82	15.64	14.58	10.36	15.98
3.	Straw Market	-0.49	9.38	4.26	5.66	2.84
4.	Cattle Market	14.50	-0.09	5.55	-3.92	8.65
5.	Total Turnover	2.15	13.40	12.11	1.72	12.32

Note: (1) CGR calculated as Antilog (b-1)*100
(2) Period: I=1983-84 to 1987-88, II=1988-89 to 1992-93, III=1993-94 to 1997-98, IV=1998-99 to 2002-03, V=1983-84 to 2002-03.

Source: As per Table 1.

Period-II

Entire picture of as seen in the first period has changed in the second period. Except Cattle Market, almost all markets were showing a positive and significant growth rates. Once again Fruits and Vegetables Market performed better in growth rate in turnover with 15.64 per cent share. Food gains Market and Straw Market have registered a better position than earlier period. The Cattle Market experienced a negative growth rate with 0.09 per cent share. Thus the total turnover showed not only a positive and significant position but also performed better position than the earlier period with 13.40 per cent share.

Period-III

A general characteristic of this period shows positive trend. Fruits and Vegetables market was not only significant once again but also recorded a highest growth rate of 14.58 per cent, followed by Food gains Market with 11.02 per cent share. Cattle Market performed better than earlier period. The total turnover of the period has increased by 12.11 per cent.

Period-IV

In the recent past, the turnover of each market has achieved fewer shares as compared to earlier period. Growth rate of Fruits and Vegetables Market has the highest share in the markets. Cattle Market and Food grains Market have a negative growth rates. The total turnover has marginally increased by 1.72 per cent.

Period-V

Diagram 1 shows annual compound growth rates turnover in the sub-markets of APMC during the period from 1983-84 to 2002-03. One of the important observations of the fifth period was positive and satisfactory. Fruits and Vegetables has recorded the highest growth rates with 15.98 per cent per annum, followed by Food grains Market with 11.20 per cent. Cattle Market has also performed significantly.

VARIATION IN FINANCIAL TURNOVER OF THE SUB-MARKETS

The variation in the financial turnover of the Sub-markets of Agriculture Produce Market Committee has been analyzed in Table 3. The tools of dispersion like minimum and maximum are used to estimate the values during the period under the study.

The tool such as coefficient of range, standard deviation, coefficient of variation and skew ness are also applied to analyze the data. It is observed from the table that, Total Turnover of APMC has high relative range of 0.76. Financial Turnover of Fruits and Vegetables market were highest coefficient of range than other commodity markets with 0.87, followed by

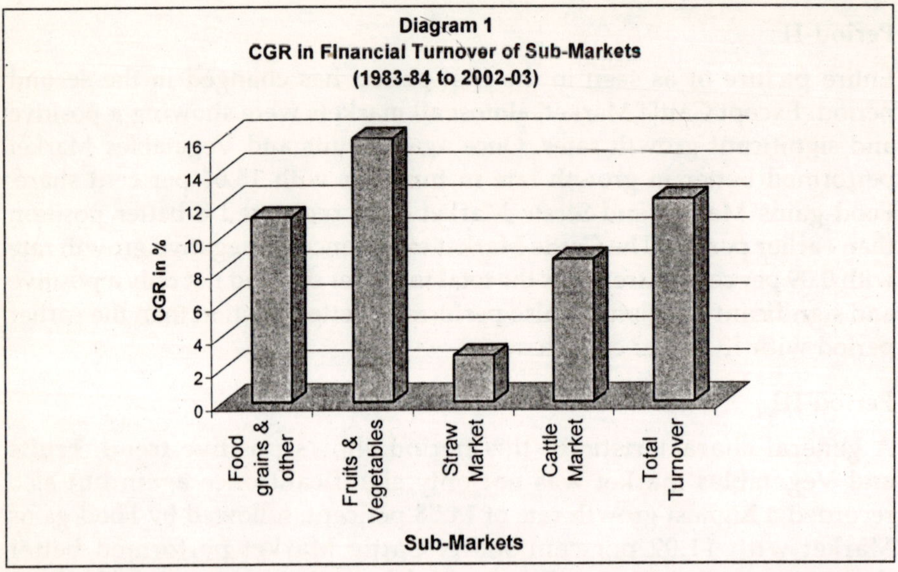

Foodgrains market with 0.75. On the other hand, Straw market has showed lowest relative range in the sub-markets with 0.39. Remaining commodity market namely, Cattle Market has showed a higher variability. The coefficient of variations of the financial turnover of Sub-markets has been estimated for the period form 1983-84 to 2002-03. Coefficient of variation is also shown in the Diagram 2.

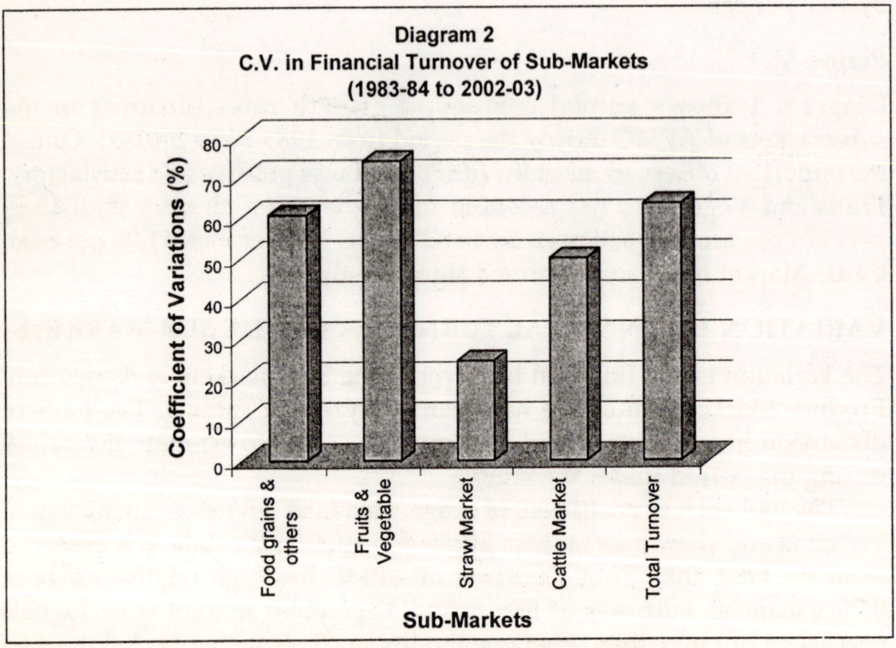

Table 3
Variations in Financial Turnover of Sub-Market of APMC

Sl. No.	Items	Range			Standard Deviation					Coefficient of Variation					
		Min.	*Max.*	*RR*	*I*	*II*	*III*	*IV*	*V*	*1st*	*2nd*	*3rd*	*4th*	*5th*	*Skew*
1.	Foodgrains & others	247491964	1726729955	0.75	31783146	87315123	136328655	196099343	476243494	11.18	17.39	15.96	13.11	60.73	0.73
2.	Fruits & Vegetables	58899808	847927904	0.87	25293229	36335219	99250640	108812681	266616895	28.55	21.81	22.30	14.77	74.05	0.59
3.	Straw Market	7986731	18236525	0.39	1361097	1860120	2428890	2535950	3044966	14.77	15.81	15.94	19.03	24.59	0.46
4.	Cattle Market	3095006	17849616	0.70	828389	648319	3039140	2109816	4580278	19.23	11.12	24.23	15.11	50.00	0.46
5.	Total Turnover	341448059	2548720245	0.76	37774437	124241064	235821415	250738283	741207648	9.78	18.10	17.72	11.09	63.58	0.63

Note:
(1) Standard Deviation: I=1983-84 to 1987-88, II=1988-89 to 1992-93, III=1993-94 to 1997-98, IV=1998-99 to 2002-03, V=1983-84 to 2002-03
(2) Coefficient of Variation: 1st=1983-84 to 1987-88, 2nd=1988-89 to 1992-93, 3rd=1993-94 to 1997-98, 4th=1998-99 to 2002-03, 5th=1983-84 to 2002-03

Source: As per Table 1.

The coefficient of variation was recorded at 63.58 per cent. Fruits and Vegetables market has registered a highest coefficient of variation among the sub-markets. Foodgrains market is next to Fruits and Vegetables market with 60.73 per cent of variation. Straw market has registered a lowest coefficient of variation than other sub-markets by 24.59 per cent. Cattle Market shows relatively higher coefficient than the Straw Market.

Distribution of financial turnover of the sub-markets in the APMC, shows a positive skewness for the entire period. Distribution in the financial turnover of Food grains market showed highly skewed with 0.73; which implies that the curve of distribution of sales has longer tail towards the right. On the other hand, Straw and Cattle Markets have a lowest skewness of 0.46. The total turnover has a lower than the Food grains but higher than other markets with 0.63; which implies that the curve of distribution of financial turnover has longer tail towards the right.

AVERAGE SHARE OFSUB-MARKETS IN TOTAL TURNOVER

The progress in the financial turnover of the market yard ultimately depends upon the performance of the sub-markets and market that determine growth prospect of market yard. Siddheshwar Market Yard consists of four sub market such as (i) Agricultural Commodities Market (ii) Fruits and Vegetables Market, (iii) Straw Market, and (iv) Cattle Market. Average share of Sub-markets in the total turnover is exhibited in Diagram 3 (A, B, C & D).

Diagram 3 (A)
Average Share of Sub-Markets
(1983-84 to 1987-88)

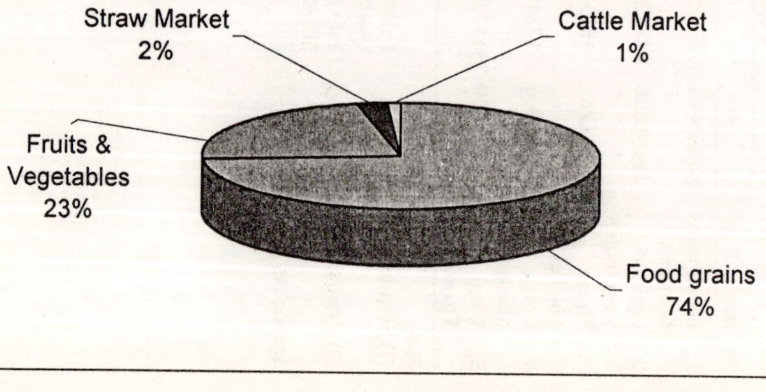

Table 4 is accounted the average share of sub-markets in total turnover. The share of food grains and other agricultural commodities in the total financial turnover of the Siddheshwar Market Yard was 73.56 percent, followed by fruits and vegetable market with a share of 22.94 per cent, straw market with a share of 2.39 percent and cattle market of 1.11 percent during the period from 1983-84 to 1987-88.

Table 4
Average Share of Sub-Markets in Total Turnover

(Figures in %)

Sl. No.	Items	Period I	Period II	Period III	Period IV	Percentage Change 1st	Percentage Change 2nd	Percentage Change 3rd	Percentage Change 4th
1.	Food grains & other	73.56	73.17	64.21	66.20	-0.53	-12.25	3.10	-10.01
2.	Fruits & Vegetable	22.94	24.27	33.70	32.59	5.80	38.85	-3.29	42.07
3.	Straw Market	2.39	1.71	1.15	0.59	-28.45	-32.75	-48.70	-75.31
4.	Cattle Market	1.11	0.85	0.94	0.62	-23.42	10.59	-34.04	-44.14
5.	Total Turnover	100	100	100	100	-	-	-	-

Note:

(1) Period: I =1983-84 to 1987-88, II=1988-89 to 1992-93, III=1993-94 to 1997-98, IV=1998-99 to 2002-03

(2) Percentage Change: 1st={(II-I)/I}*100, 2nd={(III-II)/II}*100, 3rd={(IV-III)/III}*100, 4th={(IV-I)/I}*100

Source: As per Table 1.

The share of food grains and other agricultural commodities has been continuously declining. It was 73.56 per cent in the first period, which reduced to 73.17per cent in the second period. It has further declined to 64.21per cent in the third period and marginally increased by 66.20

Diagram 3 (B)
Average Share of Sub-Markets
(1988-89 to 1992-93)

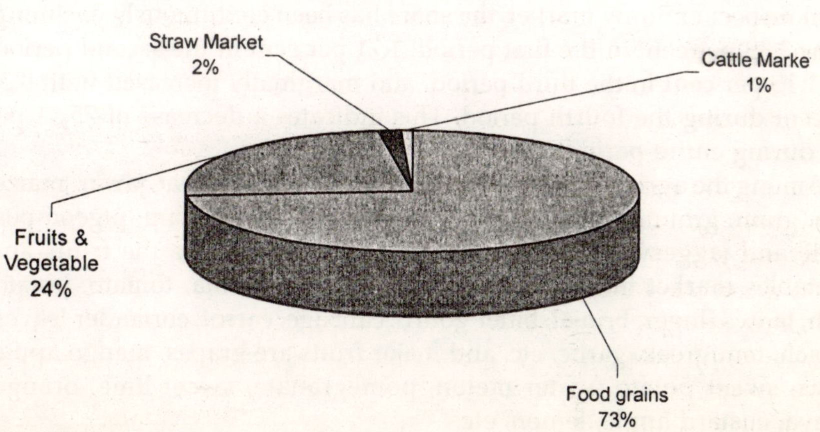

per cent during the fourth period. Thus it indicates a decrease of 10.01 per cent during entire period. While the share of fruits and vegetables market in the total turnover has increased. It was 22.94 per cent in the first period, which increased to 24.27 per cent in the second period and further increased to 33.70 per cent in the third period, and in the recent past it has marginally declined to 32.59 per cent, which indicate an increase of 42.07 per cent during the entire period.

In the case of Cattle market, the relative share of total financial turnover has declined from 1.11 percent to 0.85 per cent during second period, marginally increased to 0.94 per cent in the third period and then reduced to 0.62 per cent in the recent past, indicating no systematic trend during1983-84 and 2002-03.

Diagram 3 (C)
Average Share of Sub-Markets
(1993-94 to 1997-98)

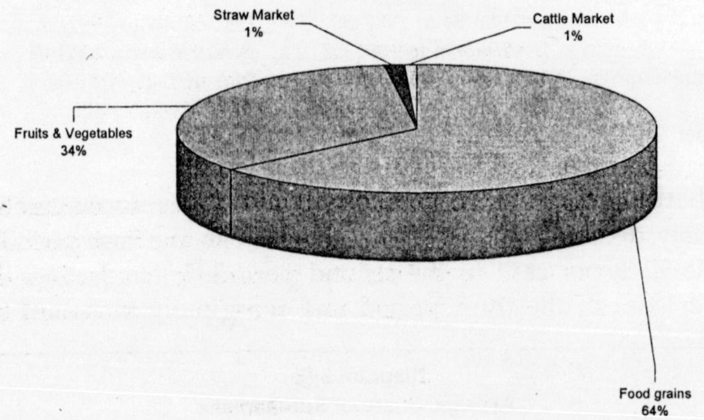

In respect of Straw market, the share has been continuously declining. It was 2.39 per cent in the first period, 1.71 per cent in the second period, and 1.15 per cent in the third period, and marginally increased with 0.59 per cent during the fourth period. This indicates a decrease of 75.31 per cent during entire period.

Among the agricultural commodities market rice, wheat, jawar, maize, bajra, gram, groundnut, sunflower, green gram, black gram, pigeon pea, chillie and jaggery are important commodities. Among the fruits and vegetables market major vegetables are onion, banana, tomato, potato, vetch, lady's finger, brinjal, bitter gourd, cabbage, carrot, coriander leaves, spinach, fenugreek, garlic, etc. and major fruits are grapes, mango apple, guava, sweet potato, water melon, pomegranate, sweet lime, orange, papaya, custard apple, lemon, etc.

Diagram 3 (D)
Average Share of Sub-Markets
(1998-99 to 2002-03)

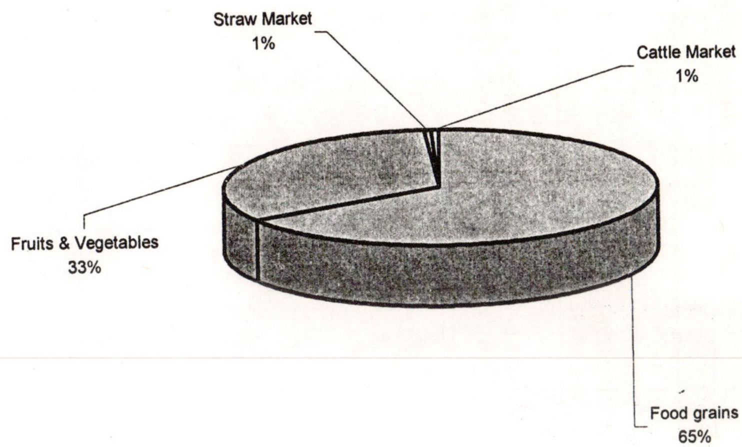

Over period of time, it has been observed that the share of each market is changing in the respect of financial turnover of the market yard.

GROWTH IN FINANCIAL TURNOVER OF APMC

In this section an attempt is made to examine the financial position of Siddheshwar Market Yard for the entire period under study. The financial position of market yard depends upon the (i) income, (ii) expenditure, (iii) surplus, (iv) permanent fund and other sources, if any. Following section deals in growth of income, expenditure, surplus and permanent funds etc.

Total Income

Table 5 accounts for the market's income of Rs. 43.11 lakh in the first period swelled to Rs.99.84 lakh in the second period thereby recording 126 per cent increase. The total income has increased to Rs. 225.44 lakh during second period. This indicates an increase of 130.41 per cent and 83.40 per cent increased only during the third period. Moreover, it has increased to Rs. 413.45 lakh during the period from 1998-99 to 2002-03. Thus it indicates an increase of 859 per cent during entire period.

Total Expenditure

Major heads of expenditure of the APMC are payments to staff, construction of Yards, buildings and other development work,

Table 5
Growth of Financial Turnover of APMC, Solapur

(Figures in Rs.)

Sl. No.	*Items*	*Period*				*Percentage Change*			
		I	*II*	*III*	*IV*	*1st*	*2nd*	*3rd*	*4th*
1.	Total Income	4311237	9784057	22543733	41344793	126.94	130.41	83.40	859.00
2.	Total Expenditure	1703574	4247051	9663062	20046495	149.30	127.52	107.45	1076.73
3.	Surplus	2607664	5537005	12880671	21298298	112.34	132.63	65.35	716.76
4.	Permanent Fund	15819006	36502813	84039327	158396949	130.75	130.23	88.48	901.31

Note:
(1) Period: I=1983-84 to 1987-88, II=1988-89 to 1992-93, III=1993-94 to 1997-98, IV=1998-99 to 2002-03
(2) Percentage Change: 1st={(II-I)/I}*100, 2nd={(III-II)/II}*100, 3rd={(IV-III)/III}*100, 4th={(IV-I)/I}*100
Source: As per Table 1.

development of sub-markets, office equipments and stationery, electricity and water bills, publicity, bank commission, dead stock, etc. For the purpose of analysis, the total expenditure is split into expenditure on staff and other expenses. The former item constitutes the single largest item of expenditure. In the case of other expenses, developmental expenditure is the biggest one. The trends of total expenditure can now be examined.

It is obvious that with growth of the market yard, its liabilities also grow by leaps and bounds. As per Table 5, Siddheshwar Market yard has spent Rs. 19.04 lakh in the first period, Rs. 42.47 lakh in the second period resulting into an increase of 149.30 per cent. The total expenditure during the third period has increased from Rs. 42.47 lakh to Rs. 96.63 lakh. An increase was to the extent of 129.52 per cent is remarkable. However it is lower than earlier period. The total expenditure of Siddheshwar Market yard has increased from Rs. 19.04 lakh to 200.46 lakh during the entire period under study. This indicates an increase of 1076.73 per cent during the period.

Surpluses

Since income of the APMC from market fee increases with the growth of the market. It plays a major role in creating surplus of income over expenditure. Even though the aggregate expenditure over time increased, aggregate income also raised at a faster rate. As such, the Siddheshwar Market Yard could generate it's own resources and in course of time accumulate huge reserves for future development programmes. Perennial surpluses help the Siddheshwar Market Yard to become self-reliant financially.

Siddheshwar Market Yard has been fortunate enough to be in surplus for last 40 years of its working. It could be seen from Table 5 that the surpluses of Siddheshwar Market Yard was Rs. 26.08 lakh in the first period and Rs. 55.37 lakh in the second resulting into an increase of 112.34 per cent. The balance with the Siddheshwar Market Yard has increased during the third period from Rs. 55.37 lakh to Rs. 128.81 lakh (132.63 per cent). The surplus of Siddheshwar Market yard has increased from Rs.26.08 lakh to Rs. 212.98 lakh during the entire study period (716.76 per cent).

Actually, during the last 40 years period, the accumulated surpluses were used for completing the development works in the premises of the market yard premises from time to time. Even then, the rate of surplus generation was more than the rate of utilization and therefore, the Siddheshwar Market Yard was able to preserve a big portion of the accumulated funds and thereby could create reserve fund.

Permanent Fund

The Permanent fund of Siddheshwar Market Yard has increased from Rs. 158.19 lakh to Rs. 365.03 lakh during the second period (130.75

per cent). This has further increased during fourth period, from Rs. 840.39 lakh to Rs. 1583.97 lakh during the fourth period (88.48 per cent). The permanent fund has increased from Rs. 158.19 lakh to Rs. 1583.97 lakh during the entire period with an increase of 901.31 per cent.

COMPOUND GROWTH RATES IN FINANCIAL TURNOVER OF APMC

The annual compound growth rates of financial turnover of APMC, Solapur is accounted in Table 6 for the period form 1983-84 to 2002-03 (See Diagram 4). The major four items of financial position of market yard namely, Income, Expenditure, Surplus, and Permanent Fund have been considered for analysis.

Table 6
Compound Growth Rates in Financial Turnover

Sl. No.	*Item*	*CGR Period*				
		I	*II*	*III*	*IV*	*V*
1.	Total Income	14.76	18.87	19.63	10.18	16.46
2.	Total Expenditure	12.01	18.56	19.67	18.04	19.70
3.	Surpluses	19.37	19.35	19.72	3.43	15.50
4.	Permanent Fund	20.21	19.34	18.03	12.58	16.90

Note: (1) CGR calculated as Antilog (b-1)*100
(2) Period: I =1983-84 to 1987-88, II=1988-89 to 1992-93, III=1993-94 to 1997-98, IV=1998-99 to 2002-03, V=1983-84 to 2002-03

Source: As per Table 1.

Period-I

Almost all items in the first period observed a positive trend. Growth rate of Permanent Fund (PF) was highest among other items of financial turnover during the period with 20.21 per cent share per annum. The Surplus stands next to the PF with 19.37 per cent. In the case of total income of APMC was greater than total expenditure during the same period. Both showed a significant growth rates.

Period-II

Comparatively a Better situation was recorded in the second period, especially in the case of Income, Expenditure and Surplus. Surplus stood at the first position among the other items with 19.35 per cent growth rate. It has increased in the case of Income and Expenditure compared to earlier period; while Expenditure, marginally differ compared to Income. On the other hand PF has recorded a significant but less than other items during the period.

Period-III

The third period showed a positive and significant growth rates in all items of financial turnover. Almost all items have achieved a better

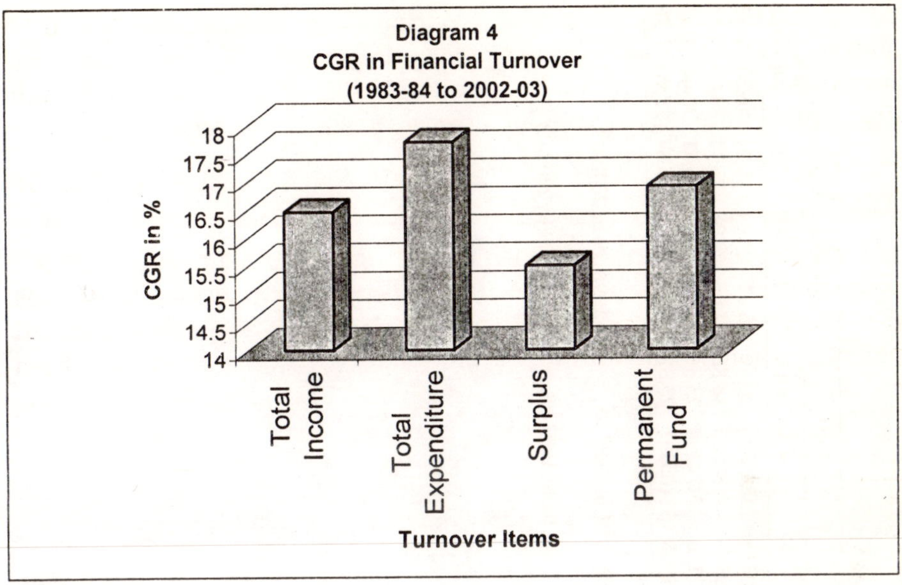

performance like that in second period. But in the case of PF, the position has changed. PF stood at the first position in this period. The range of all items in growth rates was observed very little with 0.4 per cent. Actual growth rates of all items were in the range of 19.63 to 18.03 per cent.

Period-IV

During the recent past the situation of growth rates of various items of financial turnover was not satisfactory. Among all the items, expenditure registered a highest growth rate with 18.04 per cent share. Total Income and PF have a significant share, but the Surplus has increased marginally by 3.43 per cent. Another important observation during the period the growth rate of expenditure was greater than income. Consequently surplus reflects at smaller side.

Period-V

A general characteristic of the entire period under study has recorded a positive as well as significant growth rates of all items. Growth rate of total expenditure has recorded a greater change than other items of financial turnover with a share of 19.70 per cent per annum. PF stands next to expenditure with 16.90 per cent share. Income and Surplus have registered a higher growth compared to fourth period. The overall performance of growth rates in financial turnover was satisfactory during the study period.

VARIATION IN FINANCIAL TURNOVER OF APMC

The variation in Financial Position of Agriculture Produce Market Committee has been analyzed in Table 7. It is observed that the Financial

Table 7
Variations in Financial Position of APMC

Sl. No.	Items	Range			Standard Deviation					Coefficient of Variation					
		Min.	*Max.*	*RR*	*I*	*II*	*III*	*IV*	*V*	*1st*	*2nd*	*3rd*	*4th*	*5th*	*Skew*
1.	Total Income	3018942	52593266	0.89	870303	2486438	5284597	6300014	14883836	20.19	25.41	23.44	15.24	76.34	0.73
2.	Total Expenditure	1327452	28957722	0.91	321318	1047919	2259051	5039376	7582285	18.86	24.67	23.38	25.14	85.05	1.14
3.	Surplus	1560857	23635544	0.88	609107	1493536	3126626	1387120	7474398	23.36	26.97	24.27	6.51	70.64	0.45
4.	Permanent Fund	10317703	197207619	0.90	4012785	8422545	19625978	26361958	57405331	25.37	23.07	23.35	16.64	77.90	0.78

Note:

(1) Standard Deviation: I=1983-84 to 1987-88, II=1988-89 to 1992-93, III=1993-94 to 1997-98, IV=1998-99 to 2002-03
V = 1983-84 to 2002-03

(2) Coefficient of Variation: 1st=1983-84 to 1987-88, 2nd=1988-89 to 1992-93, 3rd=1993-94 to 1997-98, 4th=1998-99 to 2002-03
5th=1983-84 to 2002-03

Source: As per Table 1.

Position of APMC has a high relative range in various items. Total Expenditure has observed a highest coefficient of range than other items with 0.91, followed by Permanent Fund with 0.90. In the case of Total Income has also showed a high relative range of financial position with 0.89, followed by Surplus with 0.88. Coefficient of variations of financial position in the APMC during 1983-84 to 2002-03 is showed in the 5th period in Table 7.

Coefficient of variation in the value transaction of financial performance has been graphed in Diagram 5.

Diagram 5
Coefficient of Variation in Financial Position of APMC
(1983-84 to 2002-03)

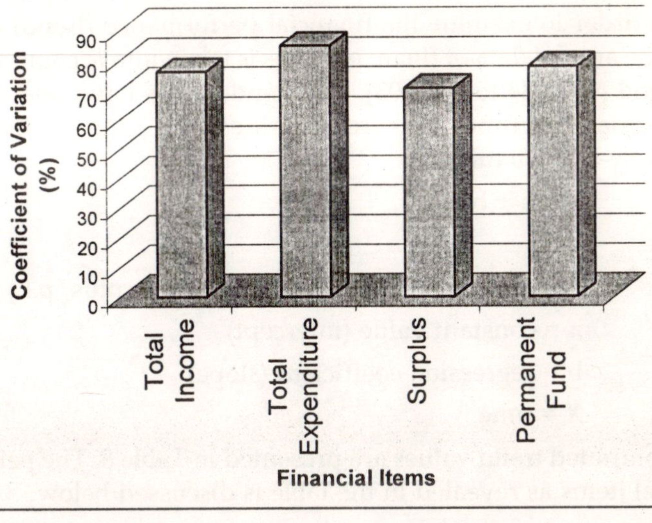

Total Expenditure registered a highest coefficient of variation than other items by 85.05 per cent. Permanent Fund is next to Total Expenditure with 77.90 per cent share. Surplus has registered a lowest coefficient of variation than other by 70.64 per cent. Total Income showed relatively higher coefficient than Surplus. Skewness of Financial Position of APMC is explained in Table 7. Distribution of almost all items of financial position of APMC showed a positive skewness for entire period. Distribution of Total Expenditure showed a highest positive skewness than other with 1.14; implying the fact that the curve of distribution of expenditure has very longer tail towards the right. In the case of Surplus the skewness is positive by 0.45; which implies that the curve of distribution of Surplus has little longer tail towards the right.

TRENDS IN FINANCIAL PERFORMANCE OF APMC

The eleventh hypothesis is taken as, "The Solapur Agricultural Produce Market Committee is financially sound during study period." For this again we considered one-sided test. The Null hypothesis is that the Solapur Agricultural Produce Market Committee is not financially sound during the study period.

$$H_0: b = 0$$

Where b is in the above notation indicate the population parameter (slope). This implies the alternative hypothesis, as the Solapur Agricultural Produce Market Committee is financially sound during study period. Explanation of alternative hypothesis is given as:

$$H_1: b > 0 \text{ (one way)}$$

We used the test statistic t on the basis of the data during the study period. In order to examine the financial performance (trend) of APMC, Solapur, the annual data of financial items is taken into account for twenty years period (1983-84 to 2002-03). The trend values have been computed by least square method. The trend values (the Line of Best Fit) are computed by the equations as:

$$Y = a + bX$$

Where,

Y = financial items (income/exp./surplus/p.f.)

a = constant value (intercept)

b = regression coefficient (slope)

X = time

The computed trend values are presented in Table 8. The performance of financial items as revealed in the table is discussed below.

Table 8
Regression Analysis of Financial Performance of APMC, Solapur

Sl. No.	*Financial Items*	*a*	*b*	*SE (b)*	*t statistic*	*r*	*r square*	*F. sig.*
1.	Total Income	-6527572	2478431	169950	14.583	0.960	0.922	0.000
2.	Total Expenditure	-3939103	1224205	113131	10.821	0.931	0.867	0.000
3.	Surplus	-2588469	1254227	77142	16.259	0.968	0.936	0.000
4.	Permanent Fund	-26605387	9551896	661237	14.446	0.959	0.921	0.000

Note: Figures of a & b in rupees.
Source: As per Table 1.

The financial items of regulated market reflect an increasing tendency during the entire period. The trend equations for financial items noticed a higher positive regression coefficient, as given below:

Total Income	Y	=	-6517572 + 2478431x
Total Expenditure	Y	=	-3939103 + 1224205x
Surplus (Balance)	Y	=	-2588469 + 1254227x
Permanent Fund	Y	=	-26605387 + 9551896x

The annual total income of regulated market has increased by Rs. 24.78 lakh while the total expenditure has increased by Rs. 12.24 lakh. The total expenditure is less than total income; therefore, the surplus of Rs. 12.54 lakh is seen. Permanent Fund also increased by Rs. 95.51 lakh, but the intercept of all financial items remained negative.

Table 8 gives the SE (b) of total turnover of various sub-markets during the study period. The tabular value of 't' at 1% level of significance for 18 degree of freedom remained at (*df*) = 1.33 (one way). The test statistic as computed with the help of twenty years annual data. Financial items noticed a greater than table value. The surplus, total income, total expenditure and Permanent Fund have noticed a very high computed 't' value of 16.259, 14.583, 14.446 and 10.821 respectively. Moreover, the F significance of all items also noticed a highly significant value of 0.000. Thus the twenty years data of financial items of the market yard provides sufficient evidence against the null hypothesis, in which the null hypothesis is rejected at 1% percent level of significance and accepts the alternative hypothesis. It means that the financial position of Solapur Agricultural Produce Market Committee has performed well during study period.

Coefficient of correlation and coefficient of determination (r^2) of financial items are also at the greater level. There is very strong relationship found between financial items and over a period of time ranging between 0.93 and 0.97, during the study period. Coefficient of determination (r^2 notation) is used to test the explanatory power of regression equations. The Surplus has high explanatory power of 0.94 or 94%. Thus it is reliable to say, that the total income, total expenditure and permanent funds have achieved a greater level of explanatory power (r^2) by 92%, 87% and 92% respectively.

The analyses indicate that there are a highly significant relationship is established between financial items and period of time. The analysis, on the whole, for income, expenditure, surplus and permanent fund, revealed that the regulated market is only positive trend but also a significant level in the market yard.

REFERENCE

Agarwal D.R. (2003), "Quantitative Methods", Vrinda Publicatios Pvt. Ltd., 3rd Revised & Enlarged Edition, Delhi.

Bhatia D.K. and Gupta Vijay (1986), "Business Statistics", Vani Educational Books, New Delhi.

Bhanumte C.S. (2001), "Functioning of Regulated Market: A Case Study of Krishi Utappanna Bazar Samitee, Solapur (Siddheshwar Market Yard)", M. Phil. Dissertation, Department of Economics, Shivaji University, Kolhapur.

Gupta S.C. (1996), "Fundamentals of Statistics", Himalaya Publishing House, New Delhi.

Memoria C.B. (1999), "Agricultural Problem of India", Kitab Mahal, New Delhi.

Monga G.S. (2000), "Mathematics and Statistics for Economics", Vikas Pub. House Pvt. Ltd., Second Revised Edition, New Delhi.

Prasad A S. (1985), "Agricultural Marketing in India", Mittal Publications, Delhi.

Reddy A.V. (1991), "Agricultural Marketing", Printwell, Jaipur.

Reddy P.I. (1995), "Marketing of Vegetables", Printwell, Jaipur.

Indian Journal of Agricultural Marketing (2002), Vol. 16, No. 2, Nagpur.

Indian Journal of Agricultural Marketing (2000), (Conference Special), Vol. 14, No. 3, Nagpur.

Sadhu and Singh (1999), "Fundaments of Agricultural Economics", Himalaya Publishing House, Bombay.

10

CONCLUSIONS AND SUGGESTIONS

INTRODUCTION

Marketing confers several benefits of immense importance on the people. The farmers' incomes go up through the highest prices they are able to get for their produce. An assured sale of produce also lowers the risks of farming to an extent. They are also able to get the right type of inputs at the right time through this very marketing system. This also raised their credit rating in the eyes of the various lending agencies. Moreover, marketing provides several avenues of employment to various types of people. The various marketing operations spread across the country and outside give rise to other activities like insurance, banking etc.

Establishment of Regulated Markets with necessary facilities can be the answer to the marketing problems of the cultivator. The main objectives of establishment of regulated markets are to ensure fair prices to producers, elimination of malpractice and providing marketing facilities, "Well Regulated Markets create in the mind of the cultivator a feeling of confidence and receiving fair play and his mood in which he is most ready to accept new ideas and strive to improve his agricultural practice".

An important contribution of the government to the improvement of agricultural marketing is the establishment of regulated markets in several parts of the country. A market committee consisting of the representatives of growers, traders, local bodies and government manage regulated Market. The market committee standardizes the various market practices and charges, keeps standard weights and ensures correct weighment. The committee issues licenses to the various market functionaries and punishes those among them who are guilty of fraudulent practices. Moreover, it constructs warehouses, rest house and the other market ancillaries. Thus, with the help of regulated market the government can avoid the defects of agricultural marketing by establishing orderly conditions within the market yard.

Keeping in view the significance of Regulated Markets emphasis was made to develop and expand agricultural regulated market in India during planning period. As a result, the number of regulated market has increased sharply. There were 283 regulated markets in 1950-51, which rose to 450 in 1955-56, indicating 59.0 percent change in the growth during 1950-56. Subsequent period showed that number of Regulated Markets increased rapidly. In 1960-61 there were 700 Regulated Markets in which further rise of 2803 had been added in 1971-72 and further addition was made by 3819 in 1980-81. Moreover, it also showed the number of Regulated Markets in India further increased to 6217 and to 7177 in 2000-01. The progress of Regulated Markets in India indicates that the overall progress of agricultural Regulated Markets indicated that agricultural Regulated Markets have been increasing in India. However, it also indicates that uneven temporal growth rates in agricultural marketing during 1950-51 to 2000-01.

The MSAMB has 7 Divisional offices at Pune, Nasik, Aurangabad, Latur, Amravati, Nagpur and Ratnagiri for proper co-ordination of the activities of all APMCs in the State. At present there are 284 APMCs with main markets and 593 sub markets. Among the districts of Maharashtra State, Solapur APMC has been selected for intensive study.

MAJOR FINDINGS OF THE STUDY

Major findings of the study are summarized as below:

1. Jowar is a main crop in this region. Consequently, in the total transaction of agricultural commodities occupy a major share among the cereals in the market during the first period with 1917.60 hundred quintals. But in the second period, it reduced to 1305.17 hundred quintals and marginally increased to 1377.23 hundred quintals in the third period and further increased with 2126.54 hundred quintals of Jowar was arrived in the market. There are ups and down in arrival of the cereals. The overall change of Jowar was recorded only 10.89 during the study period.

2. Rice performance of arrival is significant. It is much better than Wheat, Jowar and Maize. The arrivals of Rice was recorded 1842.45 hundred quintals during first period (1983-84 to 1987-88), which raised to 2563.95 hundred quintals during second period (1988-89 to 1992-93) and in the third period (1993-94 to 1997-98) it has marginally raised by 2974.32 hundred quintals and rapid increase to 5077.78 hundred quintals during the fourth period (1998-99 to 2002-03). Thus in relative terms, it showed arrival of Rice increased by 39.16 per cent during first period, which raised marginally by 16.01 per cent in the second period, which rapidly increased to

70.72 per cent during the third period. Rice is very highly performance among the cereal crops as well as other crops in the fourth period (i.e. 175.60 per cent). The main reason of better performance of Rice is not only due to arrival from surrounding area but the arrival muffusil area of from Andra Pradesh and Karnataka state.

3. Among the pulses, Pigeon Pea is important crops than other pulses like Gram, Black Gram and Green Gram. It occupies a major share in the market. In first period, 459.29 hundred quintals of Pigeon Pea was arrived in the market, which has reduced to 343.53 hundred quintals in the second period and further declined to 187.57 hundred quintals in the third period and significantly increased to 341.78 hundred quintals in the fourth period. But overall change was negative during the study period.
4. In the case of Apple, Banana, Grapes, Guava, Mango, Papaya and Watermelon there is ups and down in the arrivals. Ber, Orange, Pomegranate and Sapota have shown tremendous improvements during the study period, but a declining trend is observed in the case of Custard Apple.
5. The overall change in the arrival of Pomegranate, Ber, Papaya and Sapota was recorded by 1390.10 per cent, 1889.78 per cent, 2504.88 per cent and 9921.68 per cent during the period referred above respectively. But in the case of Banana, Custard Apple, Mango, and Watermelon negative growth rates were observed during the period from 1983-84 to 2002-03.
6. Onion occupies major share among the vegetables in the market. During the first period by 3177 hundred quintals of Onion was arrived. It has increased in the second period by 4827 hundred quintals, further continued to increase by to 10446 hundred quintals in the third period and 15425 hundred quintals in the fourth period.
7. Most of the vegetables showed a better position in arrival namely; Tomato, Potato, Brinjal, Coriander Leaves, Fenugreek, and Green Chilies. But Chuka, Garlic and Hemp recorded a negative performance during the study period.
8. CGR in arrival of Jaggery increased by 6.74 per cent per annum during 1983-84 to 2002-03, followed by Rice (6.34 per cent), Wheat (6.07 per cent), Maize (2.57 per cent), Black gram (1.94 per cent), Gram (0.91 per cent), and Jowar (0.51 per cent).
9. The performance of Sapota and Papaya were relatively impressive during the study period. Arrival of Sapota has increased by 36.24 per cent and arrival of Papaya has increased by 32.29 per cent

during 1983-84 to 2002-03. Ber has also recorded a significant performance in arrivals with 24.31 per cent growth rate, followed by Pomegranate (15.84 per cent), Orange (11.00 per cent).

10. CGR in arrival of vegetables, potato has recorded highest growth rate among the vegetable crops. Potato increased by 12.59 per cent per annum during the entire period of 20 years.
11. Onion is less perishable vegetable than other. It has registered a remarkable growth rate of 11.47 per cent during the study period. Arrival of tomato has increased by 10.79 per cent per annum during the same period. The three vegetables namely Potato, Tomato and Onion have registered two-digit growth rate.
12. In the recent period (1998-99 to 2002-03) except Banana, almost all fruits have recorded an increasing trend in the value transaction. Pomegranate has recorded the first rank among the fruits with Rs. 192.25 lakhs. Apple has achieved second rank in value transaction among all fruits by Rs. 160.46 lakhs.
13. The most prominent change observed in the value transaction was of Cauliflower with 3420.61 per cent between 1983-84 to 1987-88 and 1998-99 to 2002-03, followed by Potato (1164.12 per cent), Spinach (1099.91 per cent).
14. CGR in value transaction of foodgrains for entire period, almost all cereal crops have recorded a positive and significant growth rates in total value transaction in the fifth period. Rice has registered highest growth rate compared to all other crops with 14.91 per cent per annum. Wheat and Jaggery were the next to Rice with a share of 14.42 per cent.
15. Almost all fruits showed a positive trend except Mango marginally by 2.02 per cent. Papaya has showed a highest growth rate among all fruits with 35.58 per cent. Pomegranate, Ber and Orange were also much more significant.
16. Entire period of the analysis showed a remarkable performance of vegetables in value transaction. Garlic has recorded a highest growth rate among all vegetables during the study period with 19.55 per cent share per annum.
17. The most prominent change observed in the price was of Green gram with 297.41 per cent between 1983-84 to 1987-88 and 1998-99 to 2002-03, followed by Black gram (269.22 per cent).
18. Overall change has reflected in the price of Custard apple with the first rank among all fruits with 1984.35 per cent of change. Banana with 379.61 per cent, Orange is next to Banana with 323.62 per cent, followed by Apple with 218.65 per cent.

19. The overall change in price behaviour is seen with Cauliflower among the vegetables with 1288.51 per cent change. Shepu is the next vegetable by 350.88 per cent change during entire period. Remaining vegetables, except Gourd and Tomato, have reflected a change between 100 to 300 per cent.
20. CGR in prices of major fruits, during 1983-84 to 2002-03, observed a positive performance. Fruits have experienced increasing growth rates in the prices. Custard apple has recorded a highest growth rate in prices among the fruits with 33.52 per cent. Banana is next to Custard apple with 20.83 per cent.
21. A general feature of the entire period has observed positive annual CGR in the prices of all vegetables. Garlic has showed highest growth rate by 18.29 per cent. Cauliflower has next to Garlic with 13.59 per cent.
22. It is observed different variability among the food grains and other commodity. Sunflower's coefficient of range in arrival is highest than other commodities with 1.
23. In case of cereals, higher variability is registered in arrivals of Bajra, Rice and Maize than Wheat and Jowar. Jowar recorded a lowest range coefficient not only in the cereals but also in the other commodities.
24. Among the cereals, Jowar has registered a lowest coefficient of variation by 29.75 per cent during the entire period. It is not only a lowest variability among cereals and pulses but also in the other commodities. Maize is a next to Jowar with 37.91 per cent. Rice and Wheat have recorded a lower coefficient of variation. Bajra showed a higher coefficient of variation of 61.88 per cent than other cereals.
25. Wheat and Capsicum has observed a positive but very less skewed like as 0.02 and 0.10 respectively. We can say in the case of Wheat, the distribution in the arrival is symmetric during the study period.
26. Coefficient of range of arrival of Sapota is highest among the fruits. Custard apple, Orange, Papaya and Pomegranate have also registered the same variability with 0.99 coefficients. Banana and Mango have recorded the same variability in arrival with 0.98 coefficients. Watermelon has showed a lowest relative range of 0.48.
27. Watermelon registered lowest coefficient of variation by 26.95 per cent among the fruits during 1983-84 to 2002-03. Guava is the next to Watermelon with 37.91 per cent variation, followed by Apple with 46.33 per cent of variations. Grapes and Lemon have also recorded a lower coefficient of variation.

28. The range coefficient of arrival of Fenugreek is higher than other Vegetables with 0.99. Garlic has next to Fenugreek with 0.96 relative range. Cauliflower, Chuka, Gourd, Onion, Potato, and Spinach have registered a higher variability. Brinjal has showed a lowest relative range of 0.25 among the vegetables.
29. Among the Vegetables, Brinjal has registered a lowest coefficient of variation by 13.53 per cent. Coriander Leaves is the next to Brinjal with 20.07 per cent. Coefficient of variation is slightly higher than the Dodaka and Coriander Leaves with 20.44 per cent.
30. Coefficient of variation in value transaction of food grains, Maize has registered the lowest coefficient of variation by 59.95 per cent. Jowar is next to Maize with 63.36 per cent. Rice and Wheat have also recorded a higher coefficient of variation in value transactions. Bajra has showed the highest coefficient of variation of 117.45 per cent.
31. Orange, Papaya and Sapota have recorded the highest coefficient of range in sales with 1 for the entire period. A value transaction in Pomegranate shows a high range coefficient among the fruits with 0.99.
32. Watermelon has registered the lowest coefficient of variation of 42.41 per cent during the period from 1983-84 to 2002-03. Guava stands next with 47.04 per cent, followed by Banana with 51.60 per cent. Custard apple, Mango and Lemon have recorded a lower coefficient of variation.
33. Sale of Cauliflower and Fenugreek have a highest range of coefficient among the Vegetables with 0.99. Garlic is next to Fenugreek with 0.97 relative ranges, followed by Shepu with 0.96. Bittergourd, Carrot, Coriander Leaves, Cucumber, Gourd, Green Chilies, Lady'sfinger, Onion, Potato, Tomato and Spinach have registered higher variability between 0.80 and 0.94.
34. C.V. in value transaction of vegetables, Sweet Potato has registered a lowest coefficient of variation by 34.65 per cent. Brinjal is next commodity with 42.47 per cent of variation. Bittergourd, Cabbage, Carrot, Coriander Leaves, Dodake, Fenugreek, Gourd, Green Chilies, Hemp, Lady's finger, Shepu and Vetch have recorded a moderate coefficient of variation between 51 and 65 per cent.
35. Distribution of sale of Vegetables shows a positive skewed Distribution in the sale of Cauliflower has reflected a very high skewed with 4.41; which implies that the curve of distribution of sale has very longer tail towards the right. Chuka, Cucumber, Sweet Potato and Potato have also a positive skewed between 1 and 1.5.

36. The total turnover has increased continuously during the study period. During first period it has recorded Rs. 38.63 crores as its annual turnover, it has increased by Rs. 68.63 crores in the second period, Rs. 133.06 crores in the third period. It has also a record of Rs. 226 crores turnover in the recent period. The total turnover has increased by 485.09 per cent during the period from 1983-84 to 1987-88 and 1998-99 to 2002-03.
37. Over a period of time the most prominent change has been observed in the total turnover of the sub-markets. Fruits and Vegetable market has a higher rate of change with 731.31 per cent, followed by Food grains market with 426.56 per cent change during 1983-84 to 1987-88 and 1998-99 to 2002-03.
38. CGR in total turnover of sub-markets, Fruits and Vegetables have recorded the highest growth rates with 15.98 per cent per annum, followed by Food grains Market with 11.20 per cent. Cattle Market has also performed significantly.
39. C.V. of Total Turnover of market yard recorded 63.58 per cent. Fruits and Vegetables market has registered a highest coefficient of variation among the sub-markets. Foodgrains market is next to Fruits and Vegetables market with 60.73 per cent of variation. Straw market has registered a lowest coefficient of variation than other sub-markets by 24.59 per cent.
40. Average share of sub-markets, food grains and other agricultural commodities. It was 73.56 per cent in the first period, which reduced to 73.17per cent in the second period. While share of fruits and vegetables market in the total turnover has increased from 22.94 to 42.07 per cent during the entire period.
41. The market's income of Rs. 43.11 lakh in the first period swelled to Rs. 97.84 lakh in the second period thereby recording 126 per cent increase. The total income has increased to Rs. 225.44 lakh during second period. This indicates an increase of 130.41 per cent and 83.40 per cent increased only during the third period. Moreover, it has increased to Rs. 413.45 lakh during the period from 1998-99 to 2002-03. Thus it indicates an increase of 859 per cent during entire period.
42. It is obvious that with growth of the market yard, its liabilities also would grow by leaps and bounds. Siddheshwar Market yard has spent Rs.17.04 lakh in the first period, Rs.42.47 lakh in the second period resulting into an increase of 149.30 per cent. The total expenditure during the third period has increased from Rs.42.47 lakh to Rs.96.63 lakh. An increase was to the extent of 127.52 per cent is remarkable.

43. During the entire period, the total expenditure of Siddheshwar Market yard has increased from Rs.17.04 lakh to 200.46 lakh during the entire period under study. This indicates an increase of 1076.73 per cent during the period.
44. Market Yard has been fortunate enough to be in surplus for last 40 years of its working. It could be seen from Table 4.29 that the surpluses of Siddheshwar Market Yard was Rs.26.08 lakh in the first period and Rs.55.37 lakh in the second resulting into an increase of 112.34 per cent. The balance with the Siddheshwar Market Yard has increased during the third period from Rs.55.37 lakh to Rs.128.81 lakh (132.63 per cent). The surplus of Siddheshwar Market yard has increased from Rs.26.08 lakh to Rs. 212.98 lakh during the entire study period (716.76 per cent).
45. A general characteristic of the entire period under study has recorded a positive as well as significant growth rates of all items. Growth rate of total expenditure has recorded a greater change than other items of financial turnover with a share of 17.70 per cent per annum. PF stands next to expenditure with 16.90 per cent share. Income and Surplus have registered a higher growth compared to fourth period.
46. Some of the commodities like Bajra, Blackgram, Capsicum, Groundnut, Jowar, Pigeon pea, Sunflower and Jaggery have noticed less than zero (between -.01 and -.55) coefficient of correlation (r). In the other ward negative relationships have noticed between arrival and price among these commodities during the study period.
47. Test statistic (t ratio) is computed with the help of sample data. Table value is 1.33 at 1% level of significance with 18 degree of freedom. Values of 't' in the case of Capsicum, Pigeon pea and Jaggery have a greater value than table value by -2.815, -1.804 and -1.94 respectively. Therefore, we can say that they are significant and the null hypothesis is rejected at level of significance of 1% per cent.
48. In the case of cereals, the computed value of 't' of Rice, Wheat, Jowar, Bajra and Maize are less than table value, moreover these cereals have a very insignificant and positive relationship noticed between arrival and price. Therefore, we can say that, the arrival is not price sensitive. It means that the difference is just due to fluctuations of sampling and the sample data do not provide us sufficient evidence against the null hypothesis, which may, therefore, be accepted.
49. Among the pulses, except Pigeon pea, table value is greater than computed value of 't' in the case of Black gram, Gram and Green

gram and the value of difference is not significant. The story of cereals apply to pulses, the sample data of above pulses do not provide us sufficient evidence against the null hypothesis.

50. Most of the Fruits have noticed the picture against the null hypothesis. Banana, Ber, Guava, Lemon, Mango, Papaya, Pomegranate, Sapota and Watermelon have noticed the greater value of computed t-statistic than table value and these value has registered between -1.618 to -5.281 (t-ratio). Moreover, the differences between prices and arrival of these fruits have noticed a highly significant. In the case of Lemon, Pomegranate and Sapota have observed a very high significant with 0.000 values.
51. Most of the Fruits have observed less coefficient of determination. Some of them have noticed a very less coefficient of determination namely, Orange and Custard apple with .011 and .024 respectively.
52. 18 out of 22 Vegetables have showed the situation against the null hypothesis. Bitter gourd, Brinjal, Cabbage, Carrot, Coriander Leaves, Cucumber, Dodaka, Fenugreek, Garlic, Green chilies, Hemp, Lady's finger, Onion, Potato, Shepu, Spinach, Tomato and Vetch have noticed a greater value of computed t-statistic than the table value and these values are seen between -1.417 to -5.775 (t-ratio). Moreover, the differences between prices and arrival of these Vegetables have noticed highly significant. Some of them namely; Brinjal, Cabbage, Carrot and Lady's finger have observed a very high significant with .000, therefore, we can say that, the sample data do provide us sufficient evidence against the null hypothesis. Therefore, the null hypothesis is rejected at 1% percent level of significance with 18 degree of freedom.
53. Many Vegetables such as; Brinjal, Cabbage Carrot and Lady's finger has reflected a high coefficient of determination between 0.519 and 0.649.
54. The arrival of food grains, among the cereals, showed an increasing tendency except Bajra during the period under study. The trend equations for the arrival of cereals are given below:

Rice	Y	=	105690 + 19597x
Wheat	Y	=	74624 + 9858x
Jowar	Y	=	162431 + 546x
Maize	Y	=	4755 + 120x

55. Among the pulses, increasing trend observed in case of Black gram and Gram by 195 and 101 quintals every year respectively. On the other hand, arrival of Pigeon pea and Green gram observed decreasing trend during the study period. The rate of decrease in arrival of Pigeon pea is relatively high when compared to the

annual decrease in arrival of Green gram. The linear equations for the arrival of pulses are given below:

Black gram	Y	=	9211 + 195x
Gram	Y	=	7842 + 101x
Pigeon pea	Y	=	49151 - 1943x
Green gram	Y	=	4649 - 183x

56. The tabular value of 't' at 1% level of significance for 18 degree of freedom is estimated at *(df)* = 1.73. For testing the test statistic (t ratio) the computed 't' values of Wheat and Rice have noticed at the greater side than the table value among the cereals with a (t-statistic) registered value of 6.038 and 5.981 respectively. Moreover, the F sig. of these cereals is also notice a highly significant level with 0.000. In the case of Jaggery, also the computed t- statistic is greater with positive value than table value with 2.933. Moreover, F sig. of arrival of Jaggery is also noticed a high significant level with 0.009. Therefore, we can say that, the data provides sufficient evidence against the null hypothesis, which means the null hypothesis is rejected at 1% per cent level of significance and accept alternative hypothesis for arrival of Wheat, Rice and Jaggery.
57. Concept of coefficient of determination (r^2 notation) is applied to test the explanatory power of regression equations. It is observed that, Wheat has high explanatory power with 0.669 during the study period, followed by Rice with 0.665 (r^2). It means that explanatory power of regression equation of Wheat is 0.67 or 67% that is 67% variation in arrival (Y) is because of variation in period (X). While explanatory power of Jowar is very less with 0.004 or 0.4%.
58. The arrival of major Fruits, (most of the fruits) showed an increasing tendency during the period under study. The trend equations for arrival of some fruits are given below, which shows a positive regression coefficient.

Apple	Y	=	163082 + 20880x
Grapes	Y	=	28743 + 5638x
Lemon	Y	=	831090 + 95132x

59. For the testing the computed test statistic (t ratio) of Apple, Ber, Grapes, Lemon, Orange, Papaya and Pomegranate have noticed a greater than table value among the Fruits with values registered (t-statistic) between 2.319 and 9.213. Moreover, the F sig. of these fruits has noticed highly significant. The Ber, Grapes and Pomegranate have registered a very high significant with 0.000. Therefore, in above case, the null hypothesis is rejected.

60. Some of the fruits, observed positive regression coefficient but noticed negative intercept value, some of these trend equations are given as:

Ber	Y	=	329221x -1663232
Pomegranate	Y	=	63719x - 322129
Sapota	Y	=	12955x - 59837

From these linear equations it is seen that, the annual arrivals of the Ber has increased by 329221 kilogram. The rate of increase in arrivals of Pomegranate was 63719 dozens. All these fruits have observed a negative intercept value during the study period.

61. It is observed that, Ber has showed high explanatory power with 0.85 during the study period, followed by Pomegranate with 0.603 (r^2). It means that explanatory power of regression equation of Ber is .85 or 85%.

62. The arrivals of Vegetables have an (19 out of 22) increasing tendency during under the study. The trend equations for some vegetables are given below, which also showed a positive regression coefficient.

Cabbage	Y	=	299722 + 63888x
Cauliflower	Y	=	430188 + 29773x
Coriander Leaves	Y	=	2342424 + 90455x

63. The tabular value of 't' at 1% level of significance for 18 degree of freedom is (*df*) = 1.73. Computed 't' values of Bitter gourd, Cabbage, Carrot, Cauliflower, Coriander Leaves, Cucumber, Dodaka, Gourd, Green Chilies, Lady's finger, Onion, Potato, Shepu, Spinach, Tomato and Vetch have (16 vegetables out of 22) noticed a greater values than the table value among the Vegetables and these value have (t-statistic) registered between 2.118 and 11.397. Moreover, the F sig. of these fruits has noticed highly significant.

64. It is observed that, Onion has showed a highest explanatory power with 0.88 during the study period among the vegetables, followed by Tomato with 0.82 (r^2). It means that explanatory power of regression equation of Onion is 0.88 or 88%

65. The value transaction of food grains, among the cereals, shows an increasing tendency during under the study. The trend equations for the value transaction of cereals are given below:

Rice	Y	=	39615210x - 105163074
Wheat	Y	=	12835395x -18844429
Jowar	Y	=	7047735x + 10584785

66. In case of processed product, Jaggery showed positive and relatively higher regression coefficient than some other commodity

in value transaction. The linear equation of Jaggery in value transaction is given below:

Jaggery Y = - 14055351 + 13509764x

But negative performance observed in case of value transaction of Groundnut. The negative trend of Groundnut is given in following equations:

Groundnut Y = 12230288 - 221075x

67. The tabular value of 't' at 1% level of significance for 18 degree of freedom is (*df*) = 1.33 (one way). For the testing the test statistic of annual data for value transaction of food grains and other commodities is computed for 't' values of Wheat, Rice, Jowar, Maize, Black gram, Gram, Green gram, Capsicum and Jaggery (9 out of 13 commodity) which are noticed a greater value than table value among all commodities and these value (t-statistic) have registered between 1.733 and 11.969.

68. In the case of Bajra, Pigeon pea, Sunflower and Groundnut, we observed the computed value of 't' is less than table value, moreover F significance of Sunflower, Bajra and Pigeon pea have noticed a very insignificant trend among all commodities by 0.983, 0.958 and 0.733 respectively. Therefore, we can say that, the twenty years data do not provide sufficient evidence against the null hypothesis, which may, therefore, be accepted.

69. The value transaction of major Fruits shows an increasing tendency except Mango during the period under study. The trend equations for value transaction of some major fruits, which noticed a higher positive regression coefficient, are given below:

Pomegranate Y = 1639591x - 8327437

Apple Y = 1072994x - 4127066

Ber Y = 933291x - 3654211

70. The tabular value of 't' at 1% level of significance for 18 degree of freedom is (*df*) = 1.33. For the testing the test statistic computed with the help of (twenty years annual) data of value transaction of fruits, we computed 't' values of Apple, Banana, Ber, Custard apple, Grapes, Guava, Lemon, Orange, Papaya, Pomegranate, Sapota and Watermelon (12 fruits out of 13) which have noticed a greater values than the table values and these values have (t-statistic) registered a range of 2.209 and 9.267. Moreover, the F significance of these fruits in the value transaction has noticed a highly significant.

71. It is remarkable to say, the computed 't' values of almost all Vegetables (22 vegetables out of 22) have noticed a greater values than table values. Among the Vegetables; Bitter gourd, Brinjal,

Cabbage, Carrot, Coriander Leaves, Dodaka, Green Chilies, Lady's finger, Onion, Spinach, Tomato and Vetch have noticed a very high computed 't' value ranging between 10.136 and 16.114 and Potato, Shepu, Cucumber, Chuka, Cauliflower, Fenugreek, Garlic, Gourd, Hemp and Sweet Potato have a 't' value ranging between 2.134 and 9.846. Moreover, the F significance of all vegetables has noticed highly significant values.

72. The total turnover of all sub-markets have observed increasing tendency during the entire period. The trend equations for total turnover of all sub-markets, which noticed higher positive regression coefficient, are given below:

Food grains & other	Y	=	-20010487 + 76594542x
Fruits & Vegetable	Y	=	-106282153 + 44412611x
Straw Market	Y	=	8900963 + 331749x
Cattle Market	Y	=	2001203 + 681971x

73. The computed 't' values of almost all sub-markets in the total turnover have noticed a greater than table values. Among the sub-markets, Food grains market and Fruits & Vegetable market have noticed a very high computed 't' value of 10.518 and 14.651 respectively.

74. The financial items of regulated market have observed increasing tendency during the entire period. The trend equations for financial items, which noticed higher positive regression coefficient, are given below:

Total Income	Y	=	-6517572 + 2478431x
Total Expenditure	Y	=	-3939103 + 1224205x
Surplus (Balance)	Y	=	-2588469 + 1254227x
Permanent Fund	Y	=	-26605387 + 9551896x

75. The test statistic as computed with the help of twenty years annual data. Financial items noticed a greater than table value. The surplus, total income, total expenditure and Permanent Fund have noticed a very high computed 't' value of 16.259, 14.583, 14.446 and 10.821 respectively. Moreover, the F of all items also noticed a highly significant value of 0.000.

SUGGESTIONS

The findings of the study are quite useful for stimulating the growth of agricultural regulating markets, which encourage ultimately, the growth of agricultural sector in India. What are required the adoption of a few market and an all-round development of both infrastructure and institutions as a model one which can expert a profound demonstration effect on the rural community and that can set in motion "revolution of rising exceptions" among the farmers. Centralization of market forces and development of regulated markets need to be the only solution. This channel is important for certain commodities and that should be strengthened. Regulated markets are highly beneficial only when it helps in centralizing market forces. But this is possible only when certain integrated marketing services are offered including facilitative services. This requires several market development programmes. It is difficult to achieve all these together. This necessitates the need for greater specificity and selectively in the approach. An individual farmer should have the option to avail any marketing services and it should be made available by regulated markets. This kind of state intervention will help in developing not only agricultural sector but in transforming the rural economy.

The ultimate goal of regulated markets should be the creation of economic, cultural and social miles, which will enable the farmer to feel satisfied. The returns many vary but what is important is the satisfaction that he derives from his participation in the marketing process. Regulated markets have a positive and exciting role to play in the next millennium; policy makers are beginning to feel the need for more information on the dynamics of regulated markets. Market should try to attract more and more quantities of commodities and maximum number of agricultural commodities. Moreover, farmers should too prefer to sale agricultural commodities in the market yard rather than private market.

State Governments may take initiative for connecting market yards with villages through all weather roads. Financing can be considered by bank for transport operators sponsored by the Market Committees to ensure faster movement of produce from the fields to the market yard. Finance can be considered for those farmers who cannot dispose their produce immediately against the warehouse receipt issued by the Market Committee.

The Market Committee should be proactive and collect and collate information on price of commodities at different centers and fix the minimum floor price for the bidders at the market yards so that the farmers do not lose in the bargain. Amenities may be provided to the sellers and bidders and other market functionaries by way of rest houses, canteen, staff quarters, etc.

For more and better production of food grains and oilseeds, market yards may consider enlarging their activities to cover marketing of agricultural inputs like seeds, fertilizers, and insecticides etc. Top priority should be given to construction of the farm-to-market roads. Market yards may be provided with godowns/warehouses/cold storages accommodate the unsold stocks depending on area specific requirements. To fetch remunerative prices to farmers, presale value addition services may be provided like pre-cleaning, grading, sorting, standardization, etc.

Flow of market information through modern media should be upgraded. To eliminate chances of faulty weighing, electronic weighing machines/weigh bridges may be provided. More attention should be given to proper grading and packing of produce particularly when it is destined for export. To keep the market yard fully appraised with latest information on prices the computer may be provided to facilitate storing and analyzing the required data. This will facilitate in future to link with all the major markets.

Increasing efficiency of existing marketing system through professional management scientific operation/handling of agricultural produce. Creation of necessary infrastructure for value addition at rural level. Development of cool chain/cold storage facilities for perishables. Shortening of marketing channel. Promoting direct marketing, thereby restructuring costs and margins and achieving vertical integration between producers and final consumers. Upgradation/improvement of wholesale markets, handling foodgrains, fruits and vegetables, floriculture, livestock, fisheries etc.

Modernization of mega markets/developing specialized physical markets, for promotion of exports, facilitating bulk buying of required standards. Strengthening/improvement in retail market chain to safeguard consumers interests. Expanding domestic quality assurance viz. Grading network to ensure purity and quality of edible products consumed by common man in daily life, from local markets. Strengthening marketing extension with special emphasis on production planning, standardization, and healthy hygienic and environment friendly package of practices right from farmer to the consumer.

Promotion of rural storage with pledge finance facilities for ensuring minimum support price benefits to the small and marginal farmers. Easy accessibility to institutional credit to meet marketing needs. Promotion of group marketing to secure price benefits based on market intelligence information. Development of facilities for quick transport and communication system for inter-market linkages, pesticide, etc. to augment their income. Forward Trading for at least selected commodities may be promoted through APMC.

Now I conclude with saying that, for more and better production of food grains and oilseeds, market yards may consider Contract Farming. There is an urgent need to provide facilities for processing because there is a great scope for processing of fruits. As it is well known, majority of agricultural products are seasonal and highly perishable and therefore need immediate disposal. But, if some of these products are processed then their sale can be postponed and there is also value addition in that. In doing so, there is increase in the employment in the economy and also makes many other marketing functions to operate efficiently and economically. There is also need for developing specialized markets for fruits and vegetables, etc. The challenges emerging in the post WTO environment necessitate the establishment of a free, vibrant, dynamic, competitive, and assimilative marketing structure and system. Recently Maharashtra State Government has passed the Model Market Act that will be implemented soon to create alternate ways of marketing.

BIBLIOGRAPHY

BOOKS

Agarwal D.R. (2003), "Quantitative Methods", Vrinda Publicatios Pvt. Ltd., 3rd Revised & Enlarged Edition, Delhi

Agrawal A.N. & Kundan Lal (1996), "Agricultural Problems of India", Vikas Publishing House, New Delhi.

Anitha H.S. (2000), "Agricultural Marketing", Mangal Deep Publications, Jaipur.

Barbara Harriss-White (1996), "A Political Economy of Agricultural Markets in South India".

Batra M.M. (1978), "Agricultural Production: Prices and Technology", Allied Publishers Bombay.

Bhatia D.K. & Gupta Vijay (1986), "Business Statistics", Vikas Publishing House Pvt. Ltd., New Delhi.

Clark and Clark (1976), "Principles of Marketing", S. Martine Press, Bombay.

Dale C. Dahl and Jerome W. Hammond (1977), Market and Price Analysis", McGraw Hill Book Company, New York.

Desai R.G. (1998), "Agricultural Economics", Himalaya Publishing House, Bombay.

Fahimuddin (1992), "State Regulation in Foodgrains Marketing", Print House, Lacknow.

Ghosh and Arbindo (1963), "Market Structure of Indian Agriculture", The World Press Pvt. Ltd., Calcutta.

Govil R.K. & Tripathi B.B. (1996), "Agricultural Economy of India", Kitab Mahal, New Delhi.

Gupta R.P. (1973), "Agricultural Prices in a Backward Economy", National Publishing House, Delhi.

Gupta S.C. (1996), "Fundamentals of Statistics, Himalaya Publishing House, New Delhi.

Harriss B. (1984), "State and Markets", Concept Publishing Company, New Delhi.

Jha Divakar (1997), "A Perspective on Co-operative Marketing", Vikas Publishing House Pvt. Ltd., New York.

Jugale V.B. (2000), "Sugarcane Pricing: Policy, Procedure & Operations", Atlantic Publishers & Distributors, New Delhi.

Kahlon A.S. and George M.V. (1985), "Agricultural Marketing and Price Polices", Allied Publishers Pvt. Ltd., New Delhi.

Kahlon A.S. and Tyagi D.S. (1983), "Agricultural Price Policy in India", Allied Publishers Pvt. Ltd., New Delhi.

Kamat G.S. (1986), "Managing Co-operative Marketing", Himalaya Publishing House, Bombay.

Kapde M.V., (1979), "Economics of Marketing Co-operatives", National Publishing House, Delhi.

Khusrao A.M. (1968), "Leading in Agricultural Development", Allied Publishers, Bombay.

Kohls R.L. and Uhl J.N. (1985), "Marketing of Agricultural Products", MacMillan Publishing Company, New York.

Kohls R.L. (1967), "Marketing of Agricultural Products", Macmillan, London.

Kulkarni K.R. (1963), "Agricultural Marketing in India", The Cooperators Book Depot, Bombay.

Mathur P.N. & Kulkarni A.K., Some Observations on the Working of Regulated Market at Ghoti Dist. Nasik.

Memoria C.B. (1999), "Agricultural Problem of India", Kitab Mahal, New Delhi.

Monga G.S. (2000), "Mathematics and Statistics for Economics", Vikas Publishing House Pvt. Ltd., New Delhi.

Nadkarni M.V., (1973), "Agricultural Prices and Development with Stability", National Publishing House, Delhi.

Natu W.R. (1962), "Regulation of Forward Markets", Asia Publishing House, Bombay.

Nayyar H. and Ramaswamy P., (1995), "Globalization and Agricultural Marketing", Rawat Publications, Jaipur.

NCAER (1969), "Structure and Behaviour of Prices of Foodgrains", N.K. Gossain and Co. Pvt. Ltd., New Delhi.

Penson J.B. Capps Oral and Rosson C.P. (1996), "Introduction to Agricultural Economics", Prentice Hall, Inc. A Simon & Schuster Company, New Jersey.

Prasad A.S. (1985), "Agricultural Marketing in India", Mittal Publications, Delhi

Puri V.K. (1992), "Elements of Business Statistics", Himalaya Publishing House, Bombay.

Rajbans Kaur (1975), "Agricultural Price Policy in Economic Development", Kalyani Publishers, Delhi.

Rangaswamy R. (2000), "A Text Book of Agricultural Statistics", New Age International (P) Limited, Publishers, New Delhi.

Reddy A.V. (1991), "Agricultural Marketing", Printwell, Jaipur

Reddy P.I. (1995), "Marketing of Vegetables", Printwell, Jaipur

Sadhu & Singh (1999), "Fundaments of Agricultural Economics", Himalaya Publishing House, Bombay.

Saxena H.M. (1988), "Rural Markets and Development", Rawat Publications, Jaipur.

Saxena H.M. (1992), "Regulated Agricultural Markets", Rawat Publications, Jaipur.

Singh G. Singh D. and Singh R. (1987), "Agricultural Marketing in India", Chugh Publications, Allahabad.

Singhal A.K. (1989), "Agricultural Marketing in India", Anmol Publications, New Delhi.

Sinha J.C. (1976), "Principles of Marketing and Salesmanship", S. Chand, Delhi.

Soni R.N. (1992), "Leading Issues in Agricultural Economics", S. Chand & Co., Delhi.

Svardstrom K.F. (1969), "Agricultural Marketing for Co-operators", Allied Publishers, Bombay.

Thomsen F.L. (1951), "Agricultural Marketing," McGraw Hill, New York.

Upendra M. (1991), "Studies in Agricultural Marketing And Size-Output Relationship", Amar Prakashan, Delhi.

Varmudy V. (2001), "Marketing of Vegetables in India", Daya Publishing House, Delhi.

Wayne Purcell (1979), "Agricultural Marketing, Systems, Coordination, Cash and Futures Prices", Reston Publishing Company Inc., Reston, Verginia.

Yadav J.S. and Yadav S.S. (1996), "Modern Trends in Agricultural Marketing", Pointer Publishers, Jaipur.

JOURNALS

Indian Journal of Agricultural Economics (2000), Vol. 55, No. 3 (Conference Number), Mumbai.

Indian Journal of Agricultural Marketing (2000), (Conference Special), Vol. 14, No. 3, Nagpur.

Indian Journal of Agricultural Marketing (2002), Vol. 16, No. 2, Nagpur.

The Bihar Journal of Agricultural Marketing (1997), (Bansil P. C., Article on, 'Regulated Market System in Meeting Urban Food'), (Silver Jubilee Special Number), Vol. V, No. 3, Patna.

The Bihar Journal of Agricultural Marketing (2000), Vol. VIII, No. 1, Patna.

The Bihar Journal of Agricultural Marketing (2000), Vol. VIII, No. 1, Jan-March, Patna.

REPORTS/ THESIS/ DISSERTATION

Agricultural Produce Market Committee, Solapur, Annual Report/Register during 1983-84 to 2002-03.

Ambapkar G.B. (1986), "Functioning of Regulated Market-A Case Study of Shahu Market Yard, Kolhapur", M. Phil Dissertation, Shivaji University, Kolhapur.

Bhanumate C.S. (2000), "Functioning of Regulated Market: A Case Study of Krishi Utappanna Bazar Samiti, Solapur (Siddheshwar Market Yard)", M.Phil. Dissertation, Shivaji University, Kolhapur.

Kulkarni B.D. (1977), "Functioning of The Regulated Markets in Solapur District with Special Reference to Groundnut, Tur and Bajra", Ph.D. Thesis, Shivaji University, Kolhapur.

Rupanawar V.D. (1993), "A Study of Agricultural Marketing and Its Impact on Rural Development (Case Study of Agricultural Marketing of the Taluka Malshiras of Solapur District)", Ph.D. Thesis, Shivaji University, Kolhapur.

WEBSITES

http: www.agmarket.nic.in/ reforms.htm.

http: www.agmarket.nic.in/ agmreforms.htm.

http: www.agmarket.nic.in/ agmarknet.pdf.

http: www.agriculturalmarketing.delhigovt.nic.in/ citi_charter.html.

http: www.agriculture_industry_india.com/ agro_programme.html.

http: www.agric.gov.ab.ca/ department/ deptdocs.nsf/ all/ apmc2626.

http: www.agric.gov.ab.ca/ department/ deptdocs.nsf/ all/ apmc2629.

http: www.agric.gov.ab.ca/ department/ deptdocs.nsf/ all/ acts4838.

http: www.agriwatch.com/ statichtml/ apmcreport.htm.

http: www.ccsindia.org/ dh_pdf/ ch_19damb.pdf.

http: www.cafarmersmakets.org.

http: www.iari.res.in/ divisions/ agril_economics.

http: www.gisdevelopment.net/ application/ agriculture/ production.htm.

http: www.indianchild.com/ agricultural_marketing_in_india_htm.

http: www.indianinfoline.com/ fmcg/ agma.html.

http: www.krishiworld.com/ html/ agri_storage1.html.

http: www.legisweb.state.wy.us/ statutes/ titles/ title1/ chapter35.htm.

http: www.mmrdamumbai.org/ projects_swm.htm.

http: www.mp.nic.in/ agriculture/ mandi.htm.

http: www.msamb.com.

http: www.msamb.com/ english/ apmc/ default.htm.

http: www.msamb.com/ english/ apmc/ profile.htm.

http: www.ncsl.org/ statefed/ agtrade.htm.

http: www.nda.agric.za/ docs/ digest2000/ digest6.htm.

http: www.pakissan.com/ english/ issues/ regulating.agrilmarkets.html.

http: www.punjab.gov.pk/ agriculture.

http: www.solapur.com.